Passing Ships

'022

Passing Ships

GORDON GRAY

AMBERLEY

This book is dedicated to my wife Doreen,
who shares my love of ships, the sea and the polar regions

Ships that pass in the night and speak each other in passing;
Only a signal shown a distant voice in the darkness;
So on the ocean of life we pass and speak one another,
Only a look and a voice; then darkness again and a silence.

– Henry Longfellow

Cover Picture. Taken from a painting in the author's collection
and with the kind permission of and thanks to the artist, Jenny
Morgan, RSMA.

First published 2011

Amberley Publishing
The Hill, Stroud
Gloucestershire, GL5 4EP

www.amberleybooks.com

Copyright © Gordon Gray, 2011

British Library Cataloguing in Publication Data.
A catalogue record for this book is available from the British Library.

ISBN 978 1 4456 0224 0

Typesetting and Origination by Amberley Publishing.
Printed in Great Britain.

Contents

Foreword	The Steamer	7
Part One	Early Voyages	9
Chapter 1	ST *Lord Lovat*	11
Chapter 2	MV *Silvana*	43
Chapter 3	TS *Sir Winston Churchill*	60
Part Two	The Royal Navy	83
Chapter 4	The Royal Navy	84
Chapter 5	HMS *Keppel*	97
Chapter 6	HMS *Puncheston*	109
Chapter 7	HMS *Nurton*	134
Chapter 8	HMS *Rhyl*	148
Part Three	Fish Dock and Polar Trips	161
Chapter 9	Wardroom to Fish Dock	162
Chapter 10	MV *Marco Polo*	177
Chapter 11	*Professor Molchanov*	200
Chapter 12	I/B *Kapitan Dranitsyn*	221
Chapter 13	MV *Stockholm*	252
Chapter 14	Three Key Elements	274
Appendix 1	The Tot	281
Appendix 2	Seasickness	283

FOREWORD

The Steamer

On a blustery, west highland summer's day in the early 1950s, a black-hulled, mail steamer ploughed its way northwards from Mallaig up through the sound of Sleat between the mainland of Scotland and the Isle of Skye. The spray from her bow wave flew high up her sides and dark smoke was tugged from her bright-red funnel by the wind. On the open deck, by the rails at the stern of the ship, a family group sat huddled in coats on the wooden benches while enjoying the majestic views on each side of the ship. In spite of the wind, the day was fine and the warm sun shone on the greens and purples of the heather-clad hills of Knoydart and deep into the dark entrance of Loch Hourn, while across to the west, on the Skye shoreline, the sun bathed the dazzling white lighthouse in light. A small boy, aged about two or three, wearing a green knitted top and blue dungarees, sat on the warm deck peering through the rails, his face smiling widely with excitement. The gentle roll of the wooden deck, the smoke blowing from the funnel, the sea splashing past in the wake, the seagulls wheeling overhead squawking furiously and the mixture of strange smells all filled him with excitement and enthralled him.

The boy was called back by his parents, as they were soon due to get off the steamer. They had to go down inside the steamer to a door near the waterline so they could get into an open boat that would take them ashore to the small coastal village of Glenelg.

A bright-red, clinker-built, open motor boat with just one man at the helm came out to the ship from the village, which was just a line of small, single-storeyed, white houses along the distant shore. The steamer slowed and turned across the wind then stopped to give a lee to the motor boat as it came alongside. A big, heavy, steel door near the steamer's waterline was opened and the people who had gathered by the door watched as the boat rolled and bobbed through the waves towards the steamer, with splashes of spray leaping from its bows. Mail, parcels and passengers for Glenelg were passed down to the man in the boat. The small boy was aware of being lifted out through the door in the solid steel hull, past the painted iron frames and huge rivets of the door and into the arms of the kindly, smiling man waiting below in the rocking, pitching boat. Above him, the shiny black hull seemed to stretch upwards like a cliff and a few faces peered over the railing way above him. Once everyone was on board, the red boat set off back to shore. From the boat the boy watched the steamer's black hull as the waters at its stern started to churn into white froth and it slowly turned and picked up speed heading for the Kyle Rhea narrows between Skye and the Mainland on its way to Kyle of Lochalsh. In one small boy a love of ships and the sea had been born.

MacBrayne steamer. (J&C McCutcheon Collection)

PART ONE

Early Voyages

Hull trawlers getting ready for another trip to the Arctic.

Hull trawler *Arctic Hunter*, H218. (J&C McCutcheon Collection)

CHAPTER 1

ST *Lord Lovat* – A Trip to Icelandic Fishing Grounds

'Oh please, just let me die.' The trawler lurched again, and then dropped into another wave trough. The deck beneath me fell away, my knees slid on the deck and I hung on tighter but my arms were too weak and I slipped. The ship's bow bit into the next wave and the bathroom deck shuddered under my cold knees as I struggled to hold onto the bowl. Icy seas rattled against the outside of the bulkhead as they washed along the deck outside. 'Why won't this ship stay still? Why am I still sick when there is no more left inside me?' Seasickness has hit me for the first time in my life and I am well into the second day of it. I feel weak and totally drained. My stomach feels as though it has been turned inside out and my skin is clammy with sweat, and yet I am cold. Nothing will stay still and all I want to do is die. What on earth am I doing here? I am on board an old Hull trawler, well out into the north Atlantic, somewhere off the Faroe Islands, and heading for the Icelandic fishing grounds and we are in the middle of a Force 8 gale. This is only day three of a planned twenty-day fishing trip with no ports of call, and I am now certain that I will never survive.

How had this happened to me? How had the small boy who had been lowered out of the streamer all those years before arrived here, at the point of death in an Atlantic gale on a rusty old trawler? What was I doing here? I was a sixteen-year-old schoolboy from a normal middle-class home in Buckinghamshire, and I was hanging onto the toilet bowl of a trawler as it lurched into another wave. Why am I not at home, or out riding my bike round the pleasant leafy, sun-filled country lanes, or playing rugby with my pals on the common, even revising for my 'O' levels? Anything but this! How had I managed to get myself into this mess?

It had really started four years earlier when I was twelve, during a stay in Hull with family friends who had two sons, Peter and Michael, who were roughly the same age as me. We spent all our days out on our bikes cycling around Hull and the surrounding countryside. One day I persuaded my pals that the three of us should go down on our bikes to St Andrew's Dock, or 'Fish Dock' as it was known locally, to look at the trawlers. I had always been fascinated by TV documentaries about life on Arctic trawlers and had read magazine articles about the dangers of the job and the roughness of the life but had never seen one. The romance of the names of the distant polar places that they went to excited me; Bear Island,

Iceland, the White Sea, Spitzbergen and Greenland. Places from adventure books and the Viking Sagas, places from the tales of polar explorers, icebergs, polar bears and Arctic whalers.

With my two friends, Pete and Mike, cycled down through Hull and found the way to the shopping hustle of Hessle Road and then through the Victorian streets of terraced houses and down through a dark, dank road tunnel that took us under the railway lines and up and out onto the docks. We got off our bikes and looked around. We found that we had entered a different world from the one we had left behind on Hessle Road at the other end of the tunnel.

High, flared, black bows of trawlers towered over us and dominated the immediate dockside scene. As we walked towards them we could see that the wide, open decks of the trawlers were littered with toolboxes, bundles of new nets, big round bobbins and shiny new coils of wire all to be stored away for the next trip. Some workmen were stowing some of the gear away below decks while another group worked on a big trawl winch. A tangle of masts and wires disappeared into the distance as vans and cars bustled and tooted their way over the black cobbles and through the dockside jumble of nets, pedestrians, ropes, bicycle racks, parked lorries, cyclists and huge coils of trawl warp. Looking across the dock at the ships on the far side you could immediately see their lovely lines. Their sweeping hull shape had evolved over many years of Arctic fishing; developed to deal with the worst that the weather could throw at them. Although they were only about 700 to 800 tons in size, these beautiful steel ships looked impregnable. As they lay still in the flat, calm waters of the Fish Dock it was impossible to imagine that such strong and powerful-looking ships could be tossed about in a storm, but of course they were. They all had high, flared bows to cut through the waves and throw off the icy, Arctic seas and above the bows the curved whaleback of the fo'c'sle, which gave protection and some shelter to the crew working on the open deck. From the whaleback, the high solid bulwarks then ran back past the gallows, a heavy steel arch from which the fishing gear was towed, to the low midships section, almost at water level to enable the net to be hauled over the side by hand. The midships area was dominated by the superstructure with the wheelhouse at the top. This jutted out forward from the main superstructure and stood high and fine above the deck; aloof and removed from it all. The wheelhouse windows seemed to stare out, far beyond the ship, oblivious to three schoolboys below, to the far horizons; as if they were looking for signs of more fish, or watching for a change in the weather. Immediately behind the wheelhouse was the funnel and then the low flat superstructure led smoothly aft to a rounded cruiser-style stern. Most of the trawlers were rust-streaked and had a battered, weathered look but the rust, dents and scratches could not disguise their fine lines and strength. In the sunshine those that had been freshly painted shone proudly as they lay waiting for their crew and the next tide so they could sail back to those exciting-sounding places in the far north.

To me it was all pure magic. Here were the ships that I had read about in the magazines, seen on the TV documentaries, where trawling was described as the most dangerous job in the world as well as being carried out in the stormiest, most remote and icy cold regions on the planet. Here on the dock were all the elements that went to make up a fishing trip to the Arctic: the trawler owners in their offices and all the shore support staff; the trawlermen themselves and the trawlers. I could see some of their names, fine proud names like *Stella Leonis*, *Cape Trafalgar*, *Lord Alexander*, *Westella* and *St Dominic*.

As we stood looking about and wondering what to do next (as well as making sure we did not get knocked into the dock by a passing lorry), I became aware of a gleaming black-hulled trawler that stood out from the rest as she was so clean and freshly painted. I walked towards her. On one of her lifebelts was her name, *Cape Otranto*, and the number H227. She had a high, white-fronted wheelhouse, which jutted out over the deck. The wheelhouse seemed to be so far above the deck that it must be like another world to be up there. As I stared, I saw an old man on board the ship. He was leaning against the bulwark by the aft accommodation. He had a weathered, wrinkled face and was smoking a pipe in the sunshine as he watched the comings and goings of the morning bustle. He wore an old blue jersey and had a scruffy flat cap on and a ragged scarf tied round his neck. I walked over and plucked up all my courage. In my southern accent I asked, 'Excuse me please, but would it be possible to see round your ship?' He seemed somewhat surprised at this, took a puff at his pipe, stood up and looked at me hard. He thought for a minute and then with a slight smile said, 'Aye, I s'pose so lad.' He took another draw on his pipe then knocked it out against the ship's side and put it in his pocket. 'Cum wi'me.' I clambered nervously over the steel bulwark and jumped down onto the main deck, calling to my two pals to follow, leaving the bikes by a bollard. I later discovered that the man was a watchman, one of many ex-trawlermen who worked as watchmen and stayed on board the trawlers when they were in dock, working twenty-four-hour shifts to keep a constant check for fires, flooding or other ship-borne problems as well as opening up locked compartments for the repair staff. He took us all round the ship.

We started in the galley. This seemed to be far too small to cater for a ship of this size. Even with the sun shining down through the skylight the galley seemed very small. It had shining steel worktops on two sides and a big black cooking range on a third as well as a number of small cupboards; but that was all. It was warm though and had a homely, warm, floury smell to it. The man told us, 'Here, when they are at sea, the cook will have to prepare and cook three meals a day for a crew of over twenty in all weathers, summer and winter. Basic food but plenty of it. If all else fails they can always eat fish!' he joked. A small wooden hatch allowed food to be passed into the bare-looking crew's mess deck while the officers ate in a separate mess with leather benches and panelled wood across the passageway. He showed us the tidy, four-man cabins down below for the crew and the single-berth officers' cabins on the main deck. The ship was warm and clean and smelt of a mixture of detergent and diesel oil and had a very secure feel about it. I remember thinking how snug the mate's cabin was, with its bunk, a little settee, a desk and its own porthole. I did not realise how little time he ever got to enjoy it. Then, the watchy took us up past the skipper's cabin, which had

MT *Cape Otranto* in her original Hudson Bros colours as seen by the author in 1962. Note the lovely lines of her hull and the proud look of her bridge. (Photo by kind permission of World Ship Society and Fleetwood Online Archive of Trawlers (FLOAT) http://float-trawlers. lancashire.gov.uk)

St Andrew's Dock, Hull, in 1962. The trawlers on the left are being prepared for sea.

a day cabin and a night cabin as well as its own bathroom. Then we went up another deck and into the wheelhouse. I stepped to the front of the wheelhouse, past the big wooden steering wheel and looked out of the windows. We could see over the whole of the wide, working deck, beyond the top of the fo'c'sle and along the dock, which now seemed a long way away. I heard myself stupidly say, 'Gosh, you get a good view from up here, don't you?' The watchy, without even looking at me, just said, 'Aye, that's what it's for, lad.' And with that he shuffled out of the wheelhouse and took us back down to the deck.

On the way he explained that the *Cape Otranto* was a brand-new ship that had just returned from her maiden voyage of twenty-one days and was ready to sail again that night to the far north. She had a tonnage of 923 tons and had been built in Beverley by cook, Gemmel & Welton. She was owned by Hudson Bros, a well-established company, which named all their trawlers after capes. She was 196 feet long and was powered by diesel-electric, a new system in those days (though I did not understand what that meant then). I was entranced, and my fascination for the trawlers that sailed from the Humber to the Arctic grew ever deeper. Little did I know then that in four years time I would be back on the Fish Dock.

Why I should have such an interest in ships is a mystery. No one in the family was connected with the sea, unless you count my maternal grandfather, who was a cabinet-maker for the famous John Brown's Shipbuilders on Clydebank and had worked on both the original *Queen Mary* and the *Queen Elizabeth*. There was no sea on my father's side. There I come from a long line of grass keepers and shepherds in Sutherland in northern Scotland. However, after my tour round the *Cape Otranto* I was determined to take my interest in trawlers further and so a couple years later I wrote to the British Trawler Federation asking if it was possible to go to sea on a trawler for a trip as a schoolboy during school holidays.

They said 'Yes'. Under their 'Pleasurer' scheme, schoolboys and youths could go to sea on the trawlers as 'Pleasurers' to find out if they liked trawlers and the life and to decide if they wanted to make a career of it. They gave me the names of some trawler owners to contact. I wrote to them all and received a letter back from a Mr Graham Hellyer, Managing Director of Hellyer Bros, one of the oldest and biggest trawler companies in Hull. He said that they were prepared to take me on a trip but I must sign an 'Insurance Indemnity Form' and be ready to go at short notice.

My parents thought I was mad. They had come from solid working-class families and spent their lives working to improve their lot and to do their best for me, private schools, and a nice home, but here I was reverting to a basic working-class environment as a holiday and treating it as a higher form of life. No wonder my mother called me an inverted snob! 'They send the ex-jailbirds out on the trawlers when they get out,' my Father told me; 'The only food on board is fish and you don't like fish'; 'Trawlers are full of thugs and layabouts'; 'You'll be seasick all the time'; 'Trawlers smell and you will come back smelling of fish'. These were just some of the many comments that were lobbed my way at home in tones of mischief and incomprehension. It only fuelled the fire. I was going to go!

One Saturday night, early in my school summer holiday, the phone rings. 'It is for you,' said my mother, 'someone called a Ship's Husband for Hellyers Brothers in Hull?' 'Hello,' I said nervously. In a gruff Yorkshire voice, the person on the other end told me to be in Hull at the offices of Hellyer Bros for nine o'clock on the Monday morning and to ask for Mr Easton as I will be sailing on the *Lord Lovat*. He also told me that I should stay at the Fisherman's Mission on the Sunday night and he would fix that for me.

Panic ensues as I rush to get my stuff ready. On the Sunday, I catch the train from King's Cross to Hull and get a taxi to the Fisherman's Mission, or 'The Mission' as everyone calls it, on Goulton Street, just off the Hessle Road. It is raining as I arrive and I am shown to my 'Cabin' by the Mission Superintendant, who is a very cheery and friendly man in a smart dark-blue suit. 'Here you are, lad, now you just settle yourself in, then come on down for your tea,' he says with a smile, then closes the door and leaves me to unpack. It is a pleasant room, with a washbasin, a radio and a big window overlooking the docks. I go downstairs. *Sing Something Simple*, a favourite Sunday night radio programme, is playing in the big mess room. We often have this on at home and a pang of homesickness hits me as I realise I won't be hearing it again for a few weeks. After a welcome supper of ham salad, a cup of tea and bread and butter, I go for a walk to see if I can still find the Fish Dock. It is now dark. I find the railway tunnel and emerge from it onto the Fish Dock. The docks look like a scene from a Sherlock Holmes film with the rain still lightly falling onto the deserted, jumbled emptiness of the docks and water drips loudly from broken gutters. My footsteps on the cobbled road echo round the tall, dark, Victorian buildings that house the trawler owner's offices and workshops as I splash through the oily, black puddles on the dockside. I try to remember the Fish Dock from my earlier visit as a twelve-year-old on that sunny summer's day as I walked·along the south side. I find the *Lord Lovat*. She looks forlorn and depressingly cold as she lies dark and silent tied up outboard of the *Kingston Andalusite*. She seems so much smaller than the *Cape Otranto*. It seems a much more alien world than the one I saw on that summer's day with Mike and Pete. I seriously wonder what I have let myself in for. There is still time to change my mind.

I awake early and check out of the Mission then set off nervously by taxi to be at Hellyers offices for a quarter to nine. The morning is fine after last night's rain and the sun is breaking through the remaining clouds; everything seems brighter. The taxi takes me past the streets of Victorian back-to-back houses that cluster around the Fish Dock. These two-up two-down houses are the homes of the deep-sea trawler men of Hull. If you live there, then you are in the fishing industry. Everyone here is, or has a relation who is, a trawlerman, or who works on the Dock. The only exceptions are the skippers and owners who live in 'big posh 'ouses out of town'. Hessle Road is the heart of the Hull fishing community and the bond between the people is so strong there that it is a world on its own, separate from the rest of Hull. They support Hull FC Rugby League team and not Hull KR from East Hull. It has been home to the port's deep-sea fishing fleet since the 1850s, when the herring shoals of the North Sea were discovered and the fishermen from Devon and Cornwall moved up to the Humber to capitalise on the harvest. Now Hull is the biggest distant-water fishing port in the world and three or more full trains of fish leave Hull every morning for London and Leeds and other northern cities in addition to the many countless lorry-loads that go by road all over the country. I am about to enter that world.

I pay off the taxi on the end of the dock and stand with my bag and take in the scene. The Fish Dock is very much alive now, and a very different place from last night. I am back in the world I had last seen four years before and am excited by it all over again. I am met by all the smells of the place; fish meal, diesel oil, paint, tar and all the other scents of working docks and ships. Noises from everywhere compete with each other; tug hooters, drilling, clattering of chains, machinery being dragged over the cobblestones. Men are calling from ship to shore as the ships are repaired, stored and made ready for sea. I make my way along the south side of the dock past the trawler company offices. The office windows on the upper floors overlook and silently monitor all that happens on the dock. I walk past groups of men gathered round doorways and dockside offices awaiting their money or to sign on for the next trip. The tall wooden doors of a workshop entrance swing open and allow me a glimpse of the dark interior scenes, the blue flashes of welding torches, the scream of grinders and the banging and clanging as vital parts are machined and fabricated for the trawlers. The dock seems full of trawlers. Most of them are berthed two and three deep. They seem to be crammed in and the dock is bursting with them. The trawlers are painted with black hulls, though some have pale grey hulls and others are a yellowy buff colour. Some have white bridge fronts and a number have bridge fronts painted with a brown wood-grain effect, which matches the universal wood-grain effect of the paint on the main superstructures. This wood-grain paint effect, I learnt, is called 'scrumbling' and is common in deep-sea trawlers and smaller fishing vessels.

This is the golden era of Britain's deep-sea trawling industry. A trawler owner only has to send a trawler down the Humber with the orders to turn left at the end and head north and he is assured of a profit, providing of course, she has a good skipper. Trawlers sail from here to the distant grounds at Iceland, Greenland, the Grand Banks off Canada, Spitzbergen and the White Sea, all of which offer a rich harvest of cod, haddock and other valuable fish such as halibut, at the right times of the year. There are people, trucks, bikes, and forklift trucks everywhere. Taxis trying to get along the dock swing round piles of gear and iron mooring bollards as they fight for the clear areas of cobbled road with trucks loaded with trawl gear and nets. Smoke and steam are rising from a number of the trawlers as crews climb on board with their bags and boxes. The black oily waters of the dock are glistening in the sunshine.

Hellyer's offices are about half way along the dock and I find the Ship's Husband's Office. Mr Easton is not about so I wait, mingling with the crews. Nervousness grips my stomach again. I feel totally out of place here, a real fish out of water. After the bravado of coming up by train, now I am in the reality of Fish

Lord Lovat at St Andrew's Fish Market on the day after she docked.

Dock on sailing day. The gulf between reading about trawlers in Arctic storms in magazines at home and the reality of actually being about to sail on one hits me hard. This is now reality. This is their world and I am a total stranger in it, I look it and feel it. How will they treat strangers? I am about to put myself totally in their hands for three weeks in an old trawler. The stories about ex-jailbirds being put on trawlers come back to me. Just as my imagination starts to work, Mr Easton arrives. He is a big man with a shiny bald head. It is obvious that he is a busy man. He is clearly 'Management' as he is wearing a suit. He walks briskly and has a stern and harassed look on his face. Before he gets into his office, people are asking him things and he is calling out sharp one-word answers as he goes into the office. He has a collection of papers in his hand and shouts at someone in the office to get a taxi to collect a Harry Marshal who has not shown up for the *Loch Eribol*. I must be a minor nuisance he can do without. Perhaps he won't notice me and I will miss the ship. I could slip away and be home again by tonight. Too late: he notices me. 'Gray is it? Got your indemnity form?' I nod. 'Leave your bag there then and go across to the Insurance Company and get your indemnity form signed off.' He waves an arm towards the end of the dock. 'Yes, Sir,' I stammer. I find my way there and get the form signed, then go back to the office. Mr Easton is still there. 'Now then, lad, get yourself aboard the *Lord Lovat*.' He takes the time to point me in the right direction. Smoke is now drifting up from the *Lord Lovat*'s funnel into the blue, summer sky. 'You report to the mate when you get on board, he'll sort you out.' It's now or never. I can still just walk away and half of me wants to but the other half drags me towards the unknown. I set off across the dockside chaos and clamber onto the *Kingston Andalusite* then across her deck to the *Lord Lovat*. I try to look as though I climb over trawler's high bulwarks with a kit bag every day of the week, and fail.

Once on board I find a big, fattish man with sandy hair standing watching me. 'And who are you?' This is the mate standing on the deck waiting as his crew arrives. 'Gordon Gray, I am a pleasurer for this trip. Mr Easton said to ask for the mate when I got on board.' I mention Mr Easton's name as though it will entitle me to an upgrade. Unfortunately, it doesn't. 'Well you've found him.' The mate seems a big, silent sort and just smiles in a friendly way but do I catch a slight question over my sanity in his eyes? He waves his arm towards a doorway. 'You'll be in the cook's cabin, down there, the cook is already on board.' Then he turns away as someone else climbs on board. I struggle down the steep wooden ladder to the lower deck and the smell of a mixture of detergent and diesel oil comes back to me. As I reach the bottom of the ladder I can see someone standing in a cabin. 'Excuse me, but where do I find the cook?' I ask hopefully. 'Come in, mate. I'm the cook.' He is a tall (about six feet), dark-haired guy, wearing a smart brown suit and a thin red tie. He is in his thirties and with a smiling, pleasant, open manner that immediately makes me warm to him. He actually reminds me a bit of Russ Conway. He shakes my hand, introducing himself as Dave. He is the cook for this trip and he starts asking me what trawlers I have been on before. 'None,' I reply. 'Oh Hell, we'll have to start from scratch with you then.' I am a bit puzzled. Dave carries on chatting and tells me that he is often referred to as Big Dave on board as the mate, who is also called Dave, is fatter and is known as 'Fat Dave', though never to his face, he warns. Big Dave is the regular cook in *Lord Lovat* and has done a number of trips in the ship. He has been told to expect a new galley boy for this trip as the previous one has 'gone ashore' to look for a shore job.

Just then, there is a noise from the wooden ladder and a small, thin boy in a loose, white T-shirt appears, dragging a battered old suitcase behind him. He looks round then comes into the cabin. He says he is the galley boy and is also called Dave. This is going to get very confusing! I have only met three of the crew and they are all called Dave. The cook looks relieved as he had assumed that I was the galley boy when I appeared, hence the questioning. The new Dave has already done a number of trips in another trawler so knows the job. He is a cheery sort, thin and with very fair skin and long, tousled, blond hair. I explain I am just a pleasurer and all is well. cook Big Dave then sits on the bench and fishes into his bag. He produces a bottle of rum and we all sit down on the benches alongside the bunks and he shares swigs of the rum between the three of us and all is well. I am 6 foot 4 inches and Big Dave looks at me then at the galley boy and says 'Bloody Hell, Dave, the pleasurer will make two of you, he may even eat you if the food doesn't last!' We share a laugh and they then start chatting about which ships they have been on and I look around my new home. It is a six-berth cabin with varnished wooden lockers and a sack mat floor covering. There are no scuttles as it is below the main deck level and mostly below the waterline. Dave indicates that I can have the bottom bunk of two on the port side as there will only be three of us in this cabin this trip. We are due to sail at about half past ten and other crew members have come down the ladder and found their berths while we have been sitting there. The ship gives a small jolt, the first sense of motion as it is moved by the tug off the berth and into the dock ready to sail out. My stomach lurches. Too late to get off now! I really want to be up on deck but the two Daves are chatting and having the odd swig of rum and I do not want to appear rude and walk out. I am saved by the skipper. He sends a crewman down with orders for me to go up to the wheelhouse.

The skipper is leaning against the wheelhouse front by an open window. He looks serious. 'Now then, you're Gordon, right?' 'Yes, Sir,' I reply. 'First thing, you don't call me Sir, or captain, I am just "the skipper", OK?' This is the first thing he says, as I get into the wheelhouse. 'No, Sir, er, I mean, Skipper,' I reply. He ignores my slip as I try and find somewhere to stand among the other people already in the small wheelhouse. The skipper's name is Ken. He is a quiet guy, medium height and build, with thinning hair slicked back and I guessed he must have been about forty or forty-five. 'Now then, Gordon, I never use my night cabin, especially on the fishing grounds, so shift your gear from down aft into my night cabin.' He points at a set of stairs at the back of the wheelhouse. 'You'll be better off there than down aft with that lot.' I assume he means his crew. I am feeling a bit overcome by the kindness that these people are showing me, first the cook and his rum, now the skipper and his cabin. Where are the jailbirds out to get me, the layabouts stealing my wallet? Maybe they will appear later? But for now I just enjoy the warmth of friendly, helpful people and the start of a big adventure. My earlier nervousness begins to die down a bit. The skipper's day cabin is connected directly to the bridge by a stairway and so is better for him to get to the wheelhouse quickly when he has to. He lives in his day cabin where there is a long upholstered bench settee on which he sleeps. His night cabin is off the day cabin.

The tug is let go and we clear through the lock and move out into the river Humber. Most of the crew are now on deck, some waving and calling to pals or family who have come down to see them off. I have found out from the cook that we are bound for Iceland. Five other trawlers are sailing on the same tide, three are heading for Iceland, one for the White Sea and one of them is bound for Greenland.

We make our way down the Humber in a long straggled line. After the busy and noisy chaos of sailing, everyone seems to vanish as we go down the river, doubtless back to their cabins and their own bottles. After clearing Spurn Head at the mouth of the Humber Estuary, we round our course up to north, aiming to pass off Flamborough Head and then heading for the Pentland Firth at the very top of Scotland. The sea is calm and the sky clear and sunny. The skipper tells me that on the first day out everyone not on watch turns in for the afternoon to lessen the pain of leaving home again. This includes the skipper. Radio Scarborough is playing 1960s pop music throughout the ship as she rolls gently up the Yorkshire coast with water sloshing quietly past the freeing ports.

By evening, the crew begins to reappear. George, the Radio Officer, or 'Sparks', introduces himself to me. George is an affable, laid-back guy in his late forties and has been a 'Sparks' on trawlers all his life. He spends the entire trip in the radio room, which also doubles as his cabin and, no matter what the weather, always seems to be wearing a maroon cardigan. The Radio Room is immediately behind the wheelhouse. After chatting for a while he says, 'Come, on I'll take you round.' He takes me all round the ship and shows me the layout and introduces me to the crew as we meet them. Some are still on their bunks sleeping or just lying reading. Most of the reading matter is western cowboy novels or 'wessies' or last week's Sunday papers. These are only read on the way out and then not touched until they are running for home. No newspapers are ever thrown away; all papers and paperbacks are shared and passed around the crew. George takes me up to the fo'c'sle, which has berths for up to twelve men but only six seamen are sleeping there on this trip. It is now silent as the men are still asleep, apart from about a dozen empty beer cans rolling gently across the deck. He also shows me his other domain; the cod liver oil boilers. 'When the cod are gutted, the livers are separated from the rest and put into baskets. After the catch has all been gutted, I then take the livers aft and put them into the cod liver oil boilers,' he explains. 'If I'm not around they keep them for me to boil later.' The boilers are situated in a compartment on the starboard side aft, not far from the galley. The boilers themselves are two large vats about five feet high and with heavy lids that can be clamped shut. The boilers have steam pipe connections from the engine room so steam can be pumped through them. 'It is my job to boil the livers, which separates the good oil from the residue. This oil is then fed off into storage tanks. I am then entitled to a share of the proceeds from the cod liver oil at the end of the trip, and every penny helps, believe you me, lad!'

At 2130 every night at sea, a radio message is sent to the owners to confirm the ship's position and course. This is relayed to all the ships in the company and is sent in code so that other companies cannot find out where our trawlers are fishing. We pass a small Russian trawler drifting just outside the twelve-mile limit. She is waiting for nightfall so she can move inside and fish illegally. Nothing seems to be done about it and the Russians are definitely not regarded as comrades on the high seas. As we pass Flamborough Head and alter course for Rattray Head in Scotland, a small school of dolphins swims past heading south. They are leaping out of the sea and racing each other, clearly enjoying the evening sunshine

I go back down to the cabin and take a look at my home for the next three weeks. The skipper's night cabin, now my cabin for the trip, is wood-panelled with the bunk running fore and aft on the inside bulkhead. On the outboard side, below a scuttle, is a locker, while a cushioned bench seat is fitted to the forward bulkhead. There is a brass ship's clock on the bulkhead and a fan which does not work. There are two scuttles, one forward looking onto the winch area in front of the superstructure and the other on the starboard side overlooking the deck. There is also a bathroom at the after end with black and white, diamond-shaped tiles and white steel bulkheads.

Lord Lovat, H148, is an oil-burning steam trawler of 713 tons and is 181 feet long and was built at Selby in 1951. In Hellyer Bros livery, she has a light-grey hull with brown scrumbling woodeffect superstructure with an ochre funnel and the company emblem of a white 'H' on a blue flag on the side. Her navigation equipment is basic: a magnetic compass, a radar set, a Decca Navigator and a Loran A radio navigation systems and an echo sounder. The days of gyro-compasses, autopilots and satellite navigation have not yet arrived. She is typical of the many distant-water trawlers built in the late 1940s and early 1950s for fishing at Iceland from Hull and Grimsby.

I sleep well that first night and awake just after seven. It is a fine, clear and sunny morning and the sun is glinting off the sea and shining through the porthole. *Lord Lovat* is rolling gently as she steams north. The crew is already out on deck setting up the trawl gear in readiness for fishing. First, they set up the fish washer. This is a large metal tank that is open at one end. It is mounted on tall legs amidships above the fish room hatch so that the open end faces aft and is a few feet forward of the fish room hatch. A hose is rigged up so that, when we are fishing, water continually flows into the tank. Then they assemble the nets. The nets are made up of a number of component parts: bellies, wings, side panels, cod end, foot ropes, head ropes, etc., and have to be built up to form the complete net. The headline with its floats and the ground rope with its big rollers or bobbins to roll over the seabed are all secured in place. These preparations carry on all morning in a happy atmosphere with the BBC Light Programme playing over the deck. Although the deck is open on all sides when we are under way it is fairly well sheltered from the wind by the high bows and whale back.

At about noon, after passing Rattray Head off the north-east tip of Aberdeenshire, not far from the fishing ports of Peterhead and Fraserburgh, we run into fog. George, the Sparks, tells me that the trawlers at Greenland are reporting that they are catching lots of fish. The *Lord Lovat* does not have the fuel capacity to get there and back and allow enough time there for a decent trip and so she is restricted to fishing at Iceland. It is a five-day steam to get to the Grand Banks and longer if they go up to Greenland and the Labrador Straits. As it is also a five-day steam home again, the skippers have to be confident of making good catches when they get there as they only have about ten days on the grounds to make a successful trip.

The skipper calls me to go and join him and George for lunch down in the officers' mess. This is a small, cosy mess, which has wood panelling on the bulkheads, very similar to the *Cape Otranto*'s and with the table taking up the whole room apart from the red leather-covered bench seats all round the side of it. Lunch is good, vegetable soup, roast beef, Yorkshire puddings, roast potatoes and cabbage. Then, there is steamed duff and custard for pudding. I had not realised that I was so hungry. My dockside nerves seem to have gone and I am feeling more confident about my time here. I haven't even felt seasick!

We are now entering the dangerous Pentland Firth; the narrow passage between Scotland and the Orkneys Islands through which the tides race; particularly at the time of the spring tides. Shipping from Europe heading for the Atlantic converges on this narrow channel with the rocky islands and skerries all around. The fog is now thicker than ever. It envelops the ship, covering everything in a heavy, wet dew, and locks us into our own tiny world, a world bounded by the wall of grey wetness about fifty yards from the ship. All sound is deadened so it feels as if we are in wet cottonwool. Entering the narrows of the Firth, an eerie feeling descends on the wheelhouse as the lookout peers out, seeing nothing but the wall of fog and the swirling waters as the tide races through the Firth. We know that we are now close to the rocky, wreck-strewn coast but we cannot see it. We can only hear a lone fog horn booming out somewhere in the fog and the plaintive hoot of our ship's fog horn warning any other ships of our presence. However, with the aid of Duncansby Head Lighthouse fog horn making fog signals of five blasts every two minutes, as well as the ship's radar, we are soon safely through. George tells me that on one of the Pentland Skerries (one of the clusters of small rocky islands in the Firth) there are the remains of an Aberdeen trawler, which was washed up in a ferocious storm in about 1965. She was not even holed and was just sitting up on the skerry.

At about seven that evening, the fog lifts and we finally see the cliffs of the Isle of Hoy to starboard and there on a parallel course and dwarfed by the cliffs is the trawler *Kingston Andalusite*, which had left the dock just behind us. As the fog goes so the wind picks up and the sea begins to sluice in through the freeing ports as she rolls along northwards.

Later that night, the wind gets up and I am woken by the change in the ship's movement. By morning the wind is up to Force 7 or 8 and the spray is being sent high over the whaleback and lashes onto the bridge windows. I do not feel good at all. I have to make a dash for the bathroom before I have properly woken up. I go back to bed and hope that this awful feeling will go away after being ill. It does not. I struggle up as I decide that I should try and keep going. Perhaps if I get up into the wheelhouse I will feel better. I lean against the bridge windows and hang on. The mate is there and looks relaxed and content with the world. He smiles at me with a knowing look. As I look out, hoping to see sunny calm seas ahead, I am hypnotised by the movement of the ship. The seas are coming from the north-east and the ship is rolling along and pitching into them with the bows swinging through 20 to 25 degrees. One moment the bow is poised high above the troughs and we were looking down on the seas, then the bow drops and sinks into the trough and the horizon is above us. Spray lashes across the windows. The skipper assures me that it will be far rougher when we are clear of the shelter of the Faeroes. I now feel even worse than I had done in my bunk and as I watch the bows once more, my stomach heaves and I make a dash below to the heads. I am experiencing my first, but by no means last, bout of seasickness.

As the day progresses and the pitching continues I feel more dreadful and think that death must be better than this. I seem to spend all day sitting on the bathroom floor. I try to keep going but whatever I do the bulkheads seem to close in on me and then a lurch of the bow as it drops into a wave sets my stomach off again. I only want one thing – to get off this thing! Nothing can convince me that I will be OK; I am definitely going to die. By nightfall I have lost a lot of strength and feel weak and terrible. I go to bed and praise the Lord that I am not expected to keep any sort of watch and so can lie and suffer my last hours in peace. I drift off into a deep sleep. The next morning, although still feeling bad I realise that I am still alive. How can that be? Perhaps the weather is improving? By the afternoon, the weather has abated and the ship is steaming along nicely. The sun is now shining again after the fog and the rough weather. By evening I am beginning to feel a little better. Somehow I have survived.

That night we arrive on the fishing grounds off south-east Iceland. After two days and eighteen hours of steaming we begin fishing. The big wooden and steel otter boards or 'Doors' are winched outboard. The doors are massive. Each is about 10 feet by 5 feet and about 3 or 4 inches thick. Made of solid baulks of timber and edged with heavy steel shoes to protect them from rocks on the seabed. A door hangs from each of the two big steel arches, or gallows, on the starboard side, one forward by the whaleback, one aft by the cod liver boiler house. The net is connected between them so that one is attached at each end of the net mouth and when the net is set the doors act like kites and 'fly' outwards in the sea keeping the net spread wide open. The net is connected to the trawl warps and the first trawl of the trip is underway. We are on Working Man's Bank, about half way between Iceland and the Faeroes. After towing the trawl net for about four hours at 4 knots the first catch is hauled and we have caught about eighty baskets of cod, a good catch to start with. A fishing vessel is losing money every minute that the nets are not on the seabed and set for catching fish. My seasickness has now begun to ease, I feel better and even manage to start thinking about food again.

We spend two days fishing in this area and catching good hauls of fish. The weather settles into a warm, sunny pattern, which cheers everyone up. When it is dull or rough the crew spends most of their time in their bunks but when it is sunny they spend any spare time on deck with a mug of tea and a cigarette and are altogether happier. By the third day the catches are not so good and the skipper makes the decision to move grounds. This is a big risk as no one knows whether better catches will be had or not. The time taken to change grounds and the cost of the fuel used will all work against the skipper if when he gets there the catches are poor. The Bosses in the office judge him only by how much he catches. We sail up nearer to Iceland and now I can see Iceland's mountains stretching along the horizon. In the days before Iceland's new fishery limits British trawlers could fish up to three miles of the coast, now we are not allowed within twelve miles of the coast. This is my first sight of the far north. Although we are still south of the Arctic Circle the sight of these snow-capped mountains is exciting. It is brilliantly clear and sunny and the mountains are sharp with every detail clear in dazzling white against the blue sky.

The skipper's knowledge of these waters is astounding. His charts have all sorts of hand-drawn alterations on them with ridges, banks, holes and fastenings all marked. He checks his chart with a big notebook that he keeps of all his trips indicating what he caught where and when and what the tides and weather conditions were. The tow is carefully plotted with the aid of electronic navigation systems such as Loran and Decca Navigator by which the skippers can calculate their position very accurately and so trawl along the edges of undersea cliffs and ridges. As the fish tend to lie in clumps feeding on the seabed, one good haul can often indicate plenty of fish in that area. When this occurs you can see the trawlers following each other round in circles as they try and fish out the area.

The VHF (a shortrange voice radio) speaker in the wheelhouse is constantly crackling away and snatches of conversations between skippers are heard all the time: '*Lord Lovat, Lord Lovat,* this is *Kingston Onyx, Kingston Onyx*, are you there Ken?' The skipper of another Hull trawler, the *Kingston Onyx*, which had sailed a week earlier than us and which we had seen in the distance earlier in the day is calling up our Skipper for a chat. The two skippers know each other well. They chat away talking about the weather. 'When did you get up to the grounds?' 'How are things at home?' All this is spoken in a slow Yorkshire way with lots of pauses in the conversation and 'Ayes' followed by more pauses. Then the other skipper starts to probe Ken about catches. 'Any good where you are, Ken?' The response is cagey, 'Oh, so, so, not much to be excited over.' 'Aye … Aye … same here.' Ken asks if they are heading for a market yet. 'Not sure, depends on the weather' (that is interpreted as the fishing is good so they would stay unless bad weather stopped them fishing. 'Where are you abouts now?' asks Ken. 'Just having a look at Hari Kari' is the reply, i.e. trying to indicate they have just arrived on that bank. They chatted on like this for about ten or fifteen minutes with no real facts or hard information being exchanged but lots of guesswork and innuendo sent and received. The skippers are always trying to kid each other into believing there are no fish where they are when in fact there are fish; it all seems a waste of time but does keep them happy chatting. However, if one skipper can con the other skipper to move away from good catches to poorer grounds and then move onto the better grounds themselves then they will. This goes on between ships in the same company as every skipper fishes for himself. Vessels from the same company do not fish as a fleet, pooling information or calling others to good grounds; they all look after themselves but keep chatting to the others from the company and in the hope of picking up a nugget of information that the others might let slip in an unguarded moment. Every skipper is only as good as his last trip. One bad one and he can find himself out of a job as the whole industry is run on a casual labour basis.

Later in the day we steam to 'Hari Kari Bank'. It is a fine day and, as we steam north, the sun lights up the dazzling white bow wave against the deep blue of the sea. The ship rolls along free at last of the restraining net, like a hiker walking after putting down a heavy rucksack. Hari Kari Bank is so named by British trawler men because it was regarded as the last resort ground on the way home to try and save a poor trip. *Kingston Onyx* is still there and as we approach we see that she is hauling her nets. The skipper keeps *Lord Lovat* upwind of the *Onyx* so he can see her starboard side. He watches through his binoculars as they haul their net aboard; they do not seem to be getting exceptional catches after all. Maybe their skipper was telling the truth? We do not find any good catches here either so after three hauls we steam back to Working Man's Bank where our first haul is sixty baskets, not bad. The day ends with a tea of hamburgers, peas and fresh baked bread rolls and jam.

The fishing continues round the clock and the weather also continues to hold. A calm high-pressure system is giving the north Atlantic a pleasant summer and we are enjoying it. We also continue to have reasonably good catches.

I spend some time chatting in the wheelhouse to the bosun, John. He is a cheery, friendly guy in his early twenties, clearly ambitious and takes his job seriously. He always has his greased hair flicked back in a classic 'DA' style like the Rock & Roll singers of the day. He has been at sea since leaving school. Like most of the crew he rolls his own cigarettes and takes great pride in being able to roll a 'ciggy' with one hand. On first joining the fishing industry he started off as a 'Deckie Learner', which is the bottom rung of the promotion ladder. He was a deckie learner for a year and then became a 'Spare Hand'. Some deckie learners take much longer to get to spare hand. After that he gradually climbed up the ladder. He became a third hand and then after more sea time and shore exams he became a bosun. The next step for him is to become a mate before reaching the final height of skipper. There is no short cut to the rank of skipper. No college diploma, officer entry or envelope of money to the owners can make you a skipper. The only way is to start at the bottom as a deckie learner and work your way from there. As a bosun his seamanship was expected to be as good as the mate's but he needed time to understudy the mate in fishing and managing the crew. However, he is qualified to take over from the mate if needed. He would take responsibility for some of the trawls to gain experience of fishing. A good worker with determination and hard work can become a skipper in six years, although this is unusual. Normally it takes about ten years. That is a lot of time at sea. To take a mate's ticket you have to have been at sea for four years. A lot of skippers will work for about ten to fifteen years as a skipper and then retire. They earn good money if they are successful; about £8,000 to £10,000 a year at 1966 rates. However, I could not find anyone on board who actually liked the job. They all said it was too hard, boring, and too long away from home; but they could not think what else they could do or even wanted to do instead. On the grounds they are either working on deck in all weathers and seasons, or sleeping as they can often be on deck for twelve to eighteen hours at a stretch. For most this is the only working life they have ever known about. Often they are the sons of trawlermen, with cousins and uncles also in the industry. From childhood they will have seen them disappear to sea for three weeks at a time and return with good pay packets. Some of the school chums will also have gone off to sea. For those that do not have the opportunity to go on from school to university then this is the natural progression from school for those on Hessle Road. At the age of fifteen or sixteen they want to be seen as equals among their peers and to have the money to flash about that a trawlerman can have when he comes back from a trip.

There are no recreational facilities on board other than playing cards or reading their western paperbacks and old newspapers. They all buy their tobacco from the bonded store on board. They all roll their own ciggies and have their own baccy pouches and matches. Most seem to stick at the job for the money but one of the spare hands, Colin, had given it up and had gone farming with an uncle for over a year. However, he found that working out in the fields on his own did not suit him and he missed his pals and the camaraderie of mess deck life on the trawlers and he soon found that the sea was dragging him back. Also, the money was better at sea than as a farm labourer. Once someone gets so far up the promotion ladder to, say, a bosun or a mate, then they feel they are past the point of no return and are too old to start again on the shore. Also they are now earning better money than they could ashore and so they tend to carry on to the end.

The noises and calls of trawling fills the days and nights. The first call is to 'Knock out the warps.' This action releases the two towing warps from a block on the starboard side aft near the after gallows which holds the two warps together while towing and they must be freed from that to allow the net to be hauled in. The steam winch hisses as it begins heaving in another haul, the trawl warp creaking and cracking under the strain as it winds itself onto the winch drum and remorselessly pulls the big trawl net back to the surface. The ship is brought round so the wind blows onto her starboard side and she drifts away from the net and does not drift over the top of it. The yells of the men as the trawl doors, which weigh over a ton each, come up from the deep and crash and bang hard against the side of the ship, then as they clear the side they shudder as they reach the top of the gallows. They then swing and bang until the seamen get chains round them to secure them. Then the foot rope, with its spherical bobbins and rollers, clatters over the side and onto the deck. The head rope, with its floats, follows and then the rest of the trawl is hauled up and heaved over the side. The cod end floats to the surface with the air in the fish and bobs about in the sea as the gulls scream and descend onto it fighting and shrieking to tear bits of fish from the net. The mate calls for the cod end to be lifted by the derrick and swung over the deck. He ducks beneath the bulging net as the water rushes out of it and he releases the cod end knot at the end of the net which stops the fish going straight through the whole net. Fish are sticking out of every mesh. The mate grapples with the cod end knot, then with a 'whoosh', the catch empties in a slithering, silvery rush into the wooden pounds accompanied perhaps by a cheer from the men if it is a good haul.

All the while, the skipper is watching from the open wheelhouse window, eyes everywhere, to spot any danger for his crew such as a stray wire getting caught up, or a big sea rolling the ship as the crew manhandle the net over the side of the ship. He is also, of course, assessing the success or failure of the haul. Not that you would ever tell from his face. It seems to remain totally impassive regardless of the haul. The skippers know that one good haul does not guarantee another. The cod end knot is retied and the net checked for any tears, then it is manhandled back over the starboard side and shot away. The trawler then takes up another tow for three or four hours while the crew set to work and begin gutting the catch.

The fishing goes on twenty-four hours a day as long as the trawler is on the grounds. The crew carries on working regardless of the weather and the time as long as there are fish to be gutted. A series of good hauls can mean that the whole crew is on deck gutting and packing for anything up to eighteen or twenty hours at a stretch. Getting the fish below and packed on ice is all that matters.

Today is my first Sunday at sea. It is just the same as any other day, no special Sunday Service or a day off for the crew. Fishing goes on round the clock seven days a week, summer or winter, Easter or Christmas. What shore factory worker would work seven days a week for twenty-one days for just one and a half days off, all the year round? To make Sundays special at sea there is a normally a special menu on the trawlers.

The food is, so far, very good. It is also very important as it is on any ship. Food is what the crew look forward to when they are stuck out on a freezing deck gutting ice-cold wet fish for hours on end, so it has to be as good as the cook can make it with the supplies he is given. A typical day's menu might be porridge, cereals, eggs, bacon, and bread for breakfast with pots of tea. Dinner (not lunch) would be soup, a roast or sausages, or fish with vegetables, Yorkshire puddings and cake or apple pie and custard. tea could be chops and tea cakes.

While there is still fresh meat then roasts are often the main meal. It varies according to what the weather will allow the cook to make and what is left that can be eaten. The meals are at set times. Breakfast is seven to eight, dinner at twelve noon and tea at six o'clock. There are two sittings during each time of half an hour each.

On Sundays, however, breakfast is the same, bacon, eggs, beans, fried bread and fried potatoes. Lunch is a full roast dinner of roast pork, stuffing, or beef with Yorkshire puddings, carrots, peas or cabbage and a steamed duff and custard for pudding. Sunday tea is normally ham and eggs with tinned fruit salad as a pudding. For most of the crew, Sunday lunch and tea is what they look forward to all week and as in all ships a good cook and good food are essential for good crew morale. Christmas is of course a bit more homely. The company puts on board Christmas puddings and turkeys as well as extra bonded stores and liquor. Trips are normally arranged so that the ship is either steaming for home or steaming off to the grounds or in port but a large number of trawlers are always on the grounds over the Christmas period.

'Big Dave', the cook, had originally gone to sea on oil tankers and had been trained as a cook in the BP Tanker Co. so was well used to time at sea, but mostly in 50,000-ton tankers rather than 700-ton Arctic trawlers. He admitted that there was a bit of a difference between the Persian Gulf and the fishing grounds off Iceland. While life on board the tankers was good and the ships were comfortable, he found that he was away from home for too long, so he left. Tankers could be at sea for months at a time as they were often diverted mid-voyage to other ports, having set off from the Gulf bound for the UK. After he left the tankers, he did a couple of trips on timber ships that brought timber to Europe from Siberia. He told me some of his tales from those trips, of the huge Russian rivers, the poverty of Siberia and of the friendliness of the people. He explained that in summer, when the ice has receded, the timber ships steam along the north coast of Russia, along the north-east Passage, and up the big rivers of the Ob and Yenisei to load timber deep in Siberia. They can only do it in summer as the sea is frozen solid for the rest of the year, but even so the Russian icebreakers are available in case the ice closes in and the ships get stuck. A change of wind in the early part of the season can bring the ice pack back onto the coast very quickly and ships can get caught out. These sounded like fantastic trips. Eventually though, as he was a Yorkshire boy, he found that the three weeks away on the Hull trawlers was as good a deal as he was going to get so he stuck with it.

Big Dave's domain is the galley, which is situated towards the after end of the accommodation area. It is small, only eight feet by eight feet and no room for more than one person to work in it at a time; especially when Dave was trying to serve up a meal. When Dave has a full meal on the go it is as hot as the boiler room. There is no airconditioning here, just one small scuttle. The cooker is a large, black, oil-fired range, which appears to be virtually uncontrollable. Nothing that Dave does to the regulators seems to make any difference. The range has two ovens and hot plates on the top with a grid of large steel 'fiddles' over it. These 'fiddles' are movable bars that the cook can use to try and secure pots on the range in bad weather and stop them sliding right off. Dave tries to make fresh bread rolls at sea whenever he can. All the dough has to be hand-kneaded in bowls while he is kneeling on the food-store deck. The food store adjoins the galley at the after end and is slightly cooler than the galley itself. He kneels on the floor to do it as there are no worktops. The bread then has to be cooked with the oven door left slightly open, otherwise it is burned to a cinder on the outside and raw dough inside. When there are strong winds they can blow out the range fires or a sudden gust can blow back down the stove pipe which causes mayhem as the pans and hot plates are sent flying off across the galley. Every evening, when he has finished clearing up after the last meal, Dave cleans the galley deck. He does this by simply boiling a large bucket of water and, while it is still boiling, throws it across the deck and under the range. He then scrubs every inch he can and hopes that the boiling water has killed off anything nasty under the range and in the darker corners. The galley boy, Dave, whose main jobs seem to be washing up and peeling potatoes, has to squat on an upturned bucket and peel the potatoes by hand; either out on deck if it is fine or in the passage outside the galley as there is no room to do it in the galley itself. Dave reckons that he loses about 2 stone a trip because of the heat in the galley combined with the fact that he says he never feels like eating the food he has prepared. Although to me the food was good, Dave says it is poor quality when compared with the food he had been used to on the tankers. He ditched all the cabbages on day three of this trip as they were bad when they were put on board.

The crew eats their meals in the crew mess, a bare, square room immediately forward of the galley. There is a slatted wooden bench that runs round all four sides. A large, fiddled table fills the rest of the space. A tiny hatch opens through to the galley for the food to be passed through. There are no pictures on the bulkheads and just one small scuttle. The crew rarely spends much time here apart from eating their meals or having a tea break when fishing. There is always a huge pot of tea on the table and often some bread or biscuits left out by the cook.

The one thing that I cannot get used to on board is the tinned milk. The crew all seem to like it and pour loads into their big china pots of tea. I find that it has a strong taste that ruins the tea, so I drink black tea. Now, years later, just the smell of tinned milk takes me back to *Lord Lovat*.

Today, the skipper sends me down into the fish room to see what goes on down there. Here the fish are packed and stored after they have been caught, gutted and cleaned. The fish room occupies about one third of the total length of the ship and stretches right across the total breadth. When a fish has been gutted it is thrown up into the washer on the deck. This large tank is open at one end and a grill chute leads from there down to the fish room hatch. Sea water is continually pouring into the washer from a hose and as the ship rolls and pitches so the fish are washed in the tank, then they roll onto the chute, the water drains off through the grills and the fish fall into the fish room. Working in the fish room is considered to be one of the best jobs, especially in winter as it is considerably warmer there than being out on deck.

When the ship leaves on a trip the fish room is filled with crushed ice from the ice factory. The fish room is arranged into pounds by fixed vertical posts and each pound can be made up at sea to form a number of shelves, each deep enough to carry a layer of fish and ice. Prime fish, such as cod, haddock and halibut, is laid on a layer of ice and a further layer of ice is put on top of the fish, then the next shelf is set up above that and so on. The lower-quality fish, such as red fish, are packed into the pounds without shelves. These are always sold off last and often go straight to the pet food factory or the fish-meal factory.

Two of the crew are given the job of stowing the catch. Charlie and Roy, who work for the mate, are responsible for the proper stowage and condition of the catch. As I climb down the ladder into the fish room I am given an axe by Roy and told to start smashing the ice that, although it came aboard in flakes, soon freezes into a solid mass. It takes hard work with a felling axe to break it back down to flakes that can be used on the shelves. The process of breaking ice for flakes also creates room for the next row of fish shelves to be set up and so it goes on until the hold is filled. Charlie and Roy are friendly guys and are happy for me to wield the axe while they stow the fish. It is clear that stowing the fish is not that easy as the layers of ice below and above the fish have to be of a certain depth for maximum preservation without crushing the fish or wasting too much space by having the ice too deep. All the time they were under pressure to keep up with the flow of fish coming down from the washer. They also have to check that the fish are properly cleaned as if the guts are accidentally left in the fish it will rot and cause fish nearby to rot too.

Most of the crewmen seem to have been given nicknames that are less than flattering. One spare hand called Wally was known as 'Soft Wally'. The deckie learner, yet another Dave, was known as 'Daft Maggot' as he was a tubby lad and not the brightest. Dave the galley boy was called 'Midget' due to his lack of height.

In spite of his small size he stood up for himself well amongst the rest of the crew. galley boys and deckie learners are prime targets for practical jokes on board and some jokes can take things a bit far. Dave the galley boy told me a story against himself when he was on his second trip the previous summer; they had gone into Akyureyri on the north coast of Iceland for repairs. It was a glorious sunny day, with sparkling, clear, blue waters. It was pretty hot for Iceland and the crew was all on deck enjoying the sunshine. They kidded Dave that he should go for a swim as the water looked really blue and inviting. He was reluctant but after some strong egging on and challenges about being a softy, he did. He dived off the ship into the harbour and by his own admission came straight back up out of the water like a torpedo. The water temperature would have been just above freezing.

On a sad note, the deckie learner, Dave, lost his life a few months later when the Hamling's-owned stern trawler *St Finbarr* was lost after an explosion and major fire off the Grand Banks on Christmas Day. A total of twelve men died that day, either due to the fire and fumes or through falling into the sea as they were being rescued. Thirteen were rescued by the stern trawler *Orsino*, which was fishing nearby and saw the flames.

After a few days on the Bill Bailey, Working Man and Hari Kari grounds we steam to Kidney Bank. There is a BBC gale warning for south-east Iceland; we could be in for more bad weather. It is the Ebor Handicap at York today and a number of the crew place bets. This is done by a telegram to their bookies at home. However, no one won any money. Like a certainty of the winners at the races, the forecast gale does not materialise either but we did have a few showers of rain.

It is an interesting day for fishing. A haul of forty baskets is deemed not too good by the skipper. He then challenges the bosun to do better and goes to his day cabin for some sleep while the bosun takes the ship on the next trawl. The bosun catches eighty baskets on his haul, much to his joy and the crew's amusement. When the skipper comes up he sets off to show that he can get a good haul too. He manages only forty baskets. He stomps off below again and leaves the mate to have a go and with orders to make sure he betters the bosun's haul. The mate then caught 120 baskets, nearly three full bags, much to everyone's amusement except the skipper's and the bosun's. It is the best haul of the trip. Three bags means that there is so much fish in the cod end that it cannot be hauled inboard in one go. With the mouth of the net safely on board, the rest of the net is left in the water full of fish; the cod end is roped off from the rest of the net then it is raised out and emptied. The cod end knot is retied then put back in the water and half of the remaining fish are brought into the cod end by hauling in on the net and the cod end filled again. This is repeated until the whole catch is emptied. Hence, three bags means three full cod ends. That night I am called out of the radio room by the mate to see the *Ross Cleveland*, which we are passing close by. She has stopped and is hauling her net on board about forty yards off our starboard beam. The crews stop working and wave to their pals on the other ship. The *Ross Cleveland* was lost with all hands, except one, in Isafjord, north-west Iceland, on 4 February 1968 after being overcome by ice in a storm and turning turtle.

The good weather continues through the trip and we are now taking this good weather for granted, with clear blue skies, calm seas and gulls around the ship. The fishing, however, is varied and we move from ground to ground in search of the 'Fish Shops' that can make a really good trip.

In the evenings I often sit in the radio room with George as I try to understand the system of 'Skeds' or 'Scheduled Broadcasts' to other trawlers and the office. George has spent most of his life on the trawlers. He explains patiently how the trawlers send their messages to the owners in Hull. If the ship is north of Wick then the ship sends a Morse message direct to Wick Radio Station in the north of Scotland. Wick then send a 'wire', a form of telegram, to the owners. If the ship is south of Wick then it uses coastal radio stations at Stonehaven, Cullercoats or Humber Radio Station.

On the grounds, one of the trawlers in the company is nominated as the 'Control Ship. It is their sparks' responsibility to contact all the company ships on the grounds and collate a 'sked' twice a day telling the company that all the trawlers are OK and where they are, what they are doing, i.e. fishing, steaming, moving grounds, dodging bad weather, etc. This is done for all the side-winders at Iceland. The trawlers at Greenland or on the Grand Banks have their own control ship and their messages are sent via Halifax, Nova Scotia or Portishead if they are in the Atlantic. The freezer trawlers have their own sked systems. Portishead Radio Station is also used by the vessels at Greenland as it is more powerful than Wick. However, Portishead is also the 'Empire Radio Station' and handles radio traffic from ships all over the Empire so it is busier and costs more.

One evening, we are sitting chatting in the radio room and George is listening to various Morse messages that are being transmitted by Wick Radio when the bosun who was on watch calls for us to go out to see a sunset. The sun slowly sinks into the sea leaving a black sea, a warm red sky and high clouds tinged with pink against a blue sky. The sunset lingers for hours, not finally fading until after midnight. During that time we watch the *Notts Forest*, a Grimsby trawler, come up over the horizon from the south, pass us and vanish away to the north. It was a very calm, peaceful night, and the Atlantic rolls gently by. The many hundreds of stars reminded me that it was across these same waters that Eric the Red led the Vikings across the Atlantic using the same stars to set up the Iceland and later the Greenland, settlements.

The trawl deck is a dangerous place and one that the skipper would only let me onto when he deemed it was safe. The heavy steel wires, or trawl warps, that hold the net are under fantastic tension when we are fishing. If the net snags on an underwater obstacle, which happens fairly often then these warps can snap. When that happens they flick back across the deck at lightning speed as the huge tensions are released. Anyone in their way has no time to escape and men have been cut in half before they even know what is happening. Sometimes a snapped warp or wire will flick and catch a man's overall or waterproof and carry him over the side. When hauling and shooting the deck is dangerous as a number of heavy wires are being let out, or held fast, as the gear is released and set. As the ship rolls across the wind and sea to allow the men to haul the net up to the ship's side, the sea can pull the net back into the sea and if hands get caught in the net then their owner will follow them over the side. There are numerous stories of trawlermen who have been washed over the side by one wave and washed back on board and dumped unceremoniously on the deck by the next wave. There are, unfortunately, stories of those who were washed over and did not get back. However, being injured by the equipment itself is the main danger. The gallows with the huge trawl doors which have to be handled during hauling and shooting, and with the main trawl warp running through them, is a favourite place to lose a finger or hand as the ton of solid timber and steel bangs up against the steel gallows inches from thick steel wire warps under tension. When the crew are gutting, the deck is lethally slippery with fish scales, offal and seawater. The crew use razor sharp knives to gut the fish and then throw the fish up into the washer. A slip here, a trip there, a rogue wave washing aboard and you can easily find yourself being gutted. The deep-sea trawling industry has always been the most dangerous occupation, way ahead of coal mining, in terms of injuries and deaths on the job. This is something that has never been recognized in the price of fish.

Helping the Sparks take the baskets of cod livers down aft to the boilers, or helping chop ice down below was about as much as a pleasurer was allowed to do. It was certainly not a place to ask the crew to stop gutting and show me how to do it. They wanted to get it done as soon as possible and get back to their bunks.

Lord Lovat off Iceland in 1970, seen from HMS *Keppel* as she slowly trawls downwind.

Lord Lovat in the swell on a winter's day off Iceland.

We have been at sea for over twelve days now and the morning finds us towing towards the north with Iceland away on the port beam. The ragged, blue snow-topped mountains lie along the horizon. The ship is in a happy mood because of the good weather and reasonable catches.

One quiet, sunny afternoon, we are towing along and Big Dave and I were sitting in the crew mess having a pot of tea. The watch on deck is replacing a net belly after the last haul as the belly of the net was torn. It has to be replaced before the net can shot again and then the old belly is repaired. Dave is telling me about both the poor quality and small quantities of food that are put on board. Trawlers did not have deep freezers on board in those days so it was either fresh or tinned food, after the fresh ran out. He says there were only ten OXO cubes to cover twenty-one men for twenty-one days; only four tins of custard powder. By now, we have run out of potatoes, peas, carrots, and custard. There is some meat left but not enough to see us home and we are very low on flour for bread. Big Dave had ditched all the cabbages after three days and now after twelve we have run out of potatoes. We will probably be away for at least another eight days. How can we have run out of a basic item like potatoes? This is alarming! However, it is the lack of custard powder that concerns me most. All that is left are a few poor joints of meat, tinned steak and, of course, fish. I asked Dave if there is any chance the skipper would go into Iceland for more food and he replies without hesitation 'No chance, but they might sack me at the end'. He tells me that Hellyers has a reputation for poor food and that no fresh fruit is ever put on board except on Christmas trips. He also tells me that he has been sacked four times from trawlers for running out of food. Is that a good thing to know I wonder?

Some of the crew wander in and sit down for a pot of tea. Colin, the Spare Hand, who had been farming and is the vocal one amongst the crew, rolls himself a ciggy and starts to quiz me as to why I am there. 'What does a posh southerner like you want to be doing on this rust bucket?' This is a logical question, but one that I suddenly find very difficult to answer. Saying 'because I wanted to see what it was like' seemed very weak. I burble about always having liked trawlers and wanting to go to the Arctic. They stare at me incomprehensively. To them there has never been any thought as to going to sea in trawlers. It is the world in which they have been brought up. It was expected of them and it is what they expected to do. Equally, they cannot comprehend someone from such a different environment and background even wanting to see what it is like. They have probably never given any thought to seeing the Arctic as a romantic, faraway place of famous explorers or of getting excited by the look of trawler's fine lines. To them it is just a job and, apart from the money, not a very good one. Why would anyone from outside the industry ever want to spend three weeks on a trawler unless they were totally mad? I am sure that this is what they think but they are decent enough not to actually say it. They change tack and ask about my school, home and whether or not I have a girlfriend. Why did I want to leave her for three weeks to come here? I could see their point. Maybe I am mad?

I keep occupied by doing odd jobs about the ship such as painting the steering box in the wheelhouse as it was badly scratched and looked scruffy against the big, varnished, wooden-spoked wheel. I polish all the bridge brass work again, which has become my main role on board. I also try and help out a bit in the galley, with Big Dave.

We are now drawing near to the end of the trip. Colin calls me aside on deck and says 'You spend a lot of time in the wheelhouse, has the skipper said anything about heading for home yet?' 'No, not a word'. Most of the crew recognise when the end of a trip is approaching by the amount of fish we are catching and a good estimate of the ships endurance. No one says anything and the skipper certainly never gives a clue to anyone. He keeps all his options open until the very end. If for example his last haul is a bumper one he may stay and fish out the 'Fish Shop' before setting off. However, I did hear the skipper and the mate, discussing which market they thought they should aim at. This is the critical issue, as to land on the same day as a lot of other trawlers means low fish prices on the market while to be the only ship landing can lead to bumper prices, especially near the weekend. Again, guesswork and intelligence combine to give a best guess. Which ships sailed in the days before us and where they are fishing; what time is high water in Hull and what day of the week will our catch be marketed? These are factors that all go into the intelligence pot. Today is Saturday and they were discussing Thursday or Friday markets. To catch Friday's market would mean docking on the Thursday morning tide as the evening tide would not give the bobbers enough time to land the catch.

The next afternoon we are towing peacefully along. Fat Dave is on watch, the skipper is turned in and most of the crew are below as the last haul has all been gutted. The cricket test match is playing on the radio in the radio room. Suddenly,

Lord Lovat from the fo'c'sle.

the ship gives a jolt. 'We have come fast!' calls Dave. 'Go and tell the skipper.' I turn and jump towards the ladder down to his cabin, but by the time I get to the top of the ladder, the skipper is already halfway up it. 'Stop Engines, Hard a starboard', he yells. 'Already there, Skipper', calls Dave. 'Knock out the warps!' yells the skipper into the intercom down to the crew's mess as the watch on deck emerge from the mess after feeling the jolt. The ship stops with the warps pointing straight out to starboard. 'Release the winch brakes', the skipper yells out of the window as the bosun runs forward. Slowly the ship eases round on to her track and then gently retraces them. The term 'Coming Fast' means that the net has snagged on an underwater object. It could be a protruding rock or a piece of wreckage. It could certainly destroy the whole net as well as lose whatever catch is in it. In bad weather, coming fast can endanger the whole ship if the net is either not cut away from the ship quickly or the ship can release the net herself. This is always the preferred action but it is not always possible. The cost of losing a complete net, trawl warps and the doors is very high and one that would need a lot of explaining back in the office. The plan is to slowly turn the ship round then tow the net backwards off the fastening, or obstruction, from the direction she towed onto it. This will certainly result in losing all of the fish already in the net but, hopefully will prevent further tearing of the net. Most of the time, it works. The loss of one haul is small compared to the cost of a complete net and ground gear. On this occasion we are lucky. The weather is calm and the net has not got itself too entangled with the obstruction. The net is hauled back in. Luckily it is not too badly damaged and the crew get it repaired and back in the water in a short time. The skipper heaves a big sigh of relief then spends some time studying the charts and marking the position of the fastening so he can avoid it next time. Then he leaves the mate to it and goes back down to finish his sleep.

A couple of days later, we are enjoying a fine and sunny morning after a good breakfast of eggs and bacon and the ship is towing along in a calm blue sea. The crew is now getting restless to know when we might stop fishing and head for home and the tension is beginning to mount. They are certain that the skipper has made up his mind but just won't tell them. As the pleasurer, I am quizzed almost hourly as to what the skipper might have said. They do not seem to believe me when I say he has told me nothing. The rumour is that we will be heading for home tonight. At about seven o'clock that evening I am in the wheelhouse with the skipper and we have just had a good haul of sixty baskets. He turns to me and says with a smile on his face 'Should we have one more tow?' 'You are the skipper, but why not, one more for luck?' I reply. He nods, still smiling. At half past ten that night we haul in a catch of fifty baskets and the skipper seems satisfied. The skipper leans out of the bridge window and yells down 'Take in the Doors.' A cheer goes up, as that is the sign that we have now finished fishing and heading for home. The big trawl boards are hoisted inboard and secured and the nets are stowed against the bulwark. The last catch of the trip is being gutted as the telegraph rings down 'Full Ahead' and we set off on a course of south-south-east. The ship gently vibrates as the propeller bites into the cold Atlantic and starts to push us towards home at full power. We do not have a full hold but the skipper has worked out that, if we catch the right market, the catch we have might fetch a good price. A holiday atmosphere descends. We have been at sea for fifteen days and now are heading for home. I spend the late evening in the wheelhouse watching the sea slide by. The skipper has turned in and begins to try and catch up on his many hours of lost sleep.

I wake at seven the next morning. It seems quiet with no winch noises or calls of the watch on deck gutting. I hear the sound of the sea rushing past as the ship rolls along, the cabin and bunk are gently vibrating and far away I can hear the deep throb of the engines. As I go up into the wheelhouse I look out and see that the south-eastern horizon ahead is dominated by a wall of rocky cliffs capped by dark mountains and cloud. 'Faeroes', said Roy who is on watch, 'They are about 60 miles away.' What a fantastic sight they are. The apparent closeness is caused by an optical illusion often seen in the Arctic that allows you to see objects much further away than you can at lower latitudes. I watch these towering cliffs through the binoculars. It is not possible to see the foot of the cliffs but the cracks and gullies on the cliff faces are plainly visible.

After breakfast, the crew begins to break down and stow the nets. The bobbins and head ropes are detached. The washer is taken down and stowed. The sun breaks through and it turns into a fine sunny day, even so the clouds hang low over the giant cliffs of the Faeroes all day and make it seem a forbidding and dangerous place. This is not an area to be caught without power on a lee shore!

A Hull trawler fishing off Iceland, winter 1970, with ice forming on deck. Believed to be
St Gerontius owned by T. Hamlings.

The cliffs are about 1,000-feet high and drop vertically down into the sea. There is no sign of any habitation and no sign of any form of shore, just sheer cliffs straight down into the Atlantic.

At about four o'clock we pass the *Kingston Sapphire*, outward bound for Iceland. She is also owned by Hellyers and we all cheer each other from the bridge. The noise brings others up from below.

By evening, the Faeroes are dropping astern and cloud still tops the mountains but the cliffs are now looking a little softer as they glow a deep red colour in the evening sun. A long north-east swell is running and seems to be giving the *Lord Lovat* an extra shove for home with each wave that rolls under her. I take the helm for an hour or so. I had had a couple of goes on the way up to Iceland but not with the stern sea. It is tricky getting the hang of it with the quartering sea lifting and turning the ship in spite of my efforts to keep her straight and not to 'Chase the lubber line'. This is easily done when you are a novice and you try and steer the compass point towards the ship rather than the ship towards the compass point. I struggle and at one point Roy calls out 'Bloody hell, Gordon will have us back at Iceland next.' 'Go the other way.' I get the hang of it after a bit more practice. Several kittiwakes sit motionless on the whaleback watching the seas go by. Others hang motionless in the air alongside the bridge, letting the wind off the ship give them all the lift they need. It is very unusual for birds to sit on ships for long periods of time as they can and do get seasick.

By now, the food situation has got worse and fish has become the main food item. A few people are starting to moan. Today we have fish again but without chips, as the potatoes have all gone. We had a stew yesterday that Big Dave concocted from whatever tins he could find in the cupboards. The flour has all gone too so there will be no more fresh bread.

In spite of this, the work continues. The mate supervises everyone, including me, to get the ship tidied up and scrubbed clean for docking. Drums of detergent are brought up from the stores and we all set to scrubbing the passageways and bathrooms, clearing out old newspapers from the mess so that the ship will be as clean and tidy as possible.

As it had been foggy on the way out I want to see the Pentland Firth on the way home so I get up at three in the morning to see it. On the starboard side we can see the street lights of Thurso as we get into the Firth. The skipper points out the various lights of Stroma, Dunnet, and Hoy, etc. Dunnet Head light, with its whitewashed cottages, looks very peaceful and clean. A small cargo ship looms up coming towards us. We can hear her engines throbbing as she heads out into the Atlantic but we can see no sign of life on board.

Dawn is breaking as we round the sheer cliffs of Duncansby Head and come back into the North Sea. We feel as if we are almost home! I see the trawler that George had told me about, the one that had been washed ashore on Stroma, which I missed seeing on the way out. It is just a rusty hull now but clearly a trawler sitting high and dry on the flat rocks. As we sail down the Scottish coast, past Kinnaird Head, Rattray Head, Fraserburgh, and Aberdeen, the work goes on of cleaning and stowing everything and getting the decks and storage racks properly squared away and making the ship spotless for entering port. All the bathrooms and heads are scrubbed out and the smell of industrial strength detergent fills the ship. I ask if the ships are ever checked when we get in and am told yes as one of the managers from the office always goes round them and if they were not properly clean the mate gets it in the neck.

That evening we find ourselves looking at about forty radar contacts dead ahead. This turns out to be a large German fishing fleet moving north. It is a very impressive sight. The Germans are regarded as good professionals in the deep-sea trawling game. Their new big freezer trawlers are bigger and, so the crew tells me, better equipped with better accommodation and better run than ours. Later that night we see the red looms of the lights of Newcastle and Sunderland over the western horizon. I wonder what people in those places are doing as we steam down the coast. Is anyone watching our lights and wondering what ship we are? I somehow doubt it. At sea you are out of sight and out of mind for those ashore.

Today is the last morning at sea. I awake early and see Spurn Point Light out of the porthole. We are almost home and about to enter the river Humber. The water is mud brown from the Estuary and flat calm as *Lord Lovat* turns into the Humber past Spurn Head Lighthouse and we slide up the wide, brown river. A light summer haze lies along the fields and it seems strange to see hedges and fields again as I watch a small brown van driving along a lane by the water. The sun shines brightly as we pass Grimsby and Immingham and finally we sail by the city of Hull itself. The light mist on the land lifts to leave a fine morning and the spires of the city are standing proud of the rest of this maritime city and its history. How many ship's crews over the centuries have returned from the Arctic to see this scene? I think of all the whalers and the trawlermen that had sailed up this river at the end of long and punishing trips to the Arctic and looked at this scene. It feels good to be back again.

We drop anchor at Killingholm in No. 1 anchorage to wait for high tide, which is due at quarter past ten. We will be the first trawler to dock. An hour later, the *Portia*, a new diesel-electric powered trawler and also owned by Hellyers, arrives and drops her anchor astern of us. I say thank you to the skipper and George, and thank the skipper for the use of his bunk. He smiles and says it has been fine on the couch. He tells me to jump ashore with the crew at the dock Head and to get on my way. After packing my few belongings I go back on deck. As the *Lord Lovat* heaves in her anchor and steams slowly towards the lock head the rest of the crew start to emerge on deck carrying their bags but I do not recognise any of them. They have all spent the morning showering, shaving and cleaning. They have changed into their smart, going-ashore suits and shining, winkle-picker shoes, and have washed and combed their hair for the first time all trip. The strong scent of after shave lotions envelops the deck. They are all chattering excitedly about going ashore and being home again; even though in two days time they will be sailing again.

The author on board *Lord Lovat*, dressed up in his 'going ashore rig' just before we docked.

At 10.30 a.m. we come alongside the pier by the dock Head. The Customs man jumps aboard. Colin shouts across the deck to him 'Watch him, mate, he's a Pleasurer and has thousands of fags in 'is bag.' The crew laugh. The Customs man looks at me, then smiles, seeing the joke. ''Ave a good trip, lad?' 'Anything else to declare, lad, other than the fags?' 'No.' 'OK, off you go.' With that I jump ashore with the others as the tug comes out of the dock and makes fast to the stern of *Lord Lovat*. The only ones left on board are those needed to help get the ship towed into the dock and up to the berth on the Market. I stand on the quayside watching as *Lord Lovat* is towed stern first through the lock and up the St Andrews Fish Dock to her berth on the market. I watch her until she disappears behind the gantry of the road bridge and the other trawlers in the dock and feel a little sad that it is now all over.

The catch will be unloaded by the bobbers during the night so it will be fresh and ready for the market which opens at seven o'clock in the morning. The crew will come down to the office at about ten o'clock to collect their pay, which depends totally on the value of the catch. Crew pay is calculated on a sliding scale applied to the whole crew from the skipper down to the deckie learner and the galley boy. As a pleasurer I was not due to get anything.

Big Dave is chatting with his taxi driver. Every trawlererman seems to have his own taxi driver who automatically comes to the dock to meet him and take him home. Big Dave gives me a lift in his taxi. He drops me off at the Mission before heading for his home up on the Yorkshire coast.

The next day I go down onto the dock and see a few of the crew by the office. They have got their 'Settlings'. Not a bad trip, but not the best, seemed to be their verdict. I say my final farewells to them as they then head off to the Subway Club on Subway Street for a few beers. I walk on up the dock looking at the trawlers getting ready to sail and reflect on the trip. It has been an eye-opener to life at sea. Whatever I do I cannot really see myself becoming a trawlerman. That, I think, is something that you are born to and is not really a career choice. In spite of that my fascination for Arctic trawlers and the life they entail is deeper than ever. I have found enough in what I have seen and learnt to know that I certainly want to do something connected with the sea and ships. Time alone will tell me what. The memories of this trip will stay with me and will never be forgotten.

I reach the end of the dock. *Lord Lovat* is still berthed on the market quay. Now everyone has gone, the fish has been landed and sold and she lies on the berth, forgotten, silent, empty and dead. However, later today she will be towed down the dock where she will be refueled, fresh ice will be loaded, new and replacement nets will be put aboard, and fresh food stores stowed. Then tomorrow night the crew will return, her boilers will be fired up, generators will hum into life, lights will go on and she will come back to life. At high tide she will sail north for the Arctic again. I wonder whether I will ever return to Hull Fish Dock and the world that revolves around it. I take a last look at *Lord Lovat*, listen to the bustle of the dock then turn and head for Hull Station. In fact, I was to return to Fish Dock and work for Hellyer Bros. But that is another story.

CHAPTER 2

MV *Silvana*,
Baltic Timber Ship – 1967

I am hot and thirsty and beginning to wonder if it is all worth it. The heat radiates up from the old rusty railway lines that stretch away disappearing in the far distance in a shimmering haze. I struggle across the weed strewn, derelict sidings with my bag. It is a hot, humid and thundery summer's day in London's Docklands. The air is still and the pink London haze acts like a lid keeping the hot air locked over the city. I am trying to find Silvertown Wharf on the Thames and it seems like hours since I came out of the railway station and started walking towards the river. I did ask a few people back at the station if they knew the way but they could not tell me and could only wave their arms across a high fence and past railway yards in the general direction of the river. The emptiness at the other side of the railway yards told me that the river must be in that direction but there was no obvious road or path to it.

The ship is due to sail this evening and I am anxious to reach it and not waste time walking all round the main roads to see if there was a proper road entrance to the wharf; so I set off in a straight line, down a side streets and across a couple of long, railway footbridges that seemed to lead me in the rough direction of the river. At the end of the path I think I can see the river but the fence stops me carrying on. Then, I spot a small hole in the fence and clamber through it onto wasteland that appears to extend to the river. By now, I am sweating heavily as I finally scramble across some more derelict railway sidings and find myself on a deserted wharf at the riverside. This should be Silvertown Wharf, or somewhere close to it, but there are no ships in sight. The swirling, muddy-brown river Thames washes past the empty quay. I must be in the wrong place, where do I go now? Should I go back and start again? I cannot decide whether to go up or downstream from here and if so will it lead me anywhere? A trickle of sweat runs down my collar. Either I am in the wrong place or the ship has already sailed! The man who had arranged the trip had said on the phone that the ship would not sail until tonight but he did not specify a time. I am about to give up, and go back the way I have come, when I spot what looks like the yellow ochre mast tops just protruding above the quay edge round the bend, about half a mile downstream. The tide is low and the mast tops are all that is visible of whatever ship is there. I pick up my bag and start off again towards the masts. As I get closer, I can see that there is a small coaster snuggly berthed against the wharf. I round the corner and can read the name on her stern. It is *Silvana*. This is her. I have found her.

I look down onto the deck; it is deserted. Maybe they have all gone ashore and I have missed them? Someone must be on board. I climb down a long, builder's ladder that is being used instead of a gangway and get on board. I walk aft to the accommodation and put my head into an open door on the port side of the superstructure and call out 'Hello!' 'Hello, Hello, come in', comes the reply in accented English. A round, smiling, ruddy face appears out of a door on my left. 'I am ze Captain and you must be Mr Gordon, Yah?' He is a very friendly, rotund German with a shiny, bald head and he obviously speaks good English. The *Silvana* is a German ship registered in Hamburg and the captain and crew are all German. The Captain, whose name I later learn is Bruno, is also a part owner of the ship. He invites me into his homely and comfortable dayroom, which reeks of cigar smoke and offers me a Willem II cigar and a beer. I decline the cigar but accept the beer gratefully. He is puffing away on his Willem II cigar. I am to become very familiar with its smell over the next couple of weeks. Somewhere below in the ship Diana Ross is singing 'Hey life, look at me' on a record player. 'Now please tell me why you want to come with us? The office said you were a schoolboy who wanted to see a timber ship. Is that right?' I explain about my love of ships and interest in timber ships and keenness to see foreign parts. After a while and much puffing of his Willem II he sighs then says, 'Yah, we will take you but you must pay for your food and cabin'. A shudder runs through me and I think of my small supply of traveler's cheques and hope he is not about to charge me cruise ship prices. He doesn't and quotes me a nominal amount of £5 a day, well within my budget. I relax and sit back now that everything is settled and I am on my way. 'We have finished ze unloading and now we must wait for ze tide to rise and for ze pilot to come: zen we go. We will be going to Falkenberg in Sweden for a cargo of sawn softwood timber and returning wiz it here to London,' he tells me. 'So you find your cabin and we will talk later.' He stands up and calls someone's name out of the cabin door.

This is all very different from Hull Fish Dock. What was it that attracted me to a small coaster sitting in the Thames? During the trip in the *Lord Lovat*, Dave the cook had told me of the times in the 1950s when he had sailed on timber ships to the north of Russia and up the big rivers that flow out from Siberia into the Arctic Ocean. The idea fascinated me and I explored it as far as I could. However, it became clear that a trip to Russia was out of the question, but in the process I did find a way to go to the Baltic and this was it.

Silvana is a smart 1,200-ton coaster. She has a black hull with a white superstructure and deep ochre masts and derricks. She has a well deck and hold at the forward end and one main hold along the rest of the deck. Aft, she has a two-deck superstructure. On the main deck is the galley, mess room and the skipper's accommodation, which consists of a day room and a night cabin. Above that is the bridge deck and radio room.

After the rigours of life on board the *Lord Lovat* a trip on a modern coaster up to the Baltic should be a cruise by comparison. Judging by the homeliness, the family photos and personal ornaments in the captain's dayroom then this is a cruise ship. However, timber ships do have a poor reputation for capsizing as the sawn timber is loaded high on the deck, creating a lot of windage.

My bunk is in a two-berth cabin on the port side aft and the seaman who has shown me down points at the upper bunk, nods and leaves me to it. Although he is friendly enough, the seaman does not speak any English and my German is non-existent. I can see this may be a quieter voyage than I had imagined. In the lower bunk there is a large hump of the back of a body. I assume it is just sleeping but dare not prod it to find out. I learned later that it is one of the engineers but I cannot recall ever seeing him awake. He was either asleep in the bunk or the bunk was empty. The cabin is clean, tidy and airy. It has a carpet, a two-seat settee, two scuttles, wardrobes and drawers. The bunks even had curtains. It seems very posh and bigger than the cook's six-man cabin in *Lord Lovat*. I put my bag on my top bunk, claiming it as my own and go back out on deck and exchange nodded greetings with some of the crew who are leaning on the rail watching the Thames slide by. Apart from the captain, no one seems to speak English. One of the crew, a tall, fair-haired guy probably a bit older than me, is trying to put the last of the wooden hatch covers on so I help him until there is a yell from aft. It is the call for tea and the Germans stop work instantly. In my excitement to find the ship I had forgotten about food, the thought of sandwiches or even biscuits makes me realise that I have not had anything since I left home this morning. When I reach the mess I meet the smell of boiled cabbage. I find that tea consists of a large plate of cold, mashed potatoes, some raw tomatoes, and a few slices of hard German rye bread. The cabbage must have been there for lunch! There is also a big pot of coffee. My heart sinks. Oh well, maybe dinner will offer something better. I say hello and offer my hand to the crew as they come into the mess but they just shake hands, nod and smile. None of them, it seems, speak English. I help myself to a couple of cups of black coffee and a couple of slices of rye bread then go up to the bridge where the captain is concerned that I have found a bunk and settled in.

The pilot comes on board at about six o'clock we set sail an hour or so later at High Water. The engines start up and the stern rope is cast off. The stern swings out into the river and as the stream takes hold of it and swings it out further as the bows swing in over the quay. A wild, screaming, jarring noise makes everyone stop dead. The captain looks at the Pilot with a startled look on his face. The screaming is coming from the bows. Have we caught a cat in the mooring line? Then, as the ship slowly moves astern under her own power, we can see that the bow has snagged an old rusty warning sign on the quay edge and bent it flat. It is so rusty the warning it had given had long since disappeared.

It is now a pleasant evening and a cooling breeze has sprung up. We motor slowly down stream and Old Father Thames drifts along with us as we slide gently by the Essex marshes and the flat lands of Kent. At Gravesend, we stop to drop the river pilot and collect the sea pilot who will take us out to Sunk Lightship off Harwich. We sail out past Tilbury with all its new container terminals. We pass Southend and its long pier, its lights, holiday makers, pubs and bingo halls that would now be getting into full swing as we sail out into the dark emptiness of the North Sea.

I feel very much a foreigner, on a foreign ship, off to foreign lands and more than a little alone. The language barrier with the crew does not help and will not enable me to mix with them very well. However, I cannot change that now, or learn German overnight so, I will have to make the best of it. If the food so far was anything to go by then I will be a hungry foreigner too.

My concerns about the crew are increased when a little later on, while I am still standing on the bridge, the bosun, a sallow skinned man with very short black hair, comes onto the bridge. I had seen him earlier on deck and noted that he seemed to have an 'attitude'. He points at me and beckons me to follow him. I silently follow him down to his cabin, where he points at an old typewriter and issues an order. 'You type letter, please.' A hand-written letter is lying by the typewriter. I pick it up and read it. It is a complaint letter, in very basic English, to the laundry company that they use in London. I tell him that I cannot type. The mere presence of a typewriter tells me that either the bosun, or somebody else on the ship does type. This fact does not deter him in his determination to get me to do it for him. 'You speaks the language', is all he says and he walks out firmly shutting the door behind him and leaving me to it. I half listened to see if he locked me in! In spite of a desire to walk out too I decide that I should try and help, so I start to teach myself to type! I manage to type the letter but it takes a while. By the time I finish, it is dark and we are well out at sea. The bosun turns out to be a pushy, arrogant guy who I do not like much, but I also discover that none of the others do either.

I am awoken by a screaming, juddering noise that is hammering through the cabin. I lie there in the dark trying to work out what is happening. It seems to be coming from the other side of the bulkhead behind my bunk. As I wake up properly I realise what it is. The ship, being unladen, is pitching heavily and the stern is lifting out of the sea and then banging back into the waves. As my bunk is above the propeller the racing prop sounds as though it is coming in through the bulkhead. Then I recognise that familiar feeling in my stomach. Seasickness is back! 'Oh no, here we go again!' I head for the bathroom. The ship is behaving like a cork but when I look out of the porthole I am annoyed to see that it is not even rough, just a bit windy with a few white-topped waves. I dress and go up on deck. I find some coffee in the mess then spend time on the bridge where, in spite of the continual Willem II smoke, the motion is much easier. The captain smiles sympathetically, 'We will soon be in the Elbe river and the ship will behave better, then we reach Kiel Canal', he reassures me.

I eat with the crew in their small mess. The meals on board are basic; tea today was fried potatoes and a pot of tea. Full stop! Breakfast tends to be something cooked, usually fried potatoes, and egg or bratwurst with thick, dark rye bread and coffee. The coffee is very good. Heaven knows how the cook manages that. Lunch is a one-course affair of hunks of bony, fatty meat, instant potatoes and stingy greens or cabbage. Not once on board did I see a decent piece of meat let alone a full joint. What my former shipmates from the *Lord Lovat* would have made of it I cannot imagine. Maybe they should do a trip in *Silvana*? That would stop any complaints about food! Afternoon tea was more dark rye bread with coffee. Jam could be obtained by yelling 'Marmalade' loudly through the hatch to the galley. The cook, poor fellow, who hardly ever said a word, was as thick as two short planks and must have been pretty deaf as well. He was ribbed by all the crew and could do nothing right in their eyes. Even so, the crew did not seem to mind the food and I wondered what they ate at home. I came to rely on tea as my main meal of the day. Dark rye bread and tinned raspberry jam with black coffee became my staple diet on board. There was also a snack for supper. This was usually of some sort of cold potatoes, though once I did see a bratwurst.

During meals, the crew chatter and giggle away in German and totally ignore me, which is not surprising. I feel the isolation keenly but keep myself amused by trying to work out what the crew are talking about, I never know exactly what they were saying but as time went on it I was able to work out what they are talking about by watching their mannerisms, body language, expressions and moods, etc. After a few days I found that my initial thoughts were often spot on. I initially thought the fair-haired boy, called Johan, who had helped me on boarding and did speak some schoolboy English, was the captain's favourite. However, I noticed that once he was behind the captain's back he talked about how stupid the captain was and that he did not like him at all. He showed himself, during the trip, to be a real creep.

By early the next afternoon, on a dull grey day, we are in a line of ships of different sizes heading up to the mouth of the Elbe. Some, like us, are heading for the Kiel Canal some for Hamburg itself, a few miles further upstream. The low, German plains lie grey and deserted, stretching away under the low clouds,

We pass two wrecks on the sand banks to port, both of them sitting high and dry, one no more that a collection of skeletal frames sticking out of the sands, the other is a solid hull, possibly a fishing vessel, lying on its side. They lie there as silent warnings to the perils of these waters. Soon after that we see the beaches of Cuxhaven, which is a fishing port and a popular holiday town, but today the beaches and dunes are all windswept and deserted. A large German stern trawler comes down the river out bound from Bremerhaven and probably heading for the Arctic. She has obviously just been overhauled as her hull is rust free and freshly painted black contrasting with the clean white superstructure. She looks workmanlike and determined as she heads out past us into the murk of the North Sea with white foam seething at her bow. The chief engineer, a big man always in white overalls and with a healthy stubble on his chin, comes rushing onto the bridge and grabs the binoculars. 'Mr Engineer, he works for twenty years in trawlers. He knows these people,' says the captain and waves with his hand towards the passing stern trawler. I tell the captain of my trip in *Lord Lovat* and he translates it for the chief. I am not sure exactly what he said but the chief stares at me, then smiles broadly and shakes my hand. From that moment on the chief took a liking to me and whenever we met he beamed at me saying 'Ah Ze Englander, Yah?'

By four o'clock we are lying off Brunsbuttel, the western entrance to the Kiel Canal, waiting to be called into the lock. The canal is 61 miles long and cuts through from the Elbe Estuary to the Baltic Sea at Kiel and saves over 280 miles of sailing round the top of Jutland in Denmark to get into the Baltic. The canal was built to meet the demands of the German Navy, who wanted a route from their new base in Kiel to the North Sea. It was built between 1877 and 1895 and widened between 1907 and 1914 to enable the German Navy's new Dreadnought-class of battleships to use it.

The pilot came aboard and we crept forward into the locks. The rain and drizzle make the lock pits a very wet and damp place. The gates close behind us, the lock is filled with water and slowly we rise up and emerge at the canal level. When the ship edge is level with the lock side the crew then rig a temporary gangway from the upper deck to shore but I am not sure why as we should be sailing out in a few minutes. Just then I catch sight of three women, one with a pram, who seem to have appeared from nowhere and are walking in a line heading along the lock side. The first two fit my mental image of German *fraus*, The first woman is small and round. She has a scarf tied round the top of her head and a determined look on her face. She must be aged about fifty. The second woman is tall, straight-backed and well-built, about the same age as the first, and she also looks fierce and is clearly following the first one. The third one is slimmer, of medium height, and younger, perhaps about thirty, and with blonde hair escaping from under her rain hat. She is pushing a pushchair. She appears better dressed than the others, although all three are wearing raincoats and rain hats. What are three women and a baby doing on a wet afternoon walking along the Kiel Canal? As they reach the ship they turn and walk over the gangway and come straight on board. What is going on here? I had heard of women visiting ships in port but these three definitely do not fit the image I had for that sort of woman. The captain sees my interest 'Not to worry, zey are family.' They are in fact the captain's wife, chief engineer's wife and the mate's wife, with her small baby. As the families all live near Hamburg; this trip through the canal presented an ideal opportunity for a social get-together. A big family party then ensues on the bridge as they all catch up on family news and gossip. A few minutes later the lock has been completely filled, the gangway is taken in, the upper gates are opened and we sail out into the sixty-one miles of the Kiel Canal. The family party then retreats below to the captain's Dayroom leaving the captain and pilot on the bridge. The captain lights a Willem II and chats to the pilot.

The low, flat, rain-dampened landscape drifts by. This depressing scenery seems to stretch along both sides of the canal; a treeless expanse, apart from a few copses of young silver birches, and not a house in sight for miles. The slow throb of the engines is the only sound. The damp atmosphere makes me feel even hungrier. I am feeling hungry most of the time now and regret not bringing my own supply of biscuits and chocolate. Just then my mind is taken off food as the family party comes back up onto the bridge for some air and I get introduced to all the wives. The grim *fraus* that I watched on the lock side have gone and pleasant, friendly, smiling ladies introduce themselves to me. However, as they know no English it is a short conversation but one with lots of smiles and nods. Even so, it is very good to be introduced to them.

The canal is busy. Ships of all types going the other way pass us in a more or less continual stream. Sometimes we have to wait with other ships in a big layby, tied up to bollard points in the layby, while a small convoy of bigger ships passes in the opposite direction. Most of the ships we see are Russian, East German or Polish. The Russians ships seem to be either brand, shiny new and smart or old rust buckets, while the Polish ones all looked well cared for.

After a ten-hour transit we pass Kiel and clear the canal and enter the Baltic Sea. The ladies had left us at Rensburg and headed for home. By morning the weather has improved a lot and it turns into a beautiful day. A big Russian freighter of about 7,000 tons comes up on our starboard side and passes us before vanishing off into the distance, presumably heading for Leningrad. She is modern, with sleek lines and is a very beautiful ship. Her hull is painted dove grey with a clean, white superstructure and a red Soviet funnel with the gold hammer and sickle gleaming in the sun.

I watch the *Silvana*'s crew at work as they scrape and paint the main deck. The ship is kept immaculate and the crew clearly has a lot of pride in their ship. However, I cannot help comparing the easy and relaxed daily routine and working hours of these German sailors with the routine followed by the trawlermen of *Lord Lovat*. Boy, do the Germans have it easy!

The next day we clear the Storebelt and the Danish islands and head north-east towards the Swedish coast. As the Danish coast recedes on the starboard quarter, the Swedish coast comes into view ahead. The land is low with rolling, wooded hills inland. The captain points towards a giant concrete grain silo dead ahead and says 'Falkenberg'. Slowly, the small port town of Falkenberg shows itself. From the sea the concrete silo dominates the scene and the town seems to huddle round its base. At about six o'clock we pass the end of a long, rough, stone breakwater stretching about half a mile out to sea. We motor slowly up into the port past the breakwater and we berth at the seaward end of the main quay, which is built along the north bank of the river Atran. There are eight other ships moored ahead of us. Mostly they are smaller than the *Silvana*, some have low superstructures and folding masts of low air draught vessels that use the European canal systems, some are bigger sea-going coasters and all are either Swedish or German. The quayside is quiet and peaceful on a lovely summer's evening as we nudge against the wall and the lines are secured. The engines are shut down, peace descends and we settle into the warm gentle atmosphere of a Swedish summer. 'This is one of my favourite ports.' The captain is standing at my elbow as I watch the scene. He carries on, 'I have been here often. Falkenberg is a small town for holidays. About 25,000 people are living here'. 'We are now mid way between Helsingborg and city of Gothenburg which is to the north.' He waves his arm over the rail. 'Timber has been shipped through here for many, many years. It comes from, how do you say, sawmills? about 30 kilometres inland, near a place called Limmared.

MV *Silvana* alongside in Falkenberg 1967. At about 1,000 tons she was a smart-looking coaster and typical in size and looks of ships in the European trades at the time.

In fact', says the captain, 'there used to be a narrow-gauge railway that ran from Limmared to the port but that finished in about 1960'. The mate appears from the bridge and stands beside us. I have hardly seen him so far on the trip as he keeps the night watches when at sea and, other than organizing the crew first thing in the morning, he spends most of the time in his cabin. He is a small, quiet man called Heidrich. He invites me to join him and some of the others for a walk ashore. 'Some men, we go to the town. You too, yah?' The captain nods his approval. 'You will enjoy, nice Swedish town.'

That night, four of us set off and, as we are walking along the dockside, two big Volvo cars pull up in front of us and four men jump out and confront us. They are clearly not taxis so what do they want? Am I to be mugged before I even get to the town? The men all flash impressive metal badges at us and in English demand that we stand still. 'Customs', Heidrich the mate whispers to me. The men frisk all of us. I am hoping that no one has any contraband as if one of the sailors has got too much tobacco or even worse, drugs, we will all be hauled into the police station. But they find nothing and we carry on into town. After walking around the quiet town we go into the Hotel Ritz for a beer, but once we realise how high the prices of Swedish beer are, we opt to have coffee and cake instead. Johan, the tall, fair-haired, drippy sailor who bad-mouthed the captain wanders off to try and chat up a blonde girl he has spotted sitting with her friend at another table. He does not get very far and so wanders off on his own and leaves us to finish our coffees. As he leaves, Heidrich mutters some undoubtedly derogatory comment in German about Johan, which makes the others laugh.

The timber loading starts the next day and is due to last all week. They start early, removing the hatch covers and checking that the hold spaces are all clear to receive the timber. For this phase, I am allowed to help out. Johan and I are sent down into the hold to get rid of any debris from the last trip. In no time at all we are engulfed in clouds of saw dust as we clear old, broken pieces of timber and wood chips out the bottom of the holds. As the morning goes on and the sun shines down into the hold it gets hotter and hotter. The chief is up on deck in his

Silvana as seen from the ship's boat. The next day the loading began.

white overalls to ensure that the derricks and winches are all working and the captain watches from the bridge wing; his round, smiling face peering through a Willem II smoke screen. The mate organises the crew so each of them knows what they will be doing during the loading. The timber, all in rough sawn planks, bound into bundles, is brought to the dockside by bright yellow forklift trucks. The bundles are of different sizes, each conforming to international 'Standard' for timber bundles. These are about 6-feet by 6-feet by 12- or 18-feet long. It all has to be stowed as tightly as possible to fill every inch of the hold and the upper deck, so loading is a long, slow process. The standards are loaded into the ship using the ship's derricks. These are proper, old-fashioned derricks with a main swinging boom, like a crane's jib. The boom is swung across the ship and over the quay by outhaul and inhaul winches connected to the end of the boom and these then hold the boom steady as the main winch lifts then lowers the timber into the hold. The working days last from 8 a.m. until 6 p.m. Now the crew start to earn their money. By evening they are very tired as the hold is a stiflingly hot and dusty place to work and heaving and wedging the timber into place is heavy work. Unfortunately, it is not an activity in which I can join as the skipper expressly forbids me from going on deck, let alone down into the hold, while loading is going on. 'Too many accidents,' he says by way of justification. I can see what he means. As it is loaded the timber bundles swing around in the breeze and bang and crash against the ship and the hatches, with some of the crew making quick dives for cover, as it is lowered down into the hold. Late in the afternoon I was watching the loading from the bridge wing. As a bundle is lowered into the hold there is a loud 'twang' and yells from the crew on deck. One of the straps securing the bundle together snaps and releases some of the heavy planks of timber, which pour from the side of the bundle down into the hold. They just miss Heidrich, who is standing by the open hatch. Luckily, the crew in the hold below jump clear and no one is hurt. It illustrates the captain's point about the dangers! The mate storms off into the timber yard to berate the foreman for the faulty strapping, while the crew clear up the loose planks.

The good weather lasts all week and the loading goes on. Day after day, during working hours the derrick swings timber inboard and the forklift trucks bring more timber to load from the timber yard behind the quay. After a couple of days, the hold still looks half empty, as it is such a vast space to fill. The ship, even though she has fine lines, is no more than a large floating box. It seems to make little difference how many bundles of timber they load, the hold does not seem to get more full. Gradually, however, it does start to appear fuller and by Thursday the hold itself is completely full. The hatch covers are replaced, then covered and secured for sea by hammering heavy wedges into the hatch edges to hold the tarpaulin covers in place.

The second phase of loading then begins. The timber is loaded onto the upper deck and over the tops of the hatches. Vertical wooden beams are set up along the side of the deck to try and keep the timber in place. The well deck forward is loaded first. Then they start to load timber across the main deck and the hold covers. When they have finished the only way forward to the fo'c'sle is to climb over the front of the bridge wings and walk over the timber itself.

One evening the crew gathers on the stern and the record player is brought up on deck and they play a few German records. They obviously do not have a big record collection on board. However, one of the records they do have is Sandie Shaw's *Puppet on a String*, which has just won the Eurovision Song Contest. At least I can join in with this one. A few holiday makers walk down to the quay in the evening and, as we sit in the sun drinking beer watching them, the holiday makers watch us.

The captain was right. Falkenberg is a pretty little town with lovely pastel-coloured wooden houses, painted in soft blue, green or red colours. Away from the main centre quiet cobbled lanes stretched away towards the nearby open countyside. During the loading I was able to get ashore and wander through these pleasant, shady, cobbled lanes and enjoy the holiday mood of the town.

By Friday lunchtime the loading is complete. The upper deck is now piled high up to a level just below the bridge windows right the way forward to the fo'c'sle. The last of the timber is being secured and the captain is getting the charts ready so we can sail as soon as all the 'securing for sea' checks have been completed. The deck-stowed timber must be stowed and lashed as tightly as possible as if it shifts in bad weather it can take the whole ship over with it. There are many examples of this type of disaster befalling timber ships and mostly it is ships carrying sawn timber in bundles like us, rather than whole logs. Sawn-timber bundles; planks of wood to you and me, are stacked like boxes on the ship's upper deck. They add a huge amount of windage to the ship as well as top weight, which is not good for the ship's stability. Quite recently, the Greek ship *Ice Prince* was hit by heavy weather in the Channel, her sawn timber cargo shifted and after losing most of the timber over the side, she herself capsized and sank off Eastbourne. The Russian ship *Sinegorsk*

Loading and stowing timber in Falkenberg. Note the man bending over in the hold as another load is swung inboard over his head.

also lost most of her sawn-timber cargo in the English Channel. Between 2001 and 2002 there were, according the UK Marine Accident Investigation Dept, at least eight incidents where timber ships, sailing from the Baltic or Russia, experienced shifting cargoes. The causes are usually that the securing lashings fail. The bundles are secured either by lashings across the top or by vertical side supports of wood or steel that are set up along the ship's side. In either case they have proved to fail and resulted in major problems. The problems are not just for the ship that loses the timber as it can develop a heavy list or even capsize and sink but the vast amount of timber floating in tight, packed masses causes a major hazard to shipping and when it washes ashore it becomes a danger to people ashore. Cargo shifting often leads to a ship losing its stability and once that had happened it is doomed.

One of the most famous incidents of a ship capsizing is that of the *Flying Enterprise*, which capsized in the English Channel in 1951. Although she was not a timber ship, she was a 6,000-ton merchant ship and she sailed on 21 December 1951 from Hamburg heading for New York with a mixed cargo and ten passengers on board. On Christmas Day, when she was well out into the Atlantic, she met a winter storm. The ship laboured in the heavy seas and a

A quiet scene in Falkenberg in summer with pastel-coloured houses and cobbled street.

crack developed across her weather deck. Soon afterwards, the cargo shifted in the holds. By 28 December, she had developed a 45-degree list. An SOS was put out and on 29 December the passengers and crew were lifted off by helicopter. All that is, except the captain, Kurt Carlsen. The salvage tug *Turmoil* arrived and stood by. The weather was still atrocious and there was nothing that the *Turmoil* could do to get a tow attached. Finally, on 4 January 1952, *Turmoil*'s Mate, Ken Dancy, was put aboard the *Flying Enterprise* to assist Captain Carlsen to get a line connected. This they somehow managed to do and a 5-inch towline was connected in spite of the list now being about 60 degrees. The *Turmoil* started to tow the ship back towards Falmouth, over 300 miles away. All this time, Captain Carlsen and Mate Dancy were living in a rolling world that was tilted over by 60 degrees and without power, heat or lights. On 10 January, the weather worsened and the tow parted. Finally, at 1522 on 10 January, twelve days after his crew had been airlifted off and after six days of trying to keep the ship alive and under tow; Capt Carlsen and Mate Dancy left the stricken ship by simply walking along the side of the, now horizontal, funnel and jumping the few feet into the sea. They were immediately picked up safely by the *Turmoil*. The *Flying Enterprise* sank less than an hour later at 1610. The newspaper photographs showed the *Flying Enterprise* as she listed over.

    We sail from Falkenberg in mid-afternoon and set off down the Kattegat back towards the Kiel Canal. Going up on deck the next morning I am greeted with a beautiful sunrise coming up astern of the ship. The sea is flat calm sea and other ships are silhouetted against the sun as we all line up to approach the Kiel Canal. A drop in the engine revs signals that we are slowing down to pick up the pilot. No sooner is he on board than suddenly the sun vanishes and a thick, cold, wet

The *Flying Enterprise* lists heavily to port as she approaches her final moments. (J&C McCutcheon Collection)

fog descends on us. The fog gets thicker and we slow down even more. Quickly the captain orders a lookout in the bows and a man full time on the radar. It is eerily quiet and we motor slowly towards the canal entrance. Suddenly, there is a yell from forward. We all look at the bow lookout. He is waving his arms at us then points out dead ahead into the fog. We try and look into the fog but see nothing. Then the pilot gives yell. As we look the bows of a smaller coaster appear out of the fog just off the port bow. The captain grabs the wheel and spins it hard to starboard to try and miss this ship. Nothing happens, but then, slowly, *Silvana* starts to respond and the bow starts to swing, but is it too late? I cannot see how it can do anything but hit us. The other ship does not seem to have seen us and is getting closer and closer. Then, very slowly she now seems to be altering course and her bow is moving down our port side. As her wheelhouse comes into view we realise that they have seen us and are altering course. We miss each other, just. Even in German, it is clear that the pilot was not too complimentary about the coaster as we were where we should have been in the waterway and the coaster was not. We straighten up our course and move on, nerve ends tingling as everyone now stares hard out into the fog ahead. We reach the locks at half-past seven. We enter just ahead of a big, grey-hulled freighter whose bow towers over our stern. Her name is *Baltrover* and she is registered in London. This is the first London-registered ship I have seen since leaving the Thames. *Baltrover* has come down from Finland and is also heading for London.

Sunrise in the Baltic as vessels converge to enter the Kiel Canal.

As we clear the locks, the fog vanishes as quickly as it had descended and the sun reappears. All day we make our way along the canal passing ship of all types but again mostly Russian, Polish and East German and, by late afternoon, we have reached the approaches to the locks at the western end. We slow right down and wait in a canal layby to be called into an empty lock once the eastbound ships currently in it have headed out into the canal. We locked out into the river Elbe and by evening we are well clear of the canal and steaming down the Elbe Estuary. The *Baltrover* picks up speed and passes us easily heading off down the Elbe at about 15 knots.

That evening, we have the most enjoyable evening of the trip. There is a glorious sunset and, with Radio Caroline playing on the radio and the sun shining into the mess room, one of the crew comes into the mess carrying a package under his arm. It looks like old firewood wrapped in newspaper. Very appropriate, considering our cargo. He lays the bundle on the table and opens the newspaper. We see that it is a dozen smoked eels. They look like a bundle of sticks about 2-3 feet long and each eel about 2 inches thick. We have them for supper. This is a first for me; the smoked eel has a delicate taste, not too fishy at all. The hard skin cracks off leaving the flesh on the backbone and the meat falls off this in chunks of solid flesh. The eels had been bought and kept for tonight by the mate who had sent one of the crew off to a local shop as we were locking out of the canal. Later, waffles also magically appeared, surely not cooked by our cook? This is the best meal I have had on board. A very pleasant mood seems to permeate the crew, maybe due to good food for a change and for me the thought that I on my way home.

Silvana had to moor up in a layby to allow this monster past.

Nevasa at Tilbury. (J&C McCutcheon Collection)

A day or so later and we are back in the Thames off Gravesend. We have to anchor and wait for the tide to turn while the sea pilot changes with the river pilot. He will take us up to our berth in the London Docks. Eventually at about ten thirty we pick up the anchor and steam up the Thames, past Tilbury where the big white B&I school ship *Nevasa* is berthed on the floating pontoon dock. We sail up past the Essex and Kent marshes then past the Royal Docks and round the Isle of Dogs and past Greenwich. Here the south shore is dominated by the magnificent Naval College, designed as a military hospital by Sir Christopher Wren, with all its colonnades and domes. It makes a wonderful sight with the Greenwich Observatory, which sits up on the hill behind. The beautiful tea clipper, *Cutty Sark* sits in her dry dock looking as magnificent as ever and reminds me that while we have been across the North Sea and into the Baltic on this trip; her normal voyage would be to China or Australia and back. We move up past the old industrial waterfront of the Thames, past the pub 'The Prospect of Whitby', and the warehouses and backstreets that Dickens would still recognise, until we reach the entrance to the Surrey Commercial Docks on the south side of the river just below Tower Bridge.

The Surrey Docks originally consisted of a network of docks that were used for ship repairs and refits. Within the Surrey Docks is the Greenland Dock, where we are to berth. It was built in 1696 as the Howland Wet Dock but renamed the Greenland Dock in 1763 as it was then being used as a base for the Arctic whalers. Later, after the whaling finished, it was used for the timber trade. Like all the old London Docks, they were built at a time when ships were much smaller and powered by sail. Large, modern, deep-sea ships are now too big to get through the locks and so ports like Tilbury and Felixstowe have developed to take today's modern, big ships.

I am happy to refuse the lunch of boiled fat and stewed cabbage leaf, knowing that within an hour or so, once we have moored and been cleared by Customs, I will be able to go and get some food in London and will and be on my way home in time for tea.

But we are not docked yet. Now comes a trickiest bit of the voyage as the pilot has to judge his turn across the tide to get the ship into the lock so that the tide running up the river with us does not push us past the dock and cause us to go aground. Gently, he cons the ship round, constantly looking at the speed of the tide in the river and then at the dock head, a wheel order to the captain, then at how fast the bow is turning, then an engine order. Bit by bit we get nearer, and as we turn across the tide we can see that it is taking us sideways up stream. Will we get to the lock entrance before we are swept past? Those on the bridge are silent as we watch powerless to do anything. The pilot has judged it perfectly, *Silvana* slowly and smoothly slides into the lock and stops. An immigration officer jumps aboard and clears the ship while we are still in the lock. We then move slowly to our berth in the small and empty Greenland Dock.

It is another warm and sunny afternoon and *Silvana* is the only ship in the dock. It is deserted and silent; no stevedores sitting eating sandwiches, no dozing dogs, nothing. The tall brick warehouses surrounding the dock watch mournfully over the scene. The only sounds are the squeaking of ropes, soft groaning and the quiet grumbles of two old rusting lighters tied up to the dockside that our wash has disturbed from their slumber. We moor up and the engines are shut down. All falls quiet again and the dock returns to silence and enjoys the peace of a warm summer's day. Tomorrow, the unloading will start and the crew will be hard at it after lunch today starting to remove all the sea lashings from the timber. A single Customs man duly arrives and clears the ship so I am now clear to go.

My timber ship trip is over. While it did not get me to Russia it did show me what life on a modern European coaster was like as well as some of the hazards of the timber ship business. However, it does not really compare with the trawling life of those in the *Lord Lovat* and her sisters. Their life is one of endless sea time, few coasts to look at, let alone ports to visit. They effectively work at least twelve hours a day, especially on the fishing grounds when it can go up to eighteen or more for days on end. Unlike the coaster's trading patterns round European ports, the trawlermen's work place is at sea in the far north with all that the Arctic weather can throw at them on their open deck, knee deep in cold, wet fish. Nonetheless, the risks of injury, and capsize in the timber trade are real enough and every year there are examples to illustrate it. The men do work hard in port even if their life at sea is easier. At least the trawlermen do not have to unload their catches in Hull. Their work finishes when they get alongside, the coaster crew's work starts when they get alongside.

I say my goodbyes to the crew who are now sitting at the stern enjoying the sunshine. I go and see the captain. After paying him and thanking him for the trip I leave him in his dayroom lighting up another Willem II. I go ashore and leave the peace of the old docks to make my way out into the hurly burly, noise and dusty dirt of a hot London afternoon and to find the nearest tube station.

CHAPTER 3

TS *Sir Winston Churchill* – Tall Ships Race 1968

What must it be like to be on board one of the 4,000-ton, four-masted barques that used to sail down into the Southern Ocean? The towering steel masts bending and trembling under the press of wet, heavy canvas; her rigging taut and singing and with all sails set as she drives down into the Roaring Forties? It must have been a rare and fantastic experience to be on one of those majestic ships as they sailed round the Horn with cargoes of nitrate from Chile or grain from Australia. Or, to be on one of the pedigree greyhounds of the sea, the clipper ships, as they raced each other back from China? Racing all the way, down through reefs and islands of the South China Sea, across the Indian Ocean, round the Cape of Good Hope and then all the way up the Atlantic. Always driving the ship and carrying as much sail as the skipper dared. Too much sail and the ship risked being dismasted, too little and he will lose the race and her cargo will not get the premium prices. Stories about ships like the four-masted barque *Moshulu*, from that fabulous book by Eric Newby, *The Last Grain Race* or, the 'Bird of Dawning' from John Masefield's book about the tea clippers, had made me want to experience sailing on the big square-rigged sailing ships and tea clippers. But now there were only a few left and certainly none sailing commercially. One or two still exist as training ships such as the Russian ships *Sedov* and *Krusenstern*, both over 3,000 tons and as majestic as ever.

I had found out earlier that trying to get a trip on a Russian ship was not possible! However, I learnt about the Sail Training Association (STA) and their tall ships the *Sir Winston Churchill* and the *Malcolm Miller*. The STA ran these ships for young people to learn the thrill and responsibility of crewing tall ships, albeit small ones. Every two years there is an international Tall Ships Race where tall ships from all over the world compete on a ten- to fourteen-day race, normally somewhere in northern Europe. The ships range from small, family cruising yachts through to two-masted schooners and ketches as well as the big three- and four-masted Russian and Norwegian training ships.

In 1968, when I am nineteen, the Race is to be from Gothenburg in Sweden out of the Baltic, across the North Sea, round Fair Isle, between the Orkney Islands and Shetland, and then back across the North Sea to the finish at Christiansand in southern Norway. I apply to join the *Sir Winston Churchill* (SWC) for the race and am delighted to find that I am accepted as a trainee. However, I cannot afford the price of the trip. As I am still at college, working at weekends alone will not begin to provide the money. A funding dispute erupts at home. If I cannot find the money then I cannot go, very simple. Where will I find the money for the trip? Eventually a compromise is reached with my parents agreeing to fund half if I can raise the other half, through working weekends and in the school holidays. This is a great relief.

To join the ship, the crews of the two ships are to be flown out by charter flight from Gatwick to Gothenburg. I check in and go through to the departure lounge and settle down and watch the world go by feeling both excited and nervous about the trip ahead and what may lie in store. My head is full of images of letting the wrong rope go: or, of getting knocked from the rigging by a stray rope. I spot a few obvious STA trainees and start to chat to a couple of guys who are going out for the *Malcolm Miller*. I then meet a guy who is going to the *Sir Winston Churchill*. He is from Exeter and called Simon. We did not realise it then but our paths would cross later on in life too. Simon was as excited as I was but seemed pretty nervous about being seasick. This is also my very first commercial flight and I am quite excited by that as well. On the flight I sit next to a guy from the *Malcolm Miller* who is training to be a licensed Thames lighterman. He is from Millwall in the docklands and his father is a lighterman. He tells me that they serve a six or seven year apprenticeship before they are qualified as a lighterman and able to work on the tugs and barges all along the Thames and throughout the London Docks. They start off by learning to row big empty barges with long oars from wharf to wharf. Some fitness regime! They have to know all the docks and wharves along the whole of the 'Tideway' as well as all the technicalities of towing a string of barges. He is into his second year and has been sent on this trip by his employers.

As we get near to Gothenburg, we are all given a chance to visit the flight deck of the Britannia aircraft and we can see the lights of Gothenburg ahead. Somewhere down there among the lights lies the SWC, where over the next three weeks our lives will be changed. It is dark when we land. Our luggage is all loaded onto buses and we are taken down to the ships. As we step on board we are allocated to either the port or starboard watch and given coloured armbands according to which watch we are in. I am told that I am in Port watch so have a red band to be worn at all times. We are also given our sleeping berth number and told to go down to the mess deck and sort ourselves out. It is chaos below with some trainees having fixed bunk berths along the side and others, like myself, having hammocks, which are to be slung across the middle of the mess deck. We are given hammocks by the bosun's mate who briefly shows us how to sling them. Then with some people still struggling to secure their hammocks and find their bags; and others trying to work out how to get into them, the call 'Pipe Down and Lights Out' is made. As it is by now about half past one in the morning, sleep is most welcome. I fall instantly asleep and dream of roaring winds and huge waves and the ship rolling; but that may just have been the hammock!

STS *Sir Winston Churchill* at anchor in Dover harbour. (J&C McCutcheon Collection)

The *Sir Winston Churchill* is a three-masted topsail schooner. That means she has fore and aft sails on all her three masts but has three square sails on her foremast as well. These are a triangular 'Raffee' above a square topsail and a big fore course set below that. She was built in 1966 by Richard Dunston's at Hessle, on the Humber, and was designed by Camper Nicholson so has a first class sailing pedigree. She displaces 333 tons and is 135-feet long and able to carry 8,738 square feet of sail. She has a small permanent crew and is able to carry 38 trainees.

The trainees seem to come from all walks of life. There are some, like me, who are still at college and who have paid for their own trip, but most are already working as trainee managers, apprentices or factory workers. Some are even lucky enough to have been sponsored by their companies to come. Their companies see this as a good character building exercise that will help to shape and mature their employees. Most of the trainees however have come because, like me, they really want to experience tall ship sailing, or in this case tall ship racing!

The next morning, after an early call we are all sitting having breakfast in the mess deck and speculating on what the day will bring. A welcoming talk from the captain perhaps; then a gentle walk round the deck in the sunshine to see the masts and ropes; then maybe we will go ashore to see Gothenburg. Our conversation is interrupted by a short, but tough looking, bullet-headed man who marches onto the mess deck. He is probably in his thirties, wearing a dazzlingly white T-shirt and spotless working trousers. His tanned biceps stretch the T-shirt

The *Malcolm Miller* coming alongside with yards manned and headsails being stowed.
(J&C McCutcheon Collection)

sleeve impressively. He has a holster of seaman's tools on his belt. The mess deck falls silent as we notice his bulging muscles and the very serious face. I decide he has not come to invite us aft for a cocktail. He walks around the mess table slowly, looking at each of us with hard experienced eyes. 'Listen to me', he barks. 'My name is Vladimir, I am the bosun, I will teach you to sail this ship. Do as I say and it will be OK.' We stop eating and stare. He speaks with a strong Russian accent 'Now clear up your meal and be on deck in three minutes.' Simon and I look at each other. 'What is this all about?' There is a moment's silence then a mad scramble for the ladder. No one wants to be last on deck for this man! We learned later that he has come from a hard school as he has spent all his life working the big four-masted training ships of the Russian Merchant marine. There is nothing he does not know about tall ships and how to sail them. He is clearly not someone with whom we should fall out.

He begins the task of teaching us all we need to know about the ship and how to work it. This is a stem to stern and truck to keel session and nothing is left out. It covers all the standing and running rigging, the masts, yards and spars, the sails and their sheets, the halyards and buntlines and how to work out what any rope does by pulling on it. We learn the helm orders, ships times by bells and the storage spaces for spare sails and rigging that we will need to find at sea. Alongside us, the same process is taking place on the *Malcolm Miller* as both ships' permanent crews try ensure the trainees know all they should know before we set of for the start line in a few days time. Then there will be no room for errors or for letting go of the wrong rope in the dark of night. It is not long before we find out what happens when you do something wrong. Our watch is being briefed by Vladimir on the foremast running rigging and we are standing by the port rail when there is a loud thump on the wooden deck behind us. We all turn round and see that a seaman's knife has landed handle first on the deck behind us with such force that it has dented the teak deck. Before we can work out where it has come from, the bosun yells 'That man! On deck, now!' at the top of his voice high into the rigging. One of the permanent crew is up in the cross trees. The unfortunate seaman gets down to the deck and receives a rollicking from the bosun the like of which I had never heard before. The bosun sends the man away and then turns on us. 'If any of you ever, ever, do anything like that I will eat you alive.' We believe him. 'If you drop anything from aloft, you yell "Below!" as loud as you can. You understand?' 'Yes, bosun', we all mumble. The man's real crime was not so much dropping the knife, although he should have had it on a lanyard attached to his belt; but not yelling 'Below' as a warning to anyone underneath. Obviously, anything, especially a knife, dropped from that height will kill any unfortunate that is in the way. With heads spinning, we finally finish at seven that night when harbour watches were set. Those of us that are off watch are mostly too tired to go ashore to explore Gothenburg. That will have to wait for another day.

The next day we are on deck early again continuing our training but we are allowed to stop and watch the *Christian Radich* motor in. She is the Norwegian three-masted, full-rigged ship. She looks magnificent, her graceful white hull and silver masts and yards gleaming in the sunshine. She motors silently past our berth then turns round and comes back to her berth just astern of us. Ensigns are duly dipped as she goes by.

In the early afternoon, the *Malcolm Miller* and the *Sir Winston Churchill* slip their moorings and head down the river. We are going to sea! We motor gently down the harbour for the start of our sea training before the race itself. As there is nothing to do we have time to stand and stare and chat to our fellow shipmates.

We find that we have come from all over the country to be on this ship for this race. There are trainees from Lancashire, Hampshire, Scotland and Birmingham

Right: Trainees on the *Sir Winston Churchill* haul away to send the sails aloft to be bent onto the yards before the training sail.

Below: The figurehead of the *Christian Radich*. (J&C McCutcheon Collection)

but we are all under the spell of Vladimir and learning to be tall ship sailors. We have yet to meet the captain but that does not seem important now.

As we approach the open sea, the giant *Gorch Foch*, the big, three-masted barque from Germany, arrives and motors past us heading for her berth. She is the biggest ship in the race and has a white hull and bright-ochre-coloured masts and yards. She is used to train the German Navy's cadets.

Once clear of the main shipping channel we start our sea training. The bosun takes charge and we are quickly organised. He then supervises us as we raise and set the sails. Soon we are sailing briskly along in a Force 3 breeze over a calm and sunny sea. Once everything is to the bosun's liking we are given ten minutes off. We stand at the stern and watch as the *Malcolm Miller*, now far off on our port beam, heads off over the horizon.

It is one of the few clear, lasting memories of the next few days as the following days and nights merge into a jumble of memories of sail changing, dark nights on deck, stumbling into deck fittings, setting up back stays, the bosun standing, yelling, pointing, his face always a grim and serious mask. I recall the different faces of other trainees, climbing into my hammock fully dressed and struggling out again feeling cold and seasick. I can still see myself hauling endlessly on ropes with the others, taking the strain, heaving in that extra inch that Vladimir always demanded.

We practice every move in the book, tacking gybing, setting square sails, changing sails, sheeting in sails as well as cleaning and polishing. There is no time to get to know anyone as it is all we can do to keep up with the action. I do, however, start to recognise the face of the boy in the hammock next to me when we meet on deck! He is called David and is from Surrey and is a management trainee sent on the trip by his company. He has a head start on us as his father has a yacht so he knows how to sail already. Even so, he is suffering along with the rest of us and as we haul again on yet another rope, all he can say is 'My dad's yacht isn't like this!'

We are sent aloft for the first time; a terrifying experience for us all. We manage to climb up the weather rigging, trying not to let the trainee above us step on our hands, not looking down, only holding the vertical shroud, not the horizontal ratlines unless we want a verbal blast from below! Ratlines can give way so holding onto them is a bad idea. Apparently, they are always OK to stand on though! We struggle onto the top-mast cross trees. As we get there we hear 'Now move out onto the yards, first man to port, second to starboard. Move. Why are you waiting?' We have then to climb round the rigging and go out onto the yards. We have no choice but to trust that the thin, wire footrope slung beneath the yard will support us all. Gingerly, we start out onto the yard, dare we let go of the standing rigging and move our hands out to the yard itself and make a grab for the fixed jackstay that runs along the top front edge of the yard? Will our feet find the footrope? What do we move first? 'Hurry Op, we have not got all day!', yells Vladimir. We are only conscious of all the empty fresh air that suddenly surrounds us. The bosun yells instructions to us from the deck below. Somehow we get

The big German sail training barque the *Gorch Foch* at anchor in Christiansund. A magnificent sight especially from sea level.

ourselves onto the yard. We desperately cling on to the yard itself as the footrope kicks and twitches beneath our feet as other trainees step onto it and others move out along it. The cold waters of the Baltic look very solid as they rush past many tens of feet below. We press our stomachs as hard as we can against the cold steel of the yard as if this will somehow glue us to it. The roll of the ship throws us first one way then the other as the masts swings across their arc of roll. The deck now seems very small and a very long way down. The bosun orders us to loosen the buntlines; lines that hold the furled sail up close to the yard. Dare we take one hand off the jackstay to try and untie the buntlines? We had to, or else! 'One hand for the ship and one for ourselves,' is the old sailors' cry, but it seems to be heavily weighted in the ship's favour! We need three hands for ourselves right now! The lines are released and the huge mass of canvas of the foresail starts to flap free, threatening to knock our feet out from under us as it does so. This task completed, we are thankfully allowed back down to the deck. With knocking knees and a feeling of satisfaction, we regain the deck. This epic adventure was carried out in daylight and it is fairly calm. What will it be like at night or if it is rough? Before we are all down on deck Vladimir is there. 'Right get onto the sheets and haul them in.' No rest here! Somewhere in all of the training we must have eaten; but I totally forget the details of that.

On the second morning, as some of us are cleaning the mess after breakfast, a boy called Howard, from the starboard watch, is sitting on the bench seat in the mess deck. We know he should be on deck and will get a rollicking if the bosun catches him. He seems very quiet and withdrawn. 'Are you OK?' When we look at him more closely he is positively pea green in colour. I have heard of people looking green about the gills, and this poor guy is the living example. 'Hell, you look terrible,' Simon says encouragingly. He is green and not just about the gills. 'Hey guys, come down and have a look at Howard.' Mischievously, we call other trainees down from on deck to come and look at him. A few minutes later the poor guy flees to the heads.

The training goes on twenty-four hours a day. With lots of tacking and gybing, which involves tightening up the mast back stays on the leeward side of the ship before she tacks and then releasing the tension in the stays on, what was the weather side and is now the lee side, after she has tacked. We are repeatedly told that if we forget that drill we risk losing a mast or two.

Our watch is on duty for the middle watch (from twelve midnight until four o'clock). We have met some heavy weather, the night is dark and it is raining hard. Someone tells us we have sailed up to the entrance to Oslo Fjord, but we see nothing. The watch is especially hard as we have to rig handy billies on the halyards to haul the sails fully home again after reefing them down. Handy billies are small sets of rope and pulleys used to get a better mechanical advantage on a bigger rope. We cannot not get enough effort onto the rope ourselves to haul the sail all the way up so we need the handy billies to help us do it. 'Haul away, come on, haul damn you!' Five of us are hauling and heaving on the rope when with a loud 'Crack'! The rope snaps and we all end up on our backsides in the

View from *Sir Winston Churchill*'s main yard as the bow sprit leads the ship onwards.

From *Sir Winston Churchill*'s main yard. It looks a long way down from up here.

The *Gorch Fock*. (J&C McCutcheon Collection)

wet scuppers. Luckily Simon is behind me so I end up sitting on top of him. He is not amused and nor is the bosun. Pointing at me he yells 'Get up and get another billy from the store.' We go down off watch just after four o'clock in the morning feeling totally exhausted. My hands, which as a student, are not used to rope work and seawater, are now blistered and sore. Simon staggers back from the bathroom groaning with seasickness. As he falls into his hammock he echoes our feelings when he calls out 'Oh, when do we get back in? I really have had enough of this! What will the race itself be like?' I take off my oilskins but leave the rest of my clothes on and climb into my hammock. No sooner do I shut my eyes than my stomach rebels. I promptly feel horribly seasick so have to climb out again to get to the heads. In the morning the seasickness is back but I dare not be seen to be ill and loafing by the bosun so I carry on as best as I can, diving for the lee rail when I need to. My blistered hands grow worse during the forenoon, as we are doing a lot of sail changing due to the bad weather and partly to train us in the changes. The bosun catches sight of my hands bleeding as the blisters have now burst and the flesh has been cut open by the ropes. He examines my hands then orders me not to do any rope work until they heal up. I suspect this is more to do with keeping the ropes clean and blood free rather than concern for my soft, fair skinned hands! This is easier said than done as gloves are an absolute no-no on board as they can easily catch in a running rope and drag your whole hand or arm into a block or round a winch. If the bosun caught anyone with them he said he would throw them overboard. We never learnt whether he meant the trainee or the gloves.

Later that day as the weather improves and the wind drops, we see the Swedish two-masters *Gladen* and *Falcon* sailing serenely down from the north looking as if they are on a pleasure cruise. We meet up with the *Malcolm Miller* again before finally sailing back into Gothenburg together. We are feeling exhausted but whereas we sailed out as totally ignorant novices, we now feel that we can sail a big sailing ship, with Vlad's help of course! *Malcolm Miller* berths first and we are to moor alongside her. Unfortunately not without incident as our captain, Captain Willoughby, misjudges his approach and we manage to smash the *Malcolm Miller*'s stern light and scratch her paintwork along the port side. The *Malcolm Miller*'s captain, a very friendly fellow, Captain Griffiths, is unimpressed. We learnt from the trainees on *Malcolm Miller* that Capt Griffiths had learnt the Christian names of all the trainees by the time they returned to Gothenburg. We had barely seen our captain as he had left all the training to the bosun and the watch-keeping to his officers, so we suspected that Captain Willoughby did not know any of our surnames, let alone Christian names.

I spend the first evening back in Gothenburg on deck watch with one of the temporary watch officers, a guy called Charles. He is a Lieutenant in the RN and one of the officers on board for the race as an officer of the watch. He does not seem to be a very happy soul and actively distances himself from the trainees. Maybe he is following his captain's example? Unfortunately, our paths would cross in later years. Simon and I chat about the training sail as we stand by the rail and watch the passers-by. Simon, now fully recovered, is a friendly party-loving guy who I would meet again at Dartmouth. In spite of his seasickness he is not regretting being here and like me had always wanted to experience tall ships. A few of us try to chat to the Swedish girls who are out sightseeing and looking at the tall ships berthed along the quay. Some of the girls are simply gorgeous and proved that the stories of beautiful blond Swedish girls are all correct. Those off watch all go to an official Tall Ship's Race Welcoming Reception somewhere in town. I turn in about one in the morning as the light Scandinavian nights make us forget the time even though we are all pretty tired.

After the rigors of the training sail we are allowed the next day off after the daily cleaning has been completed. After lunch three of us go to an outdoor swimming pool and lido complex that has offered free tickets to race competitors. There is Bob, a big friendly lad from Rochdale, who is in 'management' in an engineering company. Bob suffered more badly from seasickness than anyone on board but in spite of that got on well with everyone on board and threw himself into any work with great gusto. Only when seasickness robbed him of his strength did he finally succumb to it and allowed himself to be sent below to recover.

Phil is a short, stocky guy with very curly fair hair. He is from Bournemouth and training to be a cabinet-maker. He is a bit of a 'cheeky chappy' always one with a comment or joke. He is very proud of his profession and woe be tide anyone who dared to call him a 'Chippy'. We all try our first saunas and as we sweat we discuss our feelings about the training trip and the race to come. Both Phil and Bob feel that the race will be much tougher than the training trip and we should expect the worst. I say that I hope the race will be easier as we will have to keep things set to keep up our speed and can't be changing everything all the time the way we were on the

Up the pole. A view of the top of the mast in the 1900s. (J&C McCutcheon Collection)

training trip. How little I knew! The weather forecast is not good either. I enjoy the sauna a lot but the other two are not too keen on it and soon go back to the outside swimming pool. However, I am not too sure about jumping into a cold plunge pool afterwards. I feel so clean that I do not want to put my clothes back on.

The next day we are put to work smartening the ship up and greasing all the running blocks and machinery as we will not have time in the race to do it. I spend the morning painting the deckhouse bulkhead. 'You drop any paint splash on my teak deck and I skin you mister!' 'Yes bosun, er, I mean, no, bosun.' It is a warm day and there are plenty of girls walking along the quay so it is good job to get, especially as I manage not to get skinned. After lunch, Bob, Phil and I go back to the Lido and take Simon along too. I have another sauna.

Gothenburg has tall ship fever. There is bright bunting out everywhere and some shops are offering free soft drinks to crew members, so we feel like returning heroes even though we have done nothing yet. In the evening we go to the Liseberg Gardens, a huge, open-air amusement and entertainment park as Georgie Fame is playing live at the outdoor theatre there. The show is great and his jazz music fills the gardens. We watch the whole show, singing along and forgetting the ordeals of our few days at sea.

The race. Today is race day. The morning is spent as usual, cleaning ship. The crowds start to build up along the quayside even though the ships are not due to sail until after lunch. The weather is glorious, another beautiful Scandinavian summer's day. Hot, sunny and windless. We slip our moorings at about 1300 to make our way down to the start line. It is a great sight. The order of ships going down the river is decided by size so it is biggest first, with *Gorch Foch* leading the way, then *Sorlandet* (another Norwegian three-master), *Christian Radich*, *Sir Winston Churchill*, *Malcolm Miller*, *Etoile* and *Belle Poule* (French) then the *Falcon* and *Gladen*.

The water is crowded with craft of all shapes and sizes; small speedboats and motor cruisers as well as yachts under engine power; and there are thousands of people cheering from the banks and beaches, houses and warehouses as we move down towards the sea. We pass under the big suspension bridge that spans the entrance to Gothenburg harbour and there are even people waving from the bridge. As we near the start line, the square-riggers let loose their square sails and become great silent ghosts drifting along in the light wind. One of the small speedboats with about half a dozen boys and girls in it roars up to our stern and the lads on board it throw us a few cans of beer which Simon manages to catch and quickly tucks into his pockets! Our watch is on duty and I am on the helm as we start to make a number of short, sharp tacks so we do not cross the start line, which is based on the Vinga Light, too early. Lots of 'Ready about', 'Set up the lee braces', 'port 20', 'Watch your course' fill the air as we jostle for position. 'Ten seconds' shouts the navigator, '5, 4, 3, 2, Now!' Silence, then, two seconds later 'Bang!' The starting gun has fired and the race has started. We cross the line a

The tall ships sail down from Gothenburg for the start of the race.

The *Christian Radich* dressed overall. (J&C McCutcheon Collection)

Two full-rigged ships, *Christian Radich* on the right, crossing the start line in the 1966 Tall Ships Race. (J&C McCutcheon Collection)

Sir Winston Churchill at speed and seen from the bowsprit.

few seconds after the gun has fired, which is pretty good given the chaos of all the small boats around as well as the other tall ships all jockeying for a good start.

Over the next hour, the small craft gradually fall astern one by one as they head for home and perhaps a few beers at a Swedish barbeque on the beach as we head out for the North Sea and the Atlantic. The late afternoon is calm and sunny as we ease slowly ahead of the *Malcolm Miller*. We can see the square riggers off to the west of us and the *Malcolm Miller* is now off the port quarter about 3 miles away. After the calm start and a lovely evening, the weather changes during the night and the race develops into non-stop action. Events again blur in the mind into a succession of watches, sail trimming, changing sail and getting some sleep whenever we could. We keep our position ahead of the *Malcolm Miller* but we are falling well behind the big square riggers who we think have headed up to the north to make the best use of the south-west wind. The wind is on our beam most of the way across the North Sea and we soon lose sight of the *Malcolm Miller*. Going aloft holds fewer fears now, especially with the bosun yelling at us from the deck telling us what to do. However, with the wind on the beam, the times when we can set the square sails are few. After a couple of days we have lost sight of all the other ships and have no real idea where we are in the race. We believe that the square riggers are well ahead but that is all.

We pass round Fair Isle on a dull and cloudy day with low clouds scudding across the hills. We catch sight of two or three lonely cottages near the shore with smoke from their chimneys being whipped away by the wind. Simon and I stop and watch as the ship rushes on. We imagine that the cottages are full of little old grannies in big rocking chairs, all busily knitting Fair Isle sweaters, sitting round a big peat fire with a nice cup of tea. Now, that would be nice. 'And perhaps a piece of your excellent fruit cake too? Thank you.'

Once clear of Fair Isle the course is set for the Skaggerak and Christiansand in Norway, and we are grateful at last for the wind coming from astern. We are soon ordered aloft again to set the square sails and then we sheet them taut and begin to really sail. We believe that we must be ahead of the *Malcolm Miller* and we now stand a good chance of beating her and winning our class.

That night on the run home the sailing is awesome. It is a wild, windy night with the clouds being blown across the sky and a bright moon that keeps coming out from between the clouds to shine on a ragged, wild and windswept sea. The wave tops are being whipped off and the spray flies horizontally across the sea. *Sir Winston Churchill* surges along down wind and down sea with all square sails set and making 17 ½ knots. For hour after hour we rush through the night, the fore and aft sails set out as far as they could go and the square sails all set on the foremast. We stand awestruck at the stern as the big seas come up out of the darkness from behind the ship and sweep underneath us; lifting first the stern then the whole ship and helping her onwards. All the while the ship yaws as the waves lift her stern and the helmsman works hard countering the yaw. The officer of the watch never takes his eyes off the sails and the rigging as they creak with the strain of the wind as it roars through the rigging. With everything set and the wind steady there is little for the watch on deck to do so a couple of us talk to the officer of the watch, Mike Critchley. Mike is the friendliest officer and takes time to explain to us what he is doing and why, how he is navigating and what he is looking out for in the sails and the wind. He is another RN officer who spent a lot of his life in sailing ships and yachts.

This is our Roaring Forties in a wool clipper running the easting down to the Horn. This is what we came for. We feel we will be in port by breakfast time and for the first time on board we do not want to go below at the end of the watch. This is what real sailing is all about and we want it to last forever. For this one night alone the trip has been worth it.

The galley is on the main deck, one deck above the mess deck and so meals from the galley have to be passed down to a duty server through a serving hatch. He stands at the hatch, takes the plated meals and then turns round and walks four paces to the mess tables. In the deck, just behind the point where the server stands at the hatch there is a trap door hatch down to the dry stores. One day, late in the race during a hurried lunch break the galley boy needs some stores and opens the hatch and shoots down into the stores. At the same time the meals are being passed down through the hatch to the trainee on serving duty. The trainee takes the plates, turns round and sets off towards the mess deck. Then he simply vanishes without a word. The two plates he was carrying are literally left hanging in mid air, *Tom and Jerry* style, for a second or two after he vanishes, then they follow him down the hatch and crash and shatter as they hit the store room deck below. This noise alerts those that had not watched the poor guy vanish, to the fact that anything is amiss! We all just stare at the hatch, no one daring to go and look down to see what carnage was there. There are no yells or screams, perhaps he is dead? Luckily and amazingly, the trainee bounced and suffered no lasting damage other than shock, but it could have been a very nasty incident. The cook was not amused as he had to produce two more meals. It did however highlight to us how easily accidents can happen at sea.

We finally cross the finishing line and arrive in Christiansand and then motor into the harbour. We are all disappointed to see that there, ahead of us on her berth already is the *Malcolm Miller*. She had picked up more wind on the way to Fair Isle than we had and so was actually ahead of us at Fair Isle. In spite of our fabulous run back through the night she still sneaked in ahead of us.

After the race there is an afternoon's inter-ship sports. These are held at some playing fields near the harbour. Being one of the smaller ships, we find that we are up against the big boys, off the big ships, who were full-time naval cadets and had been at sea and in training for months in the big heavy ships and so are much fitter than we are. However, we enter into the spirit of things as no Norwegian or German crew is going to say we are soft!

In the tug of war we easily beat the Swedish ship *Gladen* in the first round. We advance with a win against the French in *Belle Poule* to find ourselves up against the *Gorch Foch* in the semi final. Their team is made up of the biggest youths on the German ship. Hand-picked from a ship's crew of over 150. Oh well, we had got this far, that was pretty good. We take up our positions and ready ourselves. To our surprise we win the first pull. We reckon that they must have all slipped or something. Form is restored on the second pull when they win easily. Now it is one all with a third pull to decide who goes into the final. We all lean back on the rope and try to dig in. The pull seems to last forever but finally after nearly collapsing twice we found the resolve and the grip to hold out and wait for the *Gorch Foch* to step back; then on the yell 'NOW' from our leader, we pull for all we are worth, catch them off balance and have them over the line before they know it. We are in the final! And who is there to meet us? - The *Malcolm Miller*. After our efforts against the Germans we are exhausted and the *Malcolm Miller* wins the final, but only after three pulls. Their team is invited onto the stage and is awarded prizes and all of them get a kiss from a beautiful Miss Christiansand. If we had known that that was a prize we would have pulled even harder! The bosun had been on board on duty and is genuinely upset that he has missed our efforts and keeps apologising for not being there. After the two weeks of him driving us as hard as he could, it is moving that he feels so emotional about our efforts and not being there to support us. It actually affects a few of us as we have not really stopped to think how committed he is to us.

We spend a few very pleasant days in Christiansand. There is not much to do but we are happy walking the streets, looking at the other ships and yachts and chatting

Going ashore in Christiansund. Myself with Bob and Phil, ready to see the sights.

to anyone who will talk to us. We drink coffees and beers, in the cafes and bars, in between cleaning ship and readying her for the easy and relaxing sail back across the North Sea to Leith. The captain calls each of us down for individual appraisals after we leave Christiansand. As we suspected after the training sail, not only did he not know our Christian names after the training sail; he still does not know our surnames after the race. This is no surprise as we are hard pushed to recognise him too. His appraisals are based totally on what the bosun and watch officers have told him.

The Sail Home

After all the efforts we had made in both the training trip and the race itself, we were looking forward to the sail back to Leith as this was going to be a gentle cruise. However, the sail home turns out to be a bit more than we have bargained for as the weather turns very nasty indeed as soon as we leave Norway. It grows into a full Force 9 and we are all on deck to reef down the few sails we are carrying. The fore and aft sails have to be reduced to about half their full size. To do this we need all hands on deck as we heave the sails down the mast to reduce their size while the wind is doing all it can to rip the wet canvas out of our hands. The canvas is like rough sheet metal, it is so taut, and it is hard and slow work. What can it have been like in the Southern ocean in winter when the sails were literally frozen stiff? Luckily in the SWC this can all be done from the deck so we do not have to risk going up into the rigging in this weather. We take in one of the jib sails and this means some scary work up in the bows where the pitching is much more pronounced and where we get hit by lumps of sea water coming over the bow as we heave and struggle to get the sails down against the screaming force of the wind. To add to the fun it is lashing with rain throughout.

The Lee Rail Club is re instated after our few days ashore in Norway. The storm builds and that night heavy seas continually smash over the bows and wash down the length of the deck. The bosun orders lifelines to be rigged along the deck so if a sea comes aboard we can grab the life line and hold on rather than get washed overboard. As we struggle with the ropes to keep the sails trimmed more than one trainee loses his feet and tumbles and pitches back aft through the scuppers in a wave of water. Provided he has not knocked himself out on any of the hard eyes or pin rail supports that line the ship's side, he then has the pleasure of spending the rest of the watch totally soaked. Some of the deck fittings are carried away by the seas and one 10-foot long timber name board is ripped off by the sea and lost without us even knowing. These name boards are heavy wooden carvings with the ship's name and decorative scrolls carved and painted on them and mounted along each bow. It is only discovered missing as we get ready to come into Leith. After two days and two nights of gale and storm force winds we finally make it to Leith where we enter harbour manning the yards. A few trainees take up positions on the squared yards as the ship enters port while the rest of us work the mooring lines on deck. Then quite suddenly it is all over.

Calm at last and heading for home into the setting sun.

We are taken to Waverley Station and catch trains to our respective homes with promises of keeping in touch. I catch the London train to Kings Cross and on the journey have time to reflect on the whole trip. There are many things I recall about the whole trip, the formation of the Lee Rail Club. Formed by and for, those of us who suffered from seasickness and named after the bosun's continual yells at those starting to heave up, 'The lee rail! The lee rail!' Bob suffered really badly from seasickness and eventually had to be seen by the doctor. Simon was also fairly badly hit for most of the race. The rest of us coped as best we could and did our watches but never strayed too far from the lee rail until things got better. Fair Isle seemed to be the turning point and after that we were OK. I remember too the dark, wet nights on deck in the bad weather with five or six of us heaving on a rope as we slipped and slid on the sea washed deck; or wrestling with fighting wet sails accompanied by the continual yells of encouragement or howls of abuse from the bosun or watch officer, depending on what we were doing and how we were doing it. The ship was raced as hard as she could be and to achieve that we all had to suffer. That was the deal. Once you are on board a ship and a part of the crew the only way to succeed is to give everything so you do not let down your shipmates who are also giving their all. At sea you achieve nothing without hard work and often more than a little suffering. You only get out of it what you put in and I think we all put in quite a lot. No one pleaded time off for seasickness, nor for minor injuries and everyone turned out whenever they were needed. It taught us about discipline and to respond instantly to clear precise orders. We learned responsibility, to look out for your shipmates and do what is necessary without question. It also taught us to work and live with others in very close proximity and in difficult conditions. None of us had ever been on a trip like this and it is something that we will all remember for a long time.

I arrived home at about seven that evening to learn from my parents that during the storm that we experienced on the way back across the North Sea, two crew members from one of the smaller 30-foot yachts that had been in the race had been washed overboard and been lost. They had sailed before us and had also tried to get back home to the UK from Norway. This had been reported on the radio in the UK but there had been nothing about how we were fairing so it had been a bit worrying time for all our families. It puts the race into true perspective. It was all meant to be fun, good for learning about the sea, learning responsibility and making friends. It was not meant to end in anyone's death. However, with the sea that is always the price you can pay and, often, it is through no fault of your own.

PART TWO

The Royal Navy

CHAPTER 4

The Royal Navy – Officer Training

With the innocence of youth and the blindness of inexperience, I set out on a route that would pitch me head first into the life of a Nelsonian seaman where I was to become the subject of a Royal Naval board of Enquiry on my very first day at sea. I had been struggling to decide which career path to take. In spite of my love for travel and the sea, vocational tests pointed to architecture as the best career for me. As I had some doubts, before embarking on a seven-year college course I went to work in an architect's office in London as an 'architectural assistant', which was basically, an office boy. The work consisted of learning to draw different scale plans of drainage systems under supervision from one of the partners, as well as making the coffees, getting rid of unwanted sales reps, and visiting the local printers two or three times a day. Unfortunately, after working in there for nine months and seeing first-hand what the daily nine to five life of the qualified architects consisted of, I was convinced that this was not really the career for me.

Having spent so many hours staring aimlessly out of windows dreaming of ships and the sea, I had seen an advert for the Royal Navy and decided to try and see if I could get in on a five-year Short Service Commission. I would then, hopefully, be able to say that I had done something of note that was recognized in civilian life and might even help me on in the world afterwards. So, one lunch time, I walked down to Whitehall and up the grand steps into Old Admiralty Building. I was met by a slightly surprised civil servant and I asked him, 'Excuse me but how do I join the Navy?' He did not seem sure, not an encouraging start, but he went away and returned with a form for me to take home and fill in. This was duly sent off. Some weeks later and after having decided that my application had been rejected, I was stunned to get a letter inviting me to the Admiralty Interview board in HMS *Sultan*, a naval shore establishment in Gosport.

The Admiralty Interview Board

This was three days of non-stop activity. The boards were run throughout the year with each board selecting two or three candidates for the next term's entry. In our batch of applicants there were about twelve to fifteen of us, all competing for two or three places at the Britannia Royal Naval College at Dartmouth, where if we were successful, we would be trained to be naval officers. Most of the activity took place in a red brick, two-storey building where we slept in a dormitory, ate in a mess room and did our written tests in the classrooms, and the oral phases of the interview process took place in a large board room on the ground floor.

The first day was spent doing written tests. These essentially were testing us for basic literacy and included mathematics and geometry, essay writing and tests on the use of English. We also did a number of psychometric tests that looked at our abilities, personality traits and attitudes. After dinner on the first night one of the officers came in and said 'You do not have to stay here all evening you know. Why don't you go to the pub for a drink? It's just down the road' 'How friendly the Navy is', we all thought. So off we all trooped down to the pub. It was not too crowded. There was a mixed group of people at one table and a couple of men on their own playing darts. Most of the men seemed to have naval haircuts, but then in Gosport so did everyone as nearly everyone was Navy. Once we had got our beers, I found myself chatting to Nick, a guy about my own age who also wanted to do a Short Service Commission and had been on a trip on the *Malcolm Miller*, though not a full Tall Ships Race. After a couple of beers, Nick and I decided to go back to the mess but a group of the others who were beginning to enjoy themselves stayed on 'just for one more beer'.

In the brief that was sent to us before we came to the board we were asked to bring swimming trunks and plimsolls. The next day we found out why. At breakfast we were all given a set of navy overalls and told to wear them over our swimming trunks. As we were being mustered by the POs, Nick nudged me in the ribs. 'Aren't they the two guys who were playing darts at the pub last night?' I looked across. They were! It was now clear that they had been in the pub, appearing to be normal pub goers, but were in fact watching us and our behavior once we were clear of HMS *Sultan*. I wondered whether those that had stayed on for another beer or three had spotted them too!

We spent the day undergoing physical leadership tests, which took place in a converted warehouse about a quarter of a mile away. For these tests we were divided into teams of six and each team had to complete a series of six timed tasks. One person in the team was nominated by the examiners as the leader for each task, but the other members were expected to contribute ideas as the task went on. Each series of tasks involved arranging a given set of equipment such as planks of wood, wooden poles, large oil drums, lengths of rope, and heavy ropes that were suspended from the roof. The team then had to design and build a route across or around an 'obstacle'. They then had to take an 'object of high value', in most cases an old ammunition box; across the imaginary obstacle in a set amount of time. For most tests there was only one way to do it and at first glance there never seemed to be enough equipment to complete the task. The nominated team leader had to work out how to rig the available equipment and then brief and lead the team in its construction. Then he had to get the 'object' and all his team over it in the time allowed.

For some tests the obstacle was a 12-foot wide by 5-foot deep tank of cold water, for others just the floor, but a floor that was deemed to be a bottomless ravine and anyone or anything that was dropped was immediately deemed to be out of the game. My

Britannia Royal Naval College sitting high above the town of Dartmouth.

swimming trunks were put to good use when I lost my balance and fell into the water tank on the second test. I was then wet and cold for the rest of the morning. On the test for which I was nominated to lead the team, we had to build a rope and plank bridge across a bottomless ravine. All the time an examining officer was yelling 'You should have finished planning it by now!' 'How much more chatting are you lot going to do?' 'You should have your bridge built by now!' 'You only have ten minutes left' Get a move on! Are you sure you have done that right?' and other such motivational shouts. I managed not to panic, and we persevered; but when we ran out of time we had not even completed the bridge, let alone got anyone across it! We were told that we had made a mistake at the beginning by misjudging the width of the gap and the length of the planks so were really doomed before we started. However, we did not lose any men down the ravine and I thought that perhaps I had shown signs of leading from the front, but even so I did not feel very optimistic about my chances of selection.

After we were allowed to dry off and change, the rest of the day was taken up with one-to-one interviews with a psychologist who probed us about our views, family, background and our personal prejudices. There was then a further group interview. In this, a team of six of us sat before the main board and were given a written brief of the problem to be solved. In our case it was set in Antarctica where a member of a small naval survey party had been badly injured in a fall down a crevasse up on a glacier. We had to decide how to get the injured man back to base. However, there were all sorts of limitations placed on us such as the helicopter's fuel, bad weather and other higher priority tasks for the helicopter. This was a free-thinking session with no nominated leader but designed, I think, to find out who in the group could or would take a lead and, with help from the team, think the problem out and persuade the others that this was the right solution. Our group seemed to deal with the problem rationally and each step was worked out and agreed and we got close to some form of a solution when the captain stopped us by saying, 'OK you seem to have a fairly good handle on this. Let's look at what you missed.'

On the last day we met the board individually and were quizzed about our reasons for being there as well as our background and future aspirations. This was perhaps the most daunting part as the board. I was sent in and found myself in a large and otherwise empty room. The board members, six officers led the captain, sat on a low stage behind a long table. In the middle of the room, and placed on its own facing the board, was an upright chair for the candidate. I was directed to sit down on the chair. I was reminded of the painting by William Yeames of the small son of a Royalist being questioned by a group of Roundhead soldiers and titled 'And when did you last see your father?' The proceedings began with a general background session and then my CV was investigated. Misleading or erroneous statements in CVs were quickly discovered and no mercy was shown if anyone tried to bull their way through. A little earlier one candidate came out almost in tears after his CV was found to contain some fiction and he was left in no doubt what the board thought about it. I was then asked to point to the correct parts of a blank map of the UK when asked where certain places were located. The same test was then done on a blank world map. The Chairman asked 'What have you done in your life that makes you feel that you are qualified to join the Royal Navy?' I recounted my trips to sea on the *Lord Lovat*, the *Silvana* and the *Sir Winston Churchill* in the Tall Ships Race. Most of the board seemed to accept that as an OK thing to do. One of the officers however did not. 'Why on earth would you want to do that?' 'A Hull trawler for goodness sake!' The implication being that a naval officer would never do such a thing. At the time I thought this was strange as surely a naval officer would and should know what life on a trawler was like but this was all part of the interview technique and was done to try and make us lose our cool. I bit my tongue and said nothing. What could I say?

The questions resumed. 'If you were to join the Royal Navy what type of ship would you like to serve in and why?' Prior to going to the interview I had no idea about the different types of naval ship. They were all just warships to me and I had not thought too much about it. However, the previous day I had noticed a large model in the main hallway of an RN County Class destroyer, (whatever that was?) and an engraved plate describing the ship and all the gunnery systems, missile and special systems with which it was fitted. When I was asked the question I tried to remember what I had read on this plaque and caused a few smiles along the board when I said in a confident voice that 'I want to serve in a County Class Destroyer because it has stabilisers, Sir.'

After three days we were sent on our way, exhausted and confused. The board gave us absolutely no indication of how we had fared and each of us was sure we had failed to get into the Royal Navy. What would I do now? Perhaps I should now try the Merchant Navy? All they said was that if in the next week to ten days we were invited for an MOD medical examination this would mean that we had passed the board and would be selected for the Royal Navy, provided that we passed the medical tests. A week or more went by with no word, but then I received a phone call from the MOD telling me that I was invited to the Services Medical Centre in London for a full medical and dental check. Following an afternoon in Empress State

Building near Earl's Court of being endlessly prodded, poked, asked to cough, 'now stand against that freezing cold X-ray machine', told to put out my tongue, cough, touch my toes, and being hit with a hammer I was allowed to get dressed. 'Right, that's all here, now just your dental check up!' Was joining the Navy really worth all this? Finally I was allowed to go! Happily, a couple of days later a letter arrived saying that barring a couple of fillings, I was fit enough for the Royal Navy!

BRNC

The Britannia Royal Naval College at Dartmouth stands proudly behind the town, overlooking the river Dart and out to sea. A few weeks later I found myself, along with over 200 others, standing on the parade ground in the front of the college. We had been brought into the college by bus from Newton Abbot Station. As I got off the bus a petty officer yelled at me 'Name and initial?' 'Gray, G.' He consulted a list, 'Right, stand over there by the green flag. Next!' Why was everyone yelling? For a naval cadet on day one it was an imposing and very intimidating scene. As we waited for everyone to be sorted I looked about my new home. I felt sure that the architect, Aston Webb, had deliberately designed the facade of the college so that all the windows and tall white towers glared critically down on us. It was as if the college was already looking for our failings and weaknesses and was keeping a logbook with all the reasons why we were are not fit to follow the great naval heroes who had trod this parade ground before us.

To our left, the gleaming white figurehead of Britannia herself, complete with her Triton, stared past us and out to sea as if we did not exist. Later we would learn that one of the biggest mistakes we could make in any written work at the college was to misspell her name. This instantly earned us the yell from the lecturer of 'Britannia with ONE "T" and TWO "N"s'. Report to Britannia, salute her and repeat 'One "T" and two "N"s twenty times!' You then had to double from the classroom to the figurehead, and stand there, alone on the parade ground, saluting and calling out 'Britannia with one "T" and two "N"s'. All the time the rest of the college watched you from the glowering windows. You only ever misspelt her name once! At the river end of the parade ground the captain of the college's house stood in its privileged and dominant position and glared suspiciously at us all. It represented somewhere we should aspire to live one day, but really without much hope as we were mere cadets and to live in the captain's house was something from another world.

A young, tall and pale sub-lieutenant, called 'SIR' to us, took charge of about forty of us and marched us to Drake Division. Nervously, we looked about us at the long corridors with polished wood floors, the endless rows of framed photos of groups of cadets who had gone before, or of naval heroes from the past, all wrapped in the smell of wood wax polish. We went across the grand double-storied quarter deck and past the library, then up endless stairs until we were told to stop in another long, dark, wooden-floored corridor. This was the part of the college that would be our home for the next year. We were a little encouraged as the sub-lieutenant not only looked younger than some of us but seemed more nervous than we did too. I was lucky to find I was in a two-berth cabin which I was to share with a friendly Londoner called Geoff Luker. He was a friendly, easy-going guy and he and I shared the cabin for six months, becoming good friends. In spite of all the rigours and constant demands of naval training, I cannot remember Geoff and I ever losing our tempers or falling out with each. He seemed to be able to take everything with a shrug and a smile and it helped me no end, as I tended to take things, perhaps, a bit too seriously. Unlike some cadets who had fathers in the Navy, or some form of naval family background, Geoff and I had none at all so we were able to help each other along as we unraveled the seemingly endless mysteries of naval life, its customs and language.

Once I had settled in, one of the first things I did was to look up an old acquaintance. At school the Combined cadet Force had a Royal Naval section as well as the army and RAF sections. After a compulsory term in the army section we were given the chance to apply to join one of the others if we wanted to. The most popular was the naval section and I applied to join. The master in charge of the naval section was a teacher called Derek who was not only my physics teacher who I knew well, but also the school swimming coach, and I was part of the school swimming team. I felt that as he was a good, fair man I had a chance, but sadly my application was rejected so I had to stay in the army section and while my pals in the naval section went off for days at sea on MFVs and visited HMS *Victory* and modern warships in Portsmouth; my army pals and I learnt how to clean rifles and crawl through hedges and wet ditches keeping our bottoms down. A few years later Derek left the school to take up a senior science lecturer's position at BRNC, Dartmouth. A couple of years after that, as a new cadet, I had great delight in knocking on his study door at Dartmouth. He opened it and the look of surprise on his face was a picture. 'Crickey, Gray! What are you doing here?' 'I live here now Sir', I replied, he looked at me a little mystified. 'But you weren't in the naval section at School!' 'No Sir, you may have rejected me, but the Queen didn't.' He smiled and invited me in for some tea.

There then followed twelve months of rigorous naval shore training. Discipline was strict and the minor punishment for failure to follow College rules was normally an early morning run at 0600. The worst crime was being late. Or 'Adrift' as the Navy called it. 'Always be there five minute early' – Unless you want an 0600 run! As the divisional chief petty officer said 'Thems' wots keen gets fell in previous!' The training was thorough and covered everything from personal fitness to navigation, from parade-ground marching drills, to rifle shooting and swimming tests. We were taken on special fire-fighting training courses and taught how to deal with major shipboard fires and oil fires in all conditions, including the dark. We experienced CS gas for riot-control training and were taught to row and sail down on the river Dart. The subject list seemed endless and the classroom subjects included mechanical and electrical marine engineering, meteorology, naval supply, administration and management, communications and the principles of Action Information Organisation, or Command and Control as it is now known, and the theory of radar, radio and sonar. We learned seamanship from the three volumes of Admiralty books, including anchor-handling using fantastic working models of a battleship fo'c'sle with all the anchor cables, windlasses and slips. We learned coastal navigation and struggled to grasp the principles of circular geometry that applied to astro-navigation. On top of that they found time to send us out onto Dartmoor for expeditions that involved rigging timber A-frames to get across rivers, camping out and navigating ourselves across the moor. We were sent up the river Dart in 30-foot motor whalers on night exercises. These were a form of treasure hunt in the dark; where the clues were hidden at various land-based locations near the river. Each crew had its own leader who determined which clues to pursue and then the rest of the crew were dispatched ashore to find the clues, then work out the correct answers that would lead on to the next location. In the process, we had to avoid the many mud banks and shallows that lurk beneath the tidal Dart just waiting to catch a cadet on a falling tide. The night rang out with the calls of cadets who had lost their boat or a crew trying to drag someone back on board from the river, as well as calls for assistance or a tow from those who had run aground.

Sleep was a treasured commodity at Dartmouth. For the first six weeks we were not allowed out of the college at all; so we had to wait until we could savour the delights of Dartmouth town. Our days started at 0630 with physical exercise of some sort, PT or a run. There were also regular early morning Morse code reading sessions using a signal lantern. Then it was breakfast, where kindly ladies provided all the food that you could eat. One lady, trying to ensure her charges did not fade away from under nourishment, told a cadet 'Now you be sure to drink all your milk, young man!' 'That's what I tell my three-year-old son' growled the twenty-three-year-old ex-rating who was now an officer cadet. The mornings were filled with classroom studies while the afternoons tended to be for boat training on the river or sport. Further classroom studies took place in the evenings. The classroom studies and homework were important as at the end of the year we all had to pass our final exams to enable us to 'Pass Out' of the college. The lecturers were either civilians, like Derek, or naval officers and all were helpful and competent. As most had been through Dartmouth themselves, they knew the struggle we were facing and were eager to help us all they could. At 1600, it was rugby training or maybe a home match. And so it continued through to dinner. After dinner you had to get the cabin ready for rounds by the duty sub-lieutenant at 1930. This meant your beds had to be correctly made, clothes had to be folded and stowed correctly, shoes clean, parade boots bulled and no dust anywhere; even on top of the door or under the bunks. If any was found or there were other faults, maybe your parade boots were not up to standard, you were given a 'Rescrub' at 2100. As long as the cabin had passed rounds homework could be fitted in after that.

In addition to the new cadets there were also a similar number of sub-lieutenants on their third year courses at the college. These were officers who had just completed their midshipman's year at sea and had returned to college for further naval training and higher education courses. They provided the college staff with an extra set of monitors to hound and chase the worthless cadets. As cadets we had to run, or double, everywhere in the college. Run to meals, run between classes, etc. This was all part of getting us fit. The fun side of this was that in our smooth-soled shoes or hob-nailed parade boots you could slide enormous distances on the wood block floors! If any sub-lieutenant caught you not running, or indeed doing anything that you should not be doing (being caught with your hands in your pocket was always a favourite), then they could and often did, impose punishments then and there. The yell of 'Double that cadet' was often heard echoing round the red brick walls and the sound lives on in the heads of all those who were its target.

One of these allowed punishments was 'Quick Changes'. The sub-lieutenant would order you to attend his cabin at say 2100 in your daily battle dress rig and parade boots and then he would tell you to report back in three minutes wearing your gym kit. Then when you got there he would say 'Right, now be back here in three minutes in full mess undress.' Panic would set in (this rig was a real bummer as you had to have your bowtie tied correctly as well!). All the while the sub-lieutenant would be standing with his watch in his hand. Then he would order you to appear in, say, your sailing rig complete with seaman's knife, clean shoes, etc. Each new rig change was designed to ensure maximum clothing being removed and maximum chaos caused in the cabin. This would go on for as long as the sub-lieutenant wanted but often for at least half an hour. By this time, and given the number of different sets of clothing you had, your cabin looked like a Chinese laundry after a typhoon had hit it. The sub-lieutenant would then say 'That's all, don't do it again. Oh, by the way, I will do rounds on your cabin in ten minutes.' Even greater panic! Failure to have all your gear re-stowed and in the correct locations could result in another Rescrub thirty minutes later when all you really wanted to do was go to bed. With any luck your cabin mate would have been there all the time helping get the right rig and putting others away as you tore them off. In hindsight, it was all great fun and mattered little in the great scheme of life, but at the time it seemed that your whole life depended on it.

Sport was a big part of college life and I was fortunate enough to get into the rugby 1st XV, which gave me a lot of extra physical training most days as well as two matches a week. It also allowed us to get out of the college to play away matches against local colleges, such as Millfield College, and local rugby clubs such as Exeter. These away games normally involved a stop for fish and chips or beer on the way back. I also discovered that being in the 1st XV enabled you to escape duty parades, like rounds, if there was a college match on. Representing the college at a major sport also counted highly in your final assessments. Bit by bit I was learning how to survive and enjoy life in a navy blue suit.

HMS *Tenby* – Sea Training

Following two terms at Dartmouth we were sent to join our first ship, HMS *Tenby*, which was one of the ships in the Dartmouth Training Squadron. This squadron consisted of three frigates each converted to take a large mess deck full of cadets. The other two ships were HMS *Scarborough* and HMS *Torquay*.

HMS *Tenby* was a Whitby-Class, or a Type 12, frigate. She had been built at Cammell Laird in 1953 and commissioned in 1955. She was 360-feet-long, was

HMS *Tenby*, a Whitby-Class frigate and part of the Dartmouth training squadron in 1970.
(J&C McCutcheon Collection)

2,600 tons and had twin screws. This class of ship was designed to be a fast escort
with an ASW (Anti-Submarine-Warfare) capability. A feature of the class was the
hull design, which gave the ships a high fo'c'sle with a sharp, flared bow to throw
the seas up and away from the ship and to enable it to continue at high speed in
bad weather. It was also designed to minimise the amount of water getting onto the
deck that could then freeze and cause icing problems in the Arctic.

Life in the mess deck was not a great deal of fun, but then it was not meant to be.
As they say in the Navy, 'If you can't take a joke, you shouldn't have joined.' There
were no portholes or natural light and no air conditioning. As in the days of Nelson
and HMS *Victory*, we slept, ate, read, got dressed, did our studying, and wrote letters
home; all in the small same cramped space as fifty other cadets. We slept in hammocks
slung directly above the fixed mess tables and benches. Each hammock touched the
ones next to it with four or five to a row. The rope lashings at each end overlapped the
lashings of the next row so that your head was only a couple of feet away from the feet
of the guy in the next row. We each were allocated a steel locker, roughly 1 metre by
½ metre by 1 metre high, which was exactly the same as those used by the ratings, in
which we had to keep everything we possessed. From our best uniform and working
rigs, sports clothes, parade boots and working shoes to our civilian clothes, training
books and midshipman's journal, as well as any personal items we might have.

There was a leading seaman living in the mess with us to oversee us and make
sure we did things properly, especially cleaning and washing up the mess tins after
meals. The first thing he showed us was how to rig and then stow our hammocks.
If done properly they were as safe as houses. If not, then you could crash down in
the night onto the mess table below. I had found hammocks to be good for sleeping
in when I was on the *Sir Winston Churchill*, and found the same in HMS *Tenby*.
Once you had mastered rigging the hammock and getting into it and sleeping on
your back, they were very comfortable. Most nights the non-stop routine of cadet
life in HMS *Tenby* was such that we fell asleep instantly as soon as we were in our
hammocks. My immediate hammock neighbour was Graeme. Graeme and I had

become friends over the months at the college and, once we were allowed to have shore leave, Graeme and I were often to be found testing the different whiskies in the Dartmouth hostelries. Graeme was a quiet guy, but bright and cheery with a very dry sense of humour. He was from Worcester Park in Surrey and had joined the Navy straight from school as a career, or general list, officer.

We all kept watches throughout the twenty-fout hours so we had to learn where everyone else slept so you could give anyone a shake in the night for their watch. It was not a popular move to wake the wrong guy. If you did and the right guy did not get his shake it was still his fault if he was late on watch.

On board we formed a part of the ship's crew and carried out the duties that the junior rates, who we replaced, would have done as well as having to carry out our practical officer's training. We were treated, as the lowest of the low. We were junior to the most junior seaman on board and regularly reminded of it.

Mortar Bombs

We sailed from Devonport for our training Cruise to the Baltic. We were all fairly excited to be at sea as naval officers, albeit very junior ones, on our way out into the big wide world and our minds were full of gorgeous Swedish blondes that we were bound to meet! On the very first full day at sea we were all sent to our action stations while the ship carried out ASW (Anti Submarine Warfare) exercises off the South coast.

My action station was in the Port Mortar Handling Room and I shared this with Bas, a fellow cadet. This was a compartment where the ASW mortars were stowed. These were large torpedo shaped items about 5 foot long and 19 inches in diameter. They were fired in a pattern of three from launchers up on the deck so that they landed in a triangular pattern round the enemy submarine and exploded to cause maximum damage. They were all painted to a colour code; some mortars were red, some green and some black, depending upon their usage. They were stored in horizontal racks that ran fore and aft along the compartment in such a way that they could be rolled onto the special lift at the after end that took them up to the Mortar Launcher compartment. The TAS (Torpedo & Anti Submarine) Petty Officer (PO) had briefed us that three of the mortars, also painted black, were set aside on the lower of two racks by the hoist. These mortars contained special calibration, test and tuning systems and they were inserted into the launch barrels and used to test and tune all the firing circuitry of the system but were never actually fired.

The job Bas and I had was to load onto the lift whatever mortars the petty officer up in the Handling Room called for. The PO simply called down the chute from the mortar bay itself, telling us which ones he wanted for the next shoot and to send them up on the lift. We were using 'Black Inert' or practice mortars on this exercise and all went well as both Bas and I were, by now, highly trained naval officers and could tell black from green and red.

After about an hour or so, and having sent up all the black ones allocated for the exercise on the main rack, the call came down the chute from the PO to 'Send up the other three'. Bas and I looked at each other. 'Which three is that?' Bas called back as we did not have any more of the black inert ones ready to send up. 'The three on the other rack' called the PO. We sent them up and heard them successfully fired in to the sea. After the exercise was concluded the PO called down for the Test Mortars to be sent up. 'Which ones are those?' we called back, both of us a little puzzled. 'The black ones on the bottom rack' he called. Bas and I looked at each other again as alarm began to strike home. Bas called back 'But we have already sent them up when you asked for them last time!' Bas has not finished his sentence when the PO burst into the Handling Room. He was, I must say, very good about it and apart from some understandable naval swearing he did not chew us out too badly. He was more concerned about going to see the Torpedo Officer to report that the only test mortars the ship had, and which were worth a considerable sum, were now on the seabed.

The torpedo officer was not so good about it. He was called Charles and was in fact the same Charles who had been the stand-offish watch officer on *Sir Winston Churchill*. Bas and I were summoned to the ops room. In front of the captain and a full ops room he openly accused Bas and I of lying and demanded that we be severely dealt with. The captain maintained a calm exterior and sent us away. A board of Enquiry was called on board ship that afternoon and both Bas and I spent the rest of our first full day at sea in the RN as subjects of the enquiry and explaining to the first lieutenant and the Engineer Officer exactly what had happened. Our stories tallied and the petty officer was good enough to admit to us and the Enquiry that perhaps we could have been confused and that his instructions could perhaps have been clearer. In the end he got the blame for not supervising us more closely as how could we, on the first visit to the mortar room, be expected to tell the difference between a black inert and a black test mortar let alone to question a direct order 'to send up the three on the other rack' from the petty officer torpedoes.

Our relationship with 'Charles' never recovered but we learned later that no one got on with him anyway, but our relations with the petty officer torpedoes did and we got on well with him for the rest of the three months we were on board and stationed down in his mortar handling room. Bas incidentally did very well, as he was a bright lad, becoming a full captain (air engineer).

Foreign Expedition

The training Squadron that term went to the Baltic, stopping at such places as Stockholm, Copenhagen and Kotka, in Finland. As part of our training we were expected to go on expeds (expeditions) during the ship's periods in port. These were just really camping trips aimed at sharpening up our initiative skills and get us out of the ship for a while. Graeme and I had planned to do one but Graeme went down with a bad sinus infection so a fellow cadet, Keith, and I decided that we would go camping in Denmark's sunny pastoral landscape for two nights during the ship's stay in Copenhagen. We submitted our proposal, which was accepted, got all the camping gear loaned to us from the ship's stores and set off with a map and wise words from our divisional officer, 'OK, off you go, you have the ship's phone number to ring if you need help don't you?' 'Yes, Sir' we replied. This was unlikely as we had no intention of going any further than the nearest half decent cheap hotel and enjoying a proper bath and a proper bed for two nights after putting up with the mess deck and hammocks for over two months. We soon found a pleasant small hotel in a back street near Copenhagen's old harbour. The hotel was very clean and friendly and we were shown to a bright, sunlit, twin-bedded room. It was ideal. We celebrated our freedom with a steak meal and probably more than a few lagers. We considered that we were not skiving, but actually on an 'Escape and Evasion' exercise as we certainly did not want to bump into any of the ship's officers over the next couple of days! On the second morning Keith had gone out for an early walk along the quay and I went along the corridor to the bathroom for a bath. As I tried to open the room door to get back in I realised with horror that I had left the key by the bed. I then spent a damp and chilly fifteen minutes in the Hotel Reception, standing patiently in a queue of guests who were checking out while dripping water all over the polished floor, and clutching a small, wet towel round my waist, so I could ask for a spare key. There was much Danish chuckling going on.

Once back on board we sat down together and wrote our reports of how friendly the farmer was to let us sleep in his field and how attractive his sheep were (well, we had been at sea for a while).

Seaboats

'Pull! Pull! damn you. Pull! you lazy shower!' These friendly words still haunt me. Every day at sea at 1600 we had Seaboat Pulling drills. The sea boat was a heavy 27-foot Monatague whaler; this was a wooden boat that took a crew of five oarsmen, a coxswain and a bowman to propel it. It was secured fore and aft to the ship's davits by two heavy manila ropes, called falls, which needed a good team of men on each one to lower and raise the boat with any degree of control. There were no winches, hydraulics or electric motors here. The exercise commenced with one part of the watch manning the boat and the other part manning the falls. The gunnery officer was in charge. He would stand one deck above us and became a fierce and friendless demon who clearly hated each and every one of us and who we all hated back with a vengeance. The falls were released from their cleats and lowering began. Each team on each fall had to lower away and make sure that the boat was lowered evenly or else they risked tipping the boat's crew twenty feet into the sea. Any mistakes by any individual resulted in the instant command 'That cadet, twenty press ups, now!' Then, as the sea boat reached the water, ideally as the top of a wave lifted the boat, the coxswain yelled 'Slip' and one of the boat's crew pulled the slip that released the falls from the boat. If the coxswain got the timing wrong and we missed the top of the wave, then the boat dropped a number of feet and hit the water with a crash that inspired the gunnery officer to even more inventive use of the English language. It also gave cadets in the boat very bruised backsides and rattled a few teeth; but no one ever seemed to worry about that. The boat swung out away from the ship's side and the boat rope was released by the bowman. The boat rope, that was attached to the sea boat's bow, was secured on board the ship well forward of the sea boat. It ensured that the sea boat moved off at the same speed as the ship, when it hit the water. At the same time, the ships engines were stopped then run slowly astern. We now had to get the oars out smartly and row round the ship, which towered above us and was still going faster than we were able to pull. All the time the ship was slowly, slowing down and as we rowed for the bow we just hoped that they had enough astern power running so that we did not get cut in two by the ship as we went round the bow. The grey, sharp-edged bows loomed over us as the coxswain tried to judge the turn. It was always a finely judged manoeuvre; either to give the bow a wide berth and use up precious time by pulling further, or try and save time and then risk getting the oars tangled up in the bow. That only brought on a tirade of abuse from above about scratching the ships paintwork; so it was best avoided. As we rowed our little hearts out the gunnery officer was following us round the fo'c'sle giving us lots of encouragement from high above. 'Pull you lazy lot! My four-year-old daughter could pull better than that' 'I bet she can, just to get away from you!' muttered the bowman! Many other such motivating words of advice were offered down to us from on high. Once safely round the bow we had to race down the other side. We all tried to pull together and look professional but we never quite seemed to succeed. By now though, the ship could even be going astern giving us further to row. In all sorts of seas we struggled through this daily hell. Hands and fingers aching as we hung onto the heavy wooden oars, backs sore, crabs being caught as we missed the water with the oar and much muttered cursing in the boat about the gunnery officer's parents and other general fun filled our late afternoons. Once round the stern it was back to the falls and the task of getting the oars in, not hitting the ship and hooking up to the falls. Each fall had a large, heavy, wooden block at the end. In the boat were two metal releasing mechanisms called the 'Robinson's Disengaging Gear'. As we approached, the two great wooden blocks swung menacingly at head level challenging us to catch them. We had to grab these things, drag them into the boat and hook each one onto the hooks on the releasing gear in the boat. Then we had to wait while the other part of the watch started to haul us and the boat back up to the top of the falls. Once we were back at the top and all was secure the gunnery officer told us how long we had taken and what a useless shower of girls we were and reassured us that we would never get a job on the Gosport Ferry. Then it was someone else's go! Every day we gleefully looked forward to this wonderful form of sado-masochism, which undoubtedly made men of us. Electric or hydraulic davits indeed! How soft are sailors today? 'Come on lads; time for a brew of tea on the mess deck'.

The tot. officers were not entitled to a daily rum ration, or the tot, as it was known. However, as officers under training we were required to witness the issue of rum that took place on board every RN ship every day at noon. This tradition ended in July 1970 after being a central part of RN life for nearly 300 years. The history of rum in the Royal Navy is covered in Appendix 1.

CHAPTER 5

HMS *Keppel* –
Midshipman's Training

After our year at Dartmouth and successfully passing the final exams, we graduated or 'Passed Out' of the college at Lord High Admiral's Divisions. This major ceremony is held annually and was normally attended by HM The Queen. This is followed, the next day, by the summer ball. It is a huge affair with bands, pop groups and discos playing in different areas all over the college. Sumptuous buffet dinners for all and every Dartmouth hotel and guest house full of parents, girlfriends and close relations. Later in the evening some of us went down into the old town and looked back up at the college. Now that we had overcome the challenges that we had been set, the college's wide imperial facade of red brick and Portland stone with its central clock tower did not seem so intimidating. It looked magnificent under the floodlights and seemed to float majestically above the surrounding trees high, up on its hill overlooking the town. The warm, soothing sounds of a Caribbean steel band playing outside on the parade ground drifted down over the town, making Dartmouth a Caribbean hot spot for the night.

We were now promoted to midshipmen and sent off for a year's solid sea training in the Fleet. Here, we would live in the wardroom with the other officers and be treated as colleagues. After the trials and indignities of life as mere cadets, we left the college excited and eager to see what being an officer at sea in the Royal Navy really meant. This next period of sea training was to cover all aspects of operating a fighting ship from learning to be the officer of the watch to working in the boiler room, understanding the practicalities of stores management and catering to learning about gunnery and anti submarine warfare as well as trying to gain our qualifications for bridge watch keeping and ocean navigation. We were also expected to learn how to become a valued member of the wardroom. Oh yes, and how to clean the bilges underneath the main boilers! This year was to put all the theory we had learnt at Dartmouth into practical application. We also had to complete task books that formed a vital part of the final Midshipman's Board exam that we had to take at the end of the year at sea.

I was fortunate in that, purely by chance, I was paired up with my good friend from Dartmouth, Graeme, for our first spell as midshipmen. We were both sent to HMS *Keppel* for the first half of our midshipman's year of training at sea.

HMS *Keppel*, a Type 14 Blackwood-class ASW frigate, turns at speed in a calm sea.
With thanks to David Page at www.navyphotos.co.uk. Also thanks to Peter Swarbrick at
peter@swarbrick.com.

HMS *Keppel* was a Type 14 frigate, one of the 12 Blackwood Class of second rate
ASW (Anti-Submarine Warfare) frigates built for the RN in the early/mid-1950s
and all named after famous RN captains. They were of 1,456 tons displacement
and 94 metres long with a beam of just 10 metres. They were designed to be single
role, anti-submarine ships and built to help address the growing Soviet submarine
threat in the north Atlantic. They were smaller and cheaper than the Type 12
frigates, such as *Tenby*. They had a single screw and were powered by a steam
turbine. They were armed with two Limbo ASW Mortars mounted aft. Although
they were essentially good sea boats, they had a terrible reputation for rolling in
any sort of a seaway. Her CO was Cdr Richard Onslow.

In the 1950s, 1960s and 1970s, Britain's main fishing efforts were in the Arctic,
especially round Iceland and the Barents Sea off northern Norway. One of HMS
Keppel's main roles was fishery protection in the Arctic. Graeme and I joined her
in her home port of Rosyth in Scotland.

We arrived on board, feeling nervous and excited but looking forward to life at
sea as a 'proper' naval officer. However, we were greeted on board by a strangely
subdued and reticent atmosphere in the wardroom. No one seemed keen to talk
to us or make us very welcome. The steward showed us where our cabins were
and left us to it. Later in the day we were called down to meet the first lieutenant.
Without preamble he began 'You are here for training. When not on duty you are

expected to be studying in your cabin and not sitting around drinking coffee in the wardroom. The wardroom is for meals and that is all. You will address every officer on board, including the sub-lieutenants, as "Sir" and will not fraternize with the senior rates. I will inspect your Task Books every week and failure to meet the required standard is totally unacceptable due to the disgrace it would bring to the ship.' This friendly greeting took us by surprise, as this was totally contrary to what we had been led to believe that life in the fleet would be like. Everyone at Dartmouth had said how much better life as a middy would be after the strict regime of the college. We believed that we would be part of the wardroom and treated as equals (well almost equal) by our fellow officers so we could learn from them.

It was also accepted that you could call sub-lieutenants and lieutenants by their Christian names. Lieutenant commanders and above were 'Sir' to everyone below them anyway. Being told not to fraternise with senior rates was also strange as we had been told that the senior rates were the guys who could help us the most in learning about the ship and completing out task books. This was not a good start. Graeme and I found ourselves on our first day aboard sitting in my cabin wondering whether we had all been told a load of rubbish at Dartmouth.

It took us a few days to find out what was happening. The correspondence officer, or Corro, was a sub-lieutenant called Simon who was one of the good guys. He took pity on us and one afternoon called us down to his office when the first lieutenant was ashore. 'The two previous midshipmen here both badly failed their boards,' he said. 'It was obvious to everyone that they would, as they had not done any work on board and had spent most of their time loafing in the wardroom or senior rates mess. The previous first lieutenant did not chase them up at all and they failed so badly that the ship has been warned by the Admiralty to buck up. The Captain took it personally and 1st Lt got a roasting for being too lax with them'. Graeme and I were now reaping the rewards of their efforts. 'I am afraid that you two will have a tough time here as the CO and Jimmy will be onto you if they think you are not doing well enough, hence this nonsense about not being seen in the wardroom.' He added, 'Personally I think it is wrong. You have just arrived from Dartmouth and should be treated as midshipmen should be and not punished for the failings of others.' The First Lieutenant, Dave Marsh, was actually a pretty good bloke but could not show us he was.

We accepted the situation as we had no choice and were effectively excluded from the wardroom. The only officers who tried to show us some companionship were Simon, and the Torpedo Officer, Tom. At first I thought Tom was a bit stand-offish as he was very much in the image of a smooth and proper naval officer, complete with white silk handkerchief in his breast pocket. However, he was also kind and helpful as well as professional. In the meantime, Graeme and I just ate our meals and went to our cabins if we were at sea; or ashore if we were alongside and not on duty. In fact, poor Graeme did not even have a cabin. We were told that accommodation was scarce in *Keppel* and while I was allocated the last spare cabin, Graeme was told he could stow his gear in my cabin but was to sleep in the sickbay.

Luckily, Graeme had a pal in the Navy who was a couple of years senior to us and who had been based in Rosyth until just recently and he knew a group of girls in Edinburgh. They were mostly physiotherapists and nurses, and he kindly introduced us to them. Therefore Graeme and I went ashore to the 'Burg' by bus most free evenings to enjoy the company of these ladies and the comforts of their Edinburgh flat and the nearby pubs; rather than the emptiness of the cabin. The girls introduced us to others in Edinburgh and our circle of friends grew. We all went out in a group to pubs or to dinners and dances in Edinburgh. Although no romantic relationships grew from these friendships, the girls' kindness provided us with a warm and reassuringly normal base whenever *Keppel* was back in Rosyth and both Graeme and I were most grateful to Maggie, Debbie and Barbara for all their kindness.

HMS *Cavalier* – Gunnery Training

As part of our midshipman's training we had to complete the section on gunnery. *Keppel* did not have a big gun, well not one that would count in the gunnery exam, so we were sent off to the famous Second World War destroyer HMS *Cavalier* which was doing a gunnery work up in Portland. HMS *Cavalier* is a fine looking, open-bridged destroyer and was still one of the fastest ships in the Navy. She also evoked a strong feeling of the last war and memories of the black and white movies about the war at sea. I always expected Kenneth More in a duffle coat to come round the corner at any moment.

She was, by our standards, a big ship too, having 2 x 4.5-inch gun turrets forward and one 4.5-inch turret aft. Our gunnery training proceeded well alongside the ships own gunnery exercises and we seemed to do OK. During the firing exercises we spent time in all the main compartments including the magazines, the gun turrets, the ops room and even the gunnery radar dome at the very top of the mast. It seems strange now to remember that the computers used for gunnery predictions were mechanical systems dating from the last war and full of cogs, rods and gears grinding round under a big, glass-topped table rather than the Laptop/PC type of systems that ships have today.

In between the gunnery exercises it was a great thrill to be on the open bridge with the ship going at speed. The open bridge was designed so that most of the wind was swept up and over the bridge rather than allowed to blow through it so it was not as windy a place as you might think. I loved to be on watch and lean over the front of the bridge, look down onto the two gun turrets and the finely-pointed bows as they sliced through the Channel throwing the seas aside in disdain. The nearest comparison I can make is that it is the difference between being in a car and on a motorbike. With an open bridge you are part of the seascape, at one with all that is out there and aware of any changes. You can hear and see things more easily, without reflections on glass windows or bulkheads getting in the way. In a closed bridge, while it may be warmer and dry, you are removed from the real world outside and isolated from the weather and other

HMS *Cavalier*, in dock at Chatham, a true warship and a fine-looking ship. She was also one of the fastest ships in the Royal Navy. (Photo with thanks to David Page at www.navyphotos.co.uk and Peter Swarbrick at peter@swarbrick.com)

ships. However, I am not sure I would be saying that if we had been in *Cavalier* in the Arctic winter as we were in *Keppel*!

Graeme and I were made welcome in *Cavalier*, being treated well by the captain and the officers in the wardroom and even getting an invitation down to the chief's mess when the training was over. We both came away feeling proud to have spent time on such a famous old ship and even better for feeling that, at least in some ships, midshipmen were treated as fellow officers. HMS *Cavalier* is now preserved in Historic Chatham Dockyard and is well worth a visit.

North Sea Storm

Back in *Keppel*, life went on. We sailed from the Forth on a fine day but with the weather forecast to be bad with a storm on its way. We were off to take part in an exercise with aircraft and submarines well out in the northern areas of the North Sea. The exercise commenced and we midshipmen were expected to witness most of the activity in the ops room. This was always difficult as the officers directly concerned in the exercise spent their time leaning across the plotting table and so it was normally impossible to see anything except their backsides and they never had time to stop and turn round to tell you what was happening so it was all a bit of a waste of time! After we had been chasing around the sea for a couple of days the weather deteriorated rapidly and seasickness took its firm hold. The sickbay attendant gave me Marzine tablets to counter it. They were supposed to dull the brain's senses to movement. They did that OK, and they also made me very, very sleepy. I spent most of the next couple of days doing nothing more than trying to stay awake. I had no idea what was going on in the exercise and cared even less. At one point I woke up to find myself standing up and literally hanging by one hand onto an overhead pipe in the ops room. I could not have been asleep for long but I had definitely been asleep on my feet. We were also tormented by the RAF Shackleton Maritime Patrol aircraft that flew low over us during their searches for signs of submarines. As we bucked and rolled in the rough seas below, they turned round at the end of their time on task and flew back to their base, for a pleasant afternoon tea with scones and jam by the fire in the mess at RAF Turnhouse. In the meantime, the weather continued to deteriorate. We were now well out in the middle of the North Sea and well clear of any shelter that the land might have offered. The winds blew down from the Arctic with nothing to break their blast and increased beyond Force 8 and were soon well into a Force 9 from the north-west and the seas quickly building up.

Early in the storm they had been lumpy and confused, as if the waves themselves were not sure which way they should be going. These would hit the ship with a loud bang on the bows that shook the ship, and knocked her out of her rhythm as she tried to make her course. The smashed wave disintegrated into a mass of spray that rose high above the bows, was caught by the wind and sent smashing against the bridge windows blocking all vision for three or four seconds before it drained off. The ship would judder as if we had hit a submerged object, and we grabbed for a hand hold as we did not know which way the ship would fall away from the wave. The sound of breaking crockery from somewhere down in the ship, often followed by a muffled curse or a yell often, accompanied the sea's attack. We could sometimes see these lumpy rogue waves coming, sometimes not, but they always seemed to catch us unawares; forcing us to grab any handhold available or risk being sent flying across the ship into any sharp projection that always seemed to be where you landed. Finally, the exercise coordinators ashore wisely decided to cancel the exercise as it was now a full Force 9 or even Storm Force 10 at times and impossible to do anything except try and stay afloat.

'May Day May Day May Day' crackled faintly from the bridge VHF loudspeaker. Instantly everyone on the bridge was silent and alert. We strained to make out the details but could not. We called the Wireless Room to pick up the call and reply if the other ship could hear us. We passed the details to the coastguard. The call came from a Scottish fishing vessel, which was in serious difficulties somewhere well to the north. We, therefore, headed off in that direction to try and see if we could help in the search. Other ships were nearer but we still responded. This was almost into the wind and sea, which were coming from the northwest. Once the wind had been blowing at Force 9 for a length of time, down the length of the Norwegian Sea and the North Sea, the waves settled into a more regular rhythm and pattern but they also grew in height. We watched from the bridge as the next wave rolled towards us, its crest level with the bridge. As the ship slipped through the trough the bows dipped under the waters of the next wave, the sea rolling gently over the

A North Sea storm sends the seas over the bows of HMS *Keppel.*

bows, trying to push her down. The ship then fought back as her buoyancy caught
and threw off the water on her bows sending a mass of water rushing back along
the fo'c'sle to smash against the front of the superstructure. She rose strongly,
lifting us up to the top of the wave. The sky was an opaque mist and the horizon a
mass of white spray where the crests had been blown off the wave tops and swept
horizontally across the top of the sea. The wind had become a screaming, vicious
roar as it tore past the ship. So the weather continued for at least another two days.
Somehow we hung on. Watches were changed and we got what sleep we could,
wedged hard in our bunks, knees against one side and backside against the other.
Luckily, the bunks were deep-sided and we had proper bunk boards that fitted onto
the front edge so we did not fall out. The galley was closed for all normal meals
and we were reduced to eating ships biscuits and the occasional 'pot mess'.

We rode the seas by steering a course at about 30 degrees off from the wind. In
this way we lessened the physical impact of the waves and the motion of the ship
as the 30- and 40-foot-high waves rolled by. The bridge was asking the engines
for 14 knots of speed but the ship could only make good 4 or 5 knots due to the
seas and weather. There was nothing we could do but keep going as by this stage
turning round across the huge seas would have been very dangerous.

As the days went on there was still no positive news on the fishing boat and a
search was continuing up north. Our ship gradually took more and more damage.
One of the emergency sound powered telephones rang on the bridge. I picked it
up. 'Bridge.' 'Sir this is Leading Seaman Jones down aft, in the after seamans mess.

The Forth Bridge has been knocked off its mounting and we cannot get forward.' 'Stay in the mess while we check it out,' I replied. The chief shipwright went to have a look. 'They are right. It is unsafe to use as it could go over the side at any time. We cannot do anything about it in this weather, as if I put a man out there we will lose him,' he reported. There were two sailors' mess decks situated right down aft. Normally, the sailors could get to the main forward area of the ship, where the galley and bridge areas were, via the open deck. In this weather that was impossible as the decks were constantly being swept by the seas as they rolled by. The alternative route, which they had been using was for them to go up onto the deckhouse roofs and come past the funnel and across a metal girder bridge, called the Forth bridge, that linked the after deckhouses to the forward part of the ship. However, the seas had smashed the securing points for the bridge and it had been shifted off its mountings and lay tilted at a crazy angle so there was no way for the seamen to get forward. So the sailors down aft were ordered to stay there for the time being. In fact they were there for about forty-eight hours surviving on whatever food they had in their mess.

The damage inflicted elsewhere on the ship was heavy. The seas broke open welded joints between the open weather deck and the vertical boiler room casing. Water flooded into the boiler room which needed constant pumping until the seas eased. The anti-submarine mortar launchers, which were normally stowed vertically, were smashed down flat, damaging their gearing in the process. The metal screens around the mortar mounts themselves were smashed and bent out of shape or broken. Then, water started to break through an emergency escape hatch on the fo'c'sle. This was at the forward end of the main passageway, at the top of an escape ladder. There was no way anyone could get out onto the fo'c'sle deck to secure it so we tried to secure it from below with rope lashings and tackles to try and keep it as tightly shut as possible. If that hatch had gone then we could have been in deep trouble as, with the ship burying her bows into the waves, she would quickly have flooded. The ship's wireless aerials were ripped off, some of the liferafts on the port side were torn off and both of the ships wooden motor boats were badly smashed up on their davits and unusable. The full power of the sea was demonstrated by the effect it had on the paintwork. Right round the forward part of the engine room casing along the main deck, where the seas had rushed and channeled themselves when they rolled aboard, all the paint had been rubbed off by the seas constantly smashing their way along the deck. Whole areas of the bulkhead, many square feet in size, were stripped back to bare metal and left shining like silver.

People used to gather outside the ops room by an aft facing door out onto the upper deck one deck above the main weather deck. From there you could not only get some fresh air into the ship, as the normal ventilation system had been shut down, but you could stand in safety and watch as the seas roared round the side of the superstructure and pounded aboard, raging across the open weather deck and smashing all in their path.

The search for the fishing vessel was finally called off and *Keppel* was told by the coast guard that she was no longer needed in the search so once the seas allowed we gingerly turned and made our way back to Rosyth. I think the captain, Richard Onslow, had spent at least forty-eight hours on the bridge through the worst of it all. It was only then as we entered the shelter of the Forth that we were able to get out on deck and view the damage. Engineers were trying to plug the broken welds and signalers were rigging temporary aerials. When we got back to Rosyth, the ship spent three weeks in dock for the damage to be repaired and a number of other alterations done to try and prevent it happening again. This was October and the ship's next two missions over the winter were to Iceland and the Norwegian Arctic.

The Arctic

Arctic Fishery Protection is one of the oldest duties that the RN is called upon to perform. Its history can be traced back to 1586. Lord Nelson himself was a midshipman on HMS *Carcass* on fishery protection duties in the Arctic in 1773 and later he was captain of HMS *Albermarle* when she was engaged on fishery protection duties. Nelson has a great deal in common with me as I also learned how to sail on the Norfolk Broads, as did he, and we were both midshipmen in the Fishery Protection Squadron. But that, I am afraid, is where the similarity ends. In the early seventies, Arctic Fishery Protection was still a major activity not least because of the outcry that had sprung up after the loss of three Hull trawlers within one week in January and February 1968. Two were lost off north-west Iceland and one in the Norwegian Sea.

That week, during exceptionally bad gales, blinding snow storms and heavy icy conditions in the area, two trawlers, the *Kingston Peridot* and the *Ross Cleveland* were seeking the shelter of Isafjord, a long fjord on the north-west tip of Iceland, as excessive ice built up on their masts and rigging. Even with all hands smashing at the ice with picks and hammers it was impossible to clear such huge amounts of solid ice. Sadly, both ships were overcome by the ice to the point where they became top heavy and capsized. That same week, a third trawler, the *St Romanus*, disappeared without trace somewhere in the Norwegian Sea. There was only one survivor from all three ships. His name was Harry Edom and he was the mate of the *Ross Cleveland*. A fourth ship, the *Notts County* from Grimsby, nearly suffered the same fate but managed to run herself aground on a beach in Iceland and all but one of her nineteen crew were rescued by the Icelandic coastguard ship *Odinn*. That week a total of fifty-seven Hull fishermen were lost, including a fifteen-year-old boy, Michael Barnes, who was on his first trip as a galley boy. This series of disasters caused a lot of questions to be asked and provisions were made to prevent it happening again. Protest groups were set up by the wives of the trawlermen. They simply wanted all fishing in the Arctic to be banned in winter. It was an understandable position to take, but it was never going to happen in spite of all the protesters' strong feelings about the safety of the trawlers, the dock head protests and TV coverage. That same winter week, over 120 men still set sail in trawlers from Hull for the Arctic in search of fish and a good payday.

HMS *Keppel* running down sea off Iceland.

Keppel's role was to provide support where we could, carry out checks of fishing gear on all ships in the area, not just British, and to monitor the activities of the Icelandic Coast Guard vessels. Two Ministry of Agriculture & Fisheries fishery inspectors sailed with us and we had a naval doctor on board for the trip. To accommodate these extra officers I was turned out of my cabin and sent to join Graeme in the sickbay. This was a small compartment with two bunks, and its own tiny bathroom with a ¾-length bath. This bath had a rickety temporary bunk rigged over the top of it. As one bunk had to be kept free at all times for any emergency, I took one of the two bunks and Graeme decided to take the bath bunk as he was much shorter than me. As we sailed further north, it became clear that the bathroom had no heating in it at all. This was fine in the North Sea but, once we got north, poor Graeme came out in the morning absolutely blue with cold. We tried tying the door open, extra blankets, etc., but none of them worked and Graeme spent the winter freezing.

In late November off northern Iceland there are twenty-four hours of darkness; a slight lightening of the southern sky told us it was about noon, but apart from that it was dark all the time. The inspectors spent time crossing to trawlers by rubber boat to check their nets and the ships' engineers occasionally went off to assist with repairs if needed. On one occasion the diving team went off to help the *Northern Gem* free a net that they had got badly tangled round their propeller. This turned out to be a much bigger job that they anticipated and took most of the day. However, a grateful crew did send them back with a boat full of fresh cod. Fresh fish and chips for tea tonight boys!

We were patrolling the Denmark Strait and a large stationary object was reported on the radar about 20 miles away. We set off to investigate. We came up to the edge of the pack ice and could see a large iceberg frozen into the pack ice. For most of us on board it was a first. It was a dark, cloudy and gloomy day and the iceberg sat about a mile away trapped in the pack ice which itself stretched off as far as we could see.

In January, we were sent to northern Norway. As we went north we saw the fantastic beauty of the Lofoten Islands in all their winter glory. Beautiful snow-covered, pointed mountains bathed in sunshine and contrasting with the black, deep, cold waters of the fjords. We stopped in the fishing port of Harstad. It was here that I managed to get myself into trouble again. I was the Officer Of the Day (OOD) so I was not able to go ashore. That evening a cocktail party had been arranged on board for local dignitaries. After the official party, an informal one developed in the wardroom. Graeme and I were grudgingly allowed to attend these functions, but only under sufferance. One of the party guests was a rather nice young lady and I wanted to escort her home. Graeme agreed to take over the duty and the young lady and I left by taxi. I saw her back to her parent's home just out of the town. They lived in a beautiful, wooden house, which was wrapped in the folds of the deep forest snow and lit by candles in the windows. After a

MT *Portia* in Isafjord in north-west Iceland. Isafjord was the scene of a double tragedy in the winter of 1967/68 when two Hull trawlers were lost due to heavy ice.

pleasant 'coffee and chat' we agreed to meet again the next day when she would show me around Harstad.

When I arrived back on board, it was well after midnight and the quartermaster told me that the first lieutenant wanted to see me in his cabin immediately I got back on board. This could only mean trouble but I could not think of anything that I had done! Dave was sitting at his desk reading. Without looking up he said 'And where are the OOD keys?' A jolt ran through me and my day collapsed. I realised instantly that they were still in my pocket. These were the keys to the main keyboard on the ship. They are always kept by the OOD and are never, ever to leave the ship. I had forgotten to hand them over to Graeme in my hurry to get ashore. 'Oh hell,' I said 'I am sorry, Sir, I forgot to hand them over.' That cost me three days stoppage of leave and killed stone dead any possibility of a budding romance with the young lady. The moral here 'Don't let your heart rule your head!'

The next day Simon called Graeme and I down to his office. 'The Admiralty have written to the ship telling you your next ships for the last six months of your Mids year. Gordon, you are going to HMS *Puncheston*.' 'A sweeper! Great! But where is it based?' Simon checked some papers. 'I am pretty sure she is based in Bahrain', he said. 'Bahrain! Oh Lord, that is the last place I wanted to go. The Arctic to the Gulf; who says the RN does not have a sense of humour?' Graeme was going to a minesweeper, HMS *Wooton*, based in HMS *Lochinvar*, just across the Forth from Rosyth, so he would be able to continue with the friendships we had developed in Edinburgh and would be much nearer Edinburgh too. 'You jammy-wot-not Graeme!'

CHAPTER 6

HMS *Puncheston* – The Gulf

I left HMS *Keppel* after our last Arctic patrol one Friday afternoon in February and caught the afternoon train to Kings Cross and on to my parent's home in Buckinghamshire. On the Sunday my parents drove me to Brize Norton, the RAF base, and on the Monday morning, I was flown out from Brize Norton in an RAF Britannia aircraft to join HMS *Puncheston* in Bahrain for the second part of my midshipman's training. I arrived in the evening but even so the heat wrapped itself around me as I went down the aircraft steps. I was met at the airport by a fellow midshipman who saw me sweating and merely said 'You wait until it gets hot in June, then temperatures are well into the 100s!'

This was in 1971 and the Gulf had few attractions and many of the states were 'dry' as well. This was long before the Gulf was the holiday destination it is now. In fact, the Gulf sweepers were what was known as a 'DQ draft', meaning that sailors who had spent time in Detention Quarters (DQs, the Navy's prison) were sent to serve in ships in the Gulf when they were released as it was thought that the excessive heat and humidity would help to calm them down and keep them out of trouble for a spell. I am not sure what the Navy thought it would do to me!

HMS *Puncheston* was a 350-ton 'Ton' class coastal minesweeper. Ton Class Minesweepers were built for coastal mine sweeping and patrol work and the ships were all named after British villages with names that ended in 'ton'. Puncheston is a village in Pembrokeshire in Wales. The ships were built of wood and non-magnetic metals to minimise their effect on magnetic mines. They also had a shallow draft to try and avoid any buoyant, moored mines. The 'Tons' had the underwater profile of a bathtub and the buoyancy of a cork and so they sat high in the water. In fact, they looked a bit like grey plastic ducks as they bobbed along as the wheelhouse structure rose up cheekily from the main fo'c'sle deck. They were not renowned as 'good seaboats'. There were, incredibly, 117 ships of the class built between 1953 and 1971. They were built in shipyards all over the country from Belfast to Beverley and from Montrose to Dartmouth. The very last one built was HMS *Wilton* and she was built of GRP by Vosper's in Southampton. She was the first warship ever to be built of GRP and proved an outstanding success that led to many more MCMVs being built of the material. Because they were so

HMS *Puncheston*, a Ton-Class minesweeper, in the Persian Gulf in 1971.

numerous they were seen all over the world and there is scarcely anyone in the RN who has not spent some time in a 'Ton' at some stage of their career.

A friend of mine who had served in oil tankers told me a story of when he was the OOW on his 30,000-ton tanker coming through the Mediterranean from Suez. They had just had two or three days of storms and gales coming up from Suez and on the morning of the third day, as the sun started break through and shine and the seas calmed and turned blue, they found themselves steaming past Valetta Harbour in Malta. At nine o'clock in the morning they spotted a line of three little Ton-class minesweepers steaming out of the harbour at full speed 'smoke coming from their funnels' and all bobbing about on the swell 'like clockwork rubber ducks looking for fun' as my friend put it. Then, they spotted his oil tanker and they started flashing their Aldis signal lights at him. 'What ship, where bound? What ship, where bound?' they flashed merrily. 'Oh Great', said the tanker captain in a tone of doom, 'We have had three days of storms while they were all tucked up in Malta; then as soon as the sun comes out it's all "What ship where bound", bloody Navy!'

In a couple of weeks I had acclimatised to the Gulf heat and, in fact, had joined at the best time as the really hot weather and high humidity was yet to come. *Puncheston* was one of a small squadron of sweepers of the 9th MSS based in Bahrain in the Gulf. The role of the squadron was to promote the UK's interests and ensure a diplomatic presence across the Gulf. It was also to try and stop illegal immigrants from India, Pakistan and other areas getting into the Gulf. The sweepers patrolled the Gulf itself and out in the Arabian Sea along the Batina Coast of Oman. There were countless small wooden fishing dhows sailing across the Arabian Sea as well as the larger boums, or cargo dhows. While most of these are now motorized, a number were still sail powered. We would send our boarding Party across and they would search the dhows. If they found suspected illegal immigrants then we would escort the dhow into port where the local authorities would deal with it. When not chasing dhows we would spend time exercising our minesweeping equipment.

There were five officers on board HMS *Puncheston*. The CO was Lieutenant Morris, who was somewhat thin on top and did not seem to display much sense of humour and seemed to regard his officers as a burden he had to bear. He was a specialist gunnery officer and loved big naval guns. He was used to being in big ships where he had 4.5- or 6-inch guns with which to play. Punchy only had two small Bofors 40mm guns and when I joined the CO appointed me as the Fo'c'sle Officer and the gunnery officer. The fo'c'sle was run by a dark and swarthy Cornish leading seaman called 'Janner' Donahue. He bore a striking resemblance to a sun-tanned Spanish pirate, was a natural leader with roguish looks and the rest of the fo'c'sle team saw him as their leader. This was his patch and he ran it his way. He was decidedly wary of this new midshipman appearing on his deck. Eventually, after a tentative start and once he realised I did know what an anchor was, we actually got on well together. The guns were looked after by the gunner, Able Seaman 'Tanzy' Lee, who was a mild, peace-loving chap who had carefully painted a small, two-fingered 'Peace' emblem on the side of the forward gun. I never worked out why the captain allowed him to leave it there but he did! Tanzy was also a member of L/S Donahue's fo'c'sle party. His job was to maintain both the guns and fire the forward one when we did gunnery exercises. My gunnery training in HMS *Cavalier* was a good general foundation but was not in any way a specialised gunnery Course. The CO spent every gunnery exercise berating me for my lack of excitement at the loud 'bangs' rather than enthusing me about gunnery or imparting any of his knowledge of calibres, ballistics and propellants to me. I always suspected that he was really just deeply frustrated with our two little guns and wished he was back in his big ships as soon as possible.

The first lieutenant was called Robert and he was pleasant and friendly. He was very tall and thin, almost gangly. He made me look robust! Robert was also a chain-smoking insomniac and unfortunately I shared a cabin with him. I regularly woke up at 2 a.m. or 3 a.m. in the morning with a raging sore throat and the taste of cigarettes in my mouth to find the cabin lights on and Robert sitting at the small desk reading a newspaper and smoking endlessly, the small stuffy cabin, just 10-feet by 6-feet full of smoke. Nothing I said would persuade him that he should go out to the wardroom to read and smoke. He was the first lieutenant and this was his cabin. End of discussion!

Our navigator was a swarthy looking and conscientious lieutenant called Graham who had a wicked twinkle in his eye most of the time. Graham was keen to get on in the Navy and his passion at the time was the bridge log books.

He demanded that these were written up exactly as he prescribed, neatly and clearly in sharp 2B pencil, with all navigation information properly shown in his formatted way. In the early days, until I had learnt all his ways, he regularly called me back to the bridge and asked me to rewrite the log in his approved manner, or to chastise me for using a blunt pencil. He was, however, one of the good guys and enjoyed a party and 'Runs Ashore'. The other midshipman was friendly, pleasant and quiet term mate from Dartmouth called Tim. Both Tim and Graham went on to become full commanders and I met them both many years later in London.

In Bahrain, the Navy's shore base was called HMS *Jufair*. This was about a mile away from where the sweepers berthed on an old floating pontoon. The pontoon had storage areas for the ship's spare gear as well as a Chinese laundry that served all the ships. Food was provided by an MOD victualling stores depot that served all the Services in Bahrain and the first lieutenant bought the food for the ship and decided with the cook what meals we would have. Meals on board tended to be on the basic (cheap) side. Rabbit stew was one of the first lieutenant's favourites!

I had been on board for about a week and was trying to acclimatise to the heat, humidity and the very sandy atmosphere of Gulf after the clean freshness of the Arctic. I was standing on deck in Bahrain when I looked across the harbour and saw a large, sleek, white-hulled cargo ship glide slowly into the main port. The funnel had the blue and red chevrons of Strick Line of London. She looked new and I could imagine the spacious, officers' accommodation with airy single cabins with big windows and a comfortable mess room and bar. To make it worse, she would be sailing out of the Gulf in a couple of day's time, back to the UK. We were here for the duration. Some years before; on the first day of my school holidays, I had gone for a general career counseling session with the British Shipping Federation in London. It was meant to be a fact-finding meeting but to my amazement they wanted me to sail the very next day on a Strick Line ship but I turned it down as I was going away on holiday and had only gone there to seek their views, not leave home that day. It was possible that I could have been on that ship but just because I wanted a few weeks holiday, here I was stuck in the Gulf for many months to come. It was not really as simple as that but the feeling was there that it could have been. 'If you can't take a joke then you shouldn't have joined' came back to mind.

Initially it seemed very hot to me even though it was February. However, as the heat increased through the summer, because we lived in it, we became used to the heat and acclimatised so it did not bother us at all. In fact, we often found the ship's primitive air conditioning was so fierce that we would go out on deck to get warm! In summer, in places like the Musandam Peninsula, the temperatures got up to 50 °C or about 130 °F and the humidity well into the 90 per cent range. One day, the ship had arranged a football match against HMS *Wiston* but the base medical officer banned it as the humidity was 92 per cent and the temperature about 38 °C. The sailors were so angry, the MO was not a popular man, banning the lad's 'footy' match indeed. Just because it was a bit hot.

The sight of a senior government official dressed in his finery of a tropical

Beautiful Oman where in places the date groves run back from the sea to the mountains.

white 'ice cream suit', complete with white tricorn hat and white plume, sitting in a small rubber inflatable and being ferried ashore was amusing. However, this was how the UK Political Resident (PR) was taken ashore to make official calls in places with no jetty. During the year, the minesweepers would take the PR, who was based in Bahrain on visits to meet the local leaders in the smaller Gulf States. He would go to meet them to try and understand their issues and problems and offer the reassurances of the UK Government. At the time, the UK's plans to withdraw from the Gulf were causing the locals some concern as they could not see who would be there to protect them from any would be belligerents once the Royal Navy left. Some of the States had set up their own defence forces such as the Trucial Oman Scouts and the Abu Dhabi Defence Force. These were manned by locals but run by ex-UK Armed Forces personnel, who worked with and trained the locals.

Man Overboard Exercises

Morris, our captain, had a nasty habit at sea of getting up at about six o'clock in the morning and wandering down aft. Without telling anyone, he would throw a life belt over the side and then hit the 'man overboard' alarm. As Officer Of the Watch (OOW) the alarm bell was by your right ear and it made you jump out of your skin. You had no idea if it was for real or just another of Morris' early morning games. Therefore, you had to treat it as real and get the ship and crew organised and try and find and recover the man or lifebuoy, whichever it turned out to be. Seconds later the CO would be up on the bridge berating you for every failing, no matter how minor, while you were in the process of turning the ship round, putting up the right flag signal, sounding the right signal with the ship's siren, getting the duty watch organised, trying to keep am eye on the 'Man' in the water, and manoeuvring the ship. After this had happened to me a couple of times I got one of the duty watch to hang about in the main passage from 5.30 a.m. and keep an eye out for the CO leaving his cabin and to let me know if he did. I was then able to warn the watch on deck, get the flag hoist organised and mentally rehearse what I had to do. It did me no good though, as I still got shouted at. In my next ship, HMS *Nurton*, training for this eventuality was done very differently and was much more successful.

Mutton Grab

In the Gulf, some local leaders rejoice in the title of Wali. We were sent to pay a visit to one of the Walis in a remote region down on the Batina coast. His local region was surrounded by mountains and was only accessible by sea so he rarely received visitors. The captain made an official call on him in the morning and the Wali kindly invited the ship's company to dinner in his fort. Apart from the duty watch everyone on board was to attend. The captain warned us to expect a 'Mutton Grab' and just to follow what the CO did. I had no idea what to expect as all we could see from the ship was a lovely wide sandy beach that swept round the whole bay in a glorious curve. Behind the beach was a thick swath of rich, green date palms that seemed to reach back to the base of the beautiful, jagged, orange-coloured mountains. The whitewashed top of a round, mud and stone fort rose up above the date trees. We went ashore by Gemini and jumped out onto the flat sands of the beach. A tall Arab in traditional long brown robes and a red and white ghutra, or head scarf, stood motionless at the head of the beach. He had a Lee Enfield .303 rifle slung over his shoulder and beckoned for us to follow him. He escorted us up through the date grove to the fort. It was now getting quite dark so it was difficult to see anything of our immediate surroundings. At the fort we were ushered in through a low, narrow doorway and then up two flights of big, wide, open wooden ladders that looked very old. These led up to a room that made up the whole width of the tower. We gathered in a group and looked about us. The walls were made of stone and dried mud and there were burning oil lamps suspended from iron brackets in the wall. The Wali was an old man but tall and straight. He was dressed in white thobes, with a white ghutra for the occasion. His weathered, brown face smiled out kindly from under his ghutra as we all shook hands with him. We were then invited to sit on the rough wooden floor around a big Arab rug.

The captain was instructed to sit beside the Wali who slipped gracefully down to the floor, his legs and feet seeming to disappear beneath him. How does he do that? We all managed to get down into some sort of sitting position on the floor with legs and feet pointing in all sorts of directions and with more than a few 'ouches' and 'aarrghs' emanating from the older members of the crew. We waited and wondered what was to come. We were offered bowls of water and a cloth in which to wash and dry our hands, and glasses of water were put out. We then noticed that there were about six other guards, all very tall and all with old Lee Enfield .303 rifles, standing behind us in the shadows and glaring intently into the middle distance. The soft, dim, flickering light from the oil lamps threw dark, motley shadows up across the guards and cast deeper shadows across the wooded rafters of the ceiling. We were totally immersed in an Arabian world that has existed unchanged for hundreds of years. This was the Arabia of the *Arabian Nights*; a world of tribal lands, feudal tribes, meagre possessions and local warfare; a world where the main commercial activity was bartering rather than using cash and where the rule of Islam and the Sharia was all. But, it was also a land where hospitality to strangers was, and still is, paramount.

After some time, a huge platter was carried up the stairs by two of the Wali's men and placed with great care on the rug before us. On the platter was the hot carcass of a sheep lying on a bed of steaming rice flavoured with sultanas, currants and spices. The scent of the spices drifted round the room mingling with the scent of the meat. The lamb was well cooked and moist chunks of tender meat were hanging, ready to eat, from the ribs of the carcass. They then brought up big side dishes of hot flat breads and dishes of different fruits; mangos, dates and melon; all of which were placed all around the sheep's platter. The head of the animal had been detached and was placed facing towards the Wali. It still had the eyes in it. We waited for the signal to begin. The Wali invited the CO to start and we all followed his lead. Being careful not to use our left hands, a definite no-no in Arab culture, as the left hand is reserved for bodily cleansing and not for eating, we took a piece of the bread with our right hand and used that to pull small pieces of flesh off the carcass. The meat was so tender it literally dropped of the bone. The food was delicious, the spiced meat tender and sweet, the rice beautifully flavoured with sultanas and currants. After the initial nervousness about what food would we be served and concerns about Arab etiquette, we all ate until we could eat no more. It was easy now to see how the term 'Mutton Grab' had originated. Towards the end of the meal the Wali muttered something in Arabic and the captain found himself being offered the sheep's eye to eat. He had clearly done this before as he did not seem to be phased by it. He took the offered eye, placed it in his mouth and swallowed it whole. The crew were impressed, well those that could watch it were. Once he had managed to swallow that he was offered a spoon with a scooping of brain from the inside of the skull. From where I was sitting this looked like runny white mince. Somehow the captain managed to get this down too and the excellent relations between the Trucial States and the UK were confirmed with big smiles and handshakes. Even the guards behind us smiled a bit.

Soon afterwards the Wali stood up. The meal was over. We said goodbye and thank you to the Wali, his kindly face still smiling out from his ghutra, and left; escorted back to the beach by two of the guards and returned to our world of the 1970s and the Royal Navy.

Passengers

One day when we were alongside in Bahrain we were told that we should expect some passengers that night and be ready to sail as soon as they were on board. That evening after dark, an army lorry pulled up at the end of the jetty and a dozen or so big, silent and very non-communicative guys in army combat gear walked swiftly down the jetty, got on board and we cast off. Each had a huge rucksack and his own rifle. They vanished into and around the ship and quickly found their own corners or bits of deck to lie on and they settled down for the night. We sailed straight away and set off for the Musandam. The Musandam peninsula is a rugged, remote and mountainous area at the northern end of the arm that forms the east side of the Gulf. Once there, they asked us to put them ashore in an isolated bay and we then sailed away leaving them on a desert shore. Their leader had told the CO that they were off on a desert survival exercise. About a fortnight later we got orders to go back to the same spot at night and pick them up. It was a difficult spot to find in the dark but as we waited, wondering if they had sent us to the wrong place or if the soldiers had not made it back we suddenly saw a coded signal flashed from the shore. They got back on board the ship and looked dirty, battered and totally exhausted. They crashed out immediately, anywhere where they could find a flat bit of deck or in the passageways. They fell asleep instantly, still clutching their rifles to their bodies and they slept most of the way back to Bahrain. I inadvertently knocked one as I passed him in the main companionway and within a nanosecond a rifle was sticking up my nose! I recoiled saying 'Sorry, sorry. It's OK.' I received a grunted 'Sorry, mate', in reply and the soldier went straight back to sleep. We went about the ship very carefully and quietly. When we got back to Bahrain they got back into their lorry and disappeared without a word back to the RAF base and airport and their base in the UK.

By chance, many years later in Kuwait, I met one of the soldiers who had been on board *Puncheston* on that trip. He told me that they were all SAS and had been on an anti-guerrilla mission in the mountains for the fourteen days they were there. They had secret orders and were living very rough for the two-week period. This happened during the time of the Oman insurgency from communist Yemen. Sultan Qaboos had just come to power, having overthrown his father in a bloodless coup in 1970, and the communists from Yemen were trying to capitalize on the changeover and disrupt things. Britain was strongly supporting the new Sultan with help from the SAS.

American Boarding Party

In 1971, unlike today, there was hardly any presence by the US Navy in the Gulf. It was very much a British sea in those days, with the minesweepers and a duty frigate always on patrol somewhere in the Gulf. However, every so often, the US Navy would send a ship into the Gulf and one day an American frigate duly arrived. We were asked to assist them in a boarding exercise so they could train their boarding party. Our CO told us all that we were not to physically resist but not to assist them either in what was termed a 'Non-Assisted boarding'. The ship was stopped and the boarding party came along side and we all tried to act like Arab fishermen. The American sailors boarded the ship and started barking orders at us. We replied. 'No understandee! No understandee!' The crew then pretended to panic and ran all round the ship hiding in lockers and generally being totally unhelpful. The Americans tried to round us all up onto the fo'c'sle but we played dumb. The boarding officer, who was a young fair-haired lieutenant, started to chase me round the ship and I led him round the deck then all the way up the mast. It was a bit of a wriggle to get to the top and onto the radar platform but I managed to do it before he caught up. On the radar platform I ducked round to the front of the mast and dropped down the 6 feet onto the top of the bridge and so back to the deck. He had got himself stuck on the ladder trying to go up and took nearly ten minutes to extricate himself from the mast ladder. All the while is CO was watching through binoculars from the frigate. Others on board were up to similar tricks. We all thought it was a great way to spend the afternoon but I don't think the USN did. The boarding officer kept getting cryptic comments and criticisms over the radio from his CO.

Eventually, however, they had all our ship's company mustered on the fo'c'sle and thought that they had finished. It was a hot sunny day and there was no shade on the fo'c'sle. Leading Seaman Donahue, our swarthy Cornishman with eyes as dark as coal, and I decided to continue the mischief and after checking there were no sea snakes around, we just dived off into the sea and swam around the ship having a good time cooling off. The USN boys were confused at first, but had had enough by then so they left us there! The poor lieutenant decided that perhaps he should have gone into banking. At one point he yelled 'These stupid "Limeys" are too much' in total frustration. However, all was done in a good spirit and there were no hard feelings. We all knew how easy it was to mess up someone else's exercise. We somehow managed to resist their kind invitation to practice our boarding party on board their ship the next day. However, when we got back alongside in Bahrain we had a few beers with them: so UK/US diplomatic relations were all OK.

Super Tankers

By now I was qualified to keep watches on the bridge alone, navigate the ship and avoid collisions, but always after calling the captain in good time when any ships appeared to be coming closer to us than about 4 miles. I had also been awarded my Astro navigation certificate which meant that I was qualified to navigate 'out of sight land'. This was mainly due to Graham's endless patience, as he supervised me, while I spent hours taking star and sun sights by sextant and then working them out as we sailed around the Gulf and Arabian Seas. This together with my Bridge Watch Keeping certificate were the main qualifications I had to get, in order to carry on and gain a promotion.

I used to love being on watch on the bridge in the peaceful early mornings and watch the sun come up and see all the fabulous sandy and rose-red colours that it changed through as it climbed above the sand-laden atmosphere of the horizon. One morning, at about 5.30 a.m., as we sailed back up the Gulf at the end of a patrol, I was enjoying the scene and dreaming of a few days alongside in Bahrain. I was startled when the intercom clicked into life. 'Bridge Wheelhouse'. 'Bridge' I responded, annoyed at the interruption of my morning reverie. 'Sir? Have you looked out of the starboard side?' It was Able Seaman Maddison, the helmsman, one deck down in the wheelhouse, calling me. I turned round to see the huge bows of a VLCC a few hundred yards off! We were being overtaken by a huge oil tanker only about half a mile away and just aft of our starboard beam. 'Oh Golly!' I said, or something similar. With the bright sunrise directly astern I had not seen the tanker against the sun. She was empty and I could clearly see the draught marks on her bow and she was so big and high out of the water that I could not see over the top of her bulbous bow. Her black hull gleamed in the sun and her white, foaming bow wave was as big as we were. Her white superstructure seemed to be miles away, set high up at the stern and I wondered if they had seen us, We were on a converging course and would collide in about another fifteen to twenty minutes. We technically had the right of way as the tanker, as the overtaking ship, had to keep clear of us. We were steering 280, or almost due west and needed to get away from this situation. It was obvious however, that she was not about to steer away or she would have done it by now. But, when a 200,000-ton tanker and 350-ton wooden minesweeper meet? No contest. It was now up to me to do something! The tanker was now far too close for me to call the CO as I should have called him when it was ten miles away at least. Luckily, the CO's cabin did not have a porthole. 'Port 5, altering 240' I ordered, then added 'Helmsman, make sure you use no more than 5 degrees of wheel'. 'Port 5, altering to 240', he answered. I did not want the ship to heel over in the turn, as she would certainly have done had the helmsman used 15 or even 10 degrees of rudder. I conned him onto the new safe course then went onto the bridge wing and waved happily to the tanker in the hope that they would realise that we had seen them and they would not blow their siren. That would have impressed the old man at half a mile as it would probably have blown him out of his bunk. We steered a parallel course as she overtook us leaving us to roll gently in her wake. I prayed that the captain would not wake up or decide to do one of his early morning strolls to the sweep deck. If he did I was for the high jump. All went calm again, the tanker gradually vanished ahead, we resumed our course, everyone in the wheelhouse kept quiet, the captain slept peacefully on and all was well. As she sailed by I studied her bridge through the binoculars but never did see anyone there. Maybe they were watching the sunrise too.

Aground

It was decided that one of the minesweepers should make a visit to a small oil camp called Dukhan, which was situated on a tiny bay midway down the west side of the Qatar peninsula. The camp was run by a group of British engineers and they had never had a visit there by an RN ship. *Puncheston* was selected to go. As we would be at anchor during the visit, a small army personnel landing craft was sent along with us to act as a tender to ferry guests on board and to get us ashore. She was ordered to follow *Puncheston* close astern as we set off on the twenty-four-hour trip down to Dukhan. The reason so few ships, if any, ever went down the west side of Qatar is that it is very shallow, full of sand bars and shoals, there are no ports or fishing villages and it has not been charted for many years. To get there meant navigating down a stretch of water that had not been sailed through by any RN ship in recent memory. The charts for the area were at best out of date and at worst totally wrong. The very latest chart corrections had been made by an RN ship some fifty years before. Navigation was therefore going to be a bit iffy.

We sailed from Bahrain one afternoon and began the passage down between the islands and the Qatar peninsula very early in the morning of the next day. I had the morning watch and took over from Graham, the navigator, at four o'clock. It was still dark as Graham showed me our position and I reconciled the 'Decca Navigator' readings (the electronic radio navigation system) with our chart position, the depth sounder readings with the chart and the weak radar echoes of the coastline. The coast of Qatar is made up of low sand and rock and is ill-defined with no clear distinguishing marks such as headlands, cliffs or bays, nor are there any navigation marks such as lighthouses or buoys down the west side.

The watch continued using the Decca Navigator system and radar fixes where possible and with continual monitoring of the depth sounder and at very slow speed. However, at about 5.30 a.m., as a soft pink and sandy dawn broke in the east I could now start to see the low, hazy, sandy land of Qatar. Just then the Decca Navigator equipment started to play up and after a couple of fixes that were less than perfect, I had one that gave me a big 'cocked hat'. In lay terms that meant that it was difficult to say exactly where we were except somewhere in a big triangle. In fact, anywhere in that triangle was a safe place to be but I did not like the sudden loss of accuracy in an area where we were also not too sure about the tidal effects between the islands. The radar was still of little use as the land was still very low and a poor radar target. I slowed the ship and sent the bosun's mate to call the navigator up to have a look. The last thing I wanted was to run the ship aground. I knew the CO would definitely take a dim view of that. There is a saying in the Navy that 'A grounding can ruin your entire day' I was fairly confident as to where we were but in view of the doubtful charts and poor radar returns and no visible landmarks, I wanted the navigator to confirm my views. Graham arrived and agreed that the Decca Navigator signal was not good, possibly due to the sunrise, which can affect the radio-based system with an effect called the diurnal effect. That occasionally happens in weak reception areas at dawn and dusk. Having agreed and confirmed our position and treating the Decca Navigator readings with caution we proceeded, but, still slowly. 'Call me if you are in doubt' called Graham as he went down the ladder.

By eight o'clock I was comfortable with the navigation again as we had reached one of the few areas where I could get a good visual fix off the land and we had fairly good radar returns off the land too and I handed over to the navigator himself for the final few miles to Dukhan.

Dukhan is on a small sandy bay and consists of a few low bungalows for the workers and a recreation club on the beach where they had a number of small sail boats. The chart showed a smooth sandy bottom right across the bay. We arrived off the bay at about 0900. From the ship we could see a wide sweep of sandy bay backed by low desert. In the distance, behind the beach, we could see the roofs of what we assumed were single-storey houses. The only building on the beach was a modest building, that reminded me of a village cricket pavilion, but which was the oil camp's recreation centre. This was it, we had arrived so let's get anchored and go and meet the people. Let the fun begin. The captain wisely decided to take the ship slowly into the bay then reverse our course out before dropping the anchor to ensure that he knew what was under the ships swinging circle when we anchored. Having sailed into the bay and turned back out, we started heading slowly to the anchoring position.

I was now on the fo'c'sle waiting for the calls from the bridge to drop the anchor. 'Coral, dead ahead, Sir!' One of the seamen called my attention to an underwater coral bank that had come into view ahead of the ship. We shouted up to the bridge 'Coral, dead ahead!' The bridge responded. 'Stop both engines. Full astern both engines,' but it was too late. The ship ran gently onto an uncharted coral shoal and stopped. We were aground. The first feeling was how strange it felt, to be on a ship when it is aground as although everything is still and stable, every feeling is telling you that this is wrong and you should not be here. How on earth can we get back into a floating situation as soon as possible?

After the initial shock, we looked up to the bridge to see the CO's reaction. The CO came down and looked at the shoal from the fo'c'sle then he dashed off, got his snorkel and then swam around and under the ship to see how badly, or not, we were aground. We were all amazed that he did this himself rather than send one of us down to look. He determined that we were grounded only at the bow and the midships and stern was floating free.

The landing craft proved our salvation. She tied up to our stern and then all the hands including the officers worked all morning to unload all the ammunition from the magazine which was deep in the bows and carry it aft and lower it by hand into the landing craft. The craft then tied up under the bow and we slowly lowered one of the anchors and all is heavy chain cable into the craft as well.

That, as well as moving other equipment within in the ship down to the stern meant that the bow now rose higher out of the water. We were still stuck. We now tried to go astern. The landing craft was thrown a towline and she started to pull us astern. Our engines were run slowly astern. At first nothing happened. Then, slowly, Punchy moved, then slid gently off the reef into deeper water. There was an audible sigh of relief from everyone. Small chunks and strips of the wooden sacrificial sheathing that covered the hull rose to the surface as we came clear. Apart from that there was no damage and we were not holed in any way. It was a really good feeling to be afloat again. We then found a safe anchorage away from the reef and tried to carry on with the visit. First, however, we had to reload everything from the landing craft and that took care of the rest of the day.

It is difficult to imagine how we would have managed if we had been on our own. I am sure we would have got her off somehow but it would have been a lot more difficult. The CO did not take it too well and retired to his cabin to write his report. He had to send the signal to the Admiralty that every CO dreads. They are the one that start with the words, 'Sir, I have the honour to report that my ship, HMS …X.., has taken the ground in position….' The rest of us, however, tried to make up for the CO's misery and had a really good run ashore and enjoyed some great hospitality that included a visit to the oil farm as well as beach parties, sailing races and dinners. The families at Dukhan did us proud and made us all most welcome, even laying on a full Sunday roast beef lunch for us. When we returned to Bahrain the ship was dry-docked and, apart from the sacrificial sheathing, no damage was found.

There was, of course, a board of Enquiry, as there is for all RN ships grounding, no matter how slight. The captain, the navigator and I were all called to attend. It was chaired by the captain of a visiting RN frigate and two other seamen officers from the base. Everything was analysed and we were questioned in detail by the board. I, as the OOW for the morning watch, had left the bridge at 0800, at least two hours before the grounding, but I was questioned closely and repeatedly about the navigation during my watch. 'Why were you using the Decca Navigator? Did you align the system at the beginning of your watch? What do you know about the Diurnal effect? What did you think when you got the cocked hat fix? Did you take another fix? Were you running the echo sounder? What was the depth of water? Why did you call the navigator? Why did you not call him earlier? Did the echo sounder reading tie in with your Decca nav. fixes? Why did you not use radar range and bearings from the land? Why did you not stop the ship?' My questionable Decca Navigator fix at five o clock was taken apart in detail. 'What reading did you get from the Decca? Did you check that the Decca Chain was set up properly?' I was shown the notebook we used on the bridge and shown my recorded readings. The chart we had used was on the table beside us. 'Transfer those readings to the chart.' I did. It still showed a cocked hat. So it went on, seemingly for hours.

I explained why I was concerned and that I had called the navigator immediately, but I still came away from the enquiry feeling that I was being blamed for putting the ship in danger and for not getting a better fix. The navigator received similar treatment but I have no idea how the captain got on as he refused ever to talk about the incident; but I heard comments were made about not using the small landing craft to check the water depths. No one was punished for the grounding partly I think because it was known we were being sent to a poorly charted area and we had not sustained any damage let alone had any injuries, etc. So all ended as well as could be expected from running an RN warship aground.

Rebel

We had a ship's dog in *Puncheston*. He was a local mongrel of the true Heinz 57 type but looked a bit like a cross between a small Alsatian and a skinny Labrador with a rich brown and white colouring. He had been found abandoned as a puppy somewhere on the island by someone in the naval base and they had brought it up. When they were posted back home they gave the dog to the ship as they did not want to have to put it in quarantine. He was called Rebel, or Rebs, and he was as soft as a pudding. The funny thing about him was that he got seasick. Rebel was an active, bouncy dog, always out and about on deck and taking an interest in what was going on, especially if he could see any local Arab fishermen in their boats at whom he could bark. He had many places about the ship that he liked to use for sleeping, most of them out on deck. The weather in the Persian Gulf is mostly good but it can get pretty nasty when the 'Shamals' blow down from north bringing dust storms with them. The sea develops into short, steep and lumpy waves that make small ships like minesweepers bounce around a bit. Whenever we left port and ran into a shamal Rebel would firstly lose interest in what was going on out on deck and then he would retire to the wardroom couch. The wardroom couch just happened to be in the middle of the ship and so moved the least in a seaway. It was also air-conditioned. He might have been a sick dog, but he was not a daft dog! Once there he put on a really pathetic 'hang dog' expression that said 'This is terrible, I have not signed on for this! I want to go ashore'. He looked at each of us accusingly as we came and went with his head hung low with this sad, sad face and big, brown, pleading eyes as though we were personally responsible for his ailment. He would stay there, sometimes for a couple of days, without eating or going on deck until the weather improved and he would then wander out on deck sniff the air, establish that all was OK again then go up to the fo'c'sle to look for fishermen. And there are people who say seasickness is all in the mind.

Dubai in the 1970s

In 1971, the Gulf was a very different place from what it is now. In those days Bahrain was the biggest and the most cosmopolitan port in the Gulf. Its wealth was originally based on pearls but this had been overtaken by oil. By 1971, its airport was the biggest in the Gulf and it was a major RAF station as well. Bahrain was

Dhows alongside Dubai Creek, a scene unchanged in decades.

seen as the most liberal of the Gulf States. The seven 'Trucial States' as they were called, situated along the south and eastern shores of the Gulf became the United Arab Emirates, or UAE, in 1971 and set off on their way to prosperity. Dubai was then a small but busy trading port with a population of less than 100,000 but was still one of the important ports in the Gulf. It did not have any holiday makers or five star hotels, high rise buildings or golf courses that are its trade mark today. Most of the local population still lived in houses made of mud and palm fronds. Trading activity focused on the creek. Most activity was on the north side of the creek, or Deira side. This was just across the creek from the Ruler's Palace and its famous wind towers that collected any breeze and channeled it down into the rooms below.

The dhows used Dubai to trans-ship and reload before taking cargoes to the upper Gulf and Iran. Sheik Rashid had started to develop Dubai port with the major dredging of the creek and the development of the new port area for deep-sea ships at Port Rashid. Gold has always been a major trading commodity in the Gulf and the Souks for gold, spices and all types of silk and other materials were found in narrow, earth-floored lanes between the building with palm fronds or plastic sheeting strung up to the walls to keep the sun off. All very unlike the paved, high roofed and brightly lit experience that the Dubai Gold Souk is now with its air-conditioned shops all awash with gold. One or two hotels were appearing, along with commercial buildings such as international banks. The airport too was just starting to be developed and a race began between the Gulf States to see who would have the best and biggest international airport. At that time all flights from Europe to and from the Far

East had to stop in the Middle East to refuel and the Gulf States wanted this revenue.

The one thing that has not changed in Dubai, however, is the creek waterfront in Deira. The big, solid teak dhows, that trade all over the Indian Ocean, the Arabian Sea and the Gulf, still operate and berth here as they have done for centuries. A new dhow harbour further up the creek has taken the majority of dhows but a large number still berth on the creek side. The sailing dhows, with their huge, curving mast that carried their single lateen sail, have now gone to be replaced by marine diesels, They moor up side by side, sometimes six or seven abreast, on the creek with their wooden prows projecting over the ones ahead. The biggest dhows can weigh up to 500 tons. The dhows are built on beaches and in shipyards all around the region and their construction methods and tools have not changed for centuries.

Sinbad the sailor came from this area. He was an Omani and sailed to China in a ship very similar to these dhows. It was an Omani navigator who helped Vasco da Gama sail across the Indian Ocean to India; so sailing is very much in the blood here. One of the pleasures of Dubai is to wander up and down the creek watching them as they load loose cargoes of absolutely everything from everywhere. The quay is full of wheelbarrows, rice, furniture, dates, sugar, washing machines, shoes, textiles, tyres, and crates of spices, cars, and drums of oil. You can find anything there. Cars, jams, sewing machines and umbrellas are all to be found lying side by side on the creek ready to be loaded. In 1972, there were sometimes nearly 200 dhows alongside the creek and twenty or thirty more on the Dubai side. Neither the creek nor the dhows have any cranes so everything is manhandled up a single gangplank. The gangplanks are single planks of wood, without any railings or ropes, let alone safety nets. The dhows are basic, no more than floating boxes so there is no real accommodation for the crew. They sleep and eat on deck. Food is cooked on an open, single primus stove; often kept in a cut-out, square biscuit tin and ablutions are carried out by squatting in a small open privy area on the stern. The crews are always cheerful and happy to have their photos taken and exchange a cheery 'Hello, Mister!' with passers-by. Dubai grew rich on the trade brought by the dhows long before oil made it mega rich.

The Musandam Peninsula

Just to the north of Dubai, is an area we visited called the Musandam. It is part of Oman. It is a spectacularly beautiful, remote and sparsely populated area of mountain desert and steep-sided fjords that stretch to the north and form the southern side of the Straits of Hormuz. Long, silent fjords twist their way deep into the peninsula between the sheer sides of the mountains, which are between 1,000 and 1,250 metres high. In summer, due to the shelter from the winds, the temperatures in the fjords can reach oven high levels. Two major fjords, the Elphinstone Inlet (Kwawr Ash Shamm) on the west side and the Malcolm Inlet

Gulf fishermen in their boat.

A fishing village in the Musandam perched on a tiny beach between the sea and the cliffs.

The still silence of the Elphinstone Inlet..

(Ghubbat Al Ghazirah) on the east coast get to within a few hundred yards of meeting each other in the middle. In fact the Elphinstone Inlet, which is over 10 miles long, is where at one time in the late nineteenth century an RN hydrographer recorded the highest known temperature on earth at that time, almost 130 °F. The heat, the humidity and the pure silence add to the intrigue of the place. The mountain ranges step away into the distance in shades of colour that vary from black and deep blue through browns and ochres to rich orange and red depending on the sun. It is totally a barren area yet clinging to the rocky shore under huge orange sandstone cliffs are tiny fishing villages where somehow they make a living out of the sea using old wooden canoes and handmade nets.

Midshipman's Board

There were six of us midshipmen in Bahrain who were due to sit our 'Mid's board' that summer. The Admiralty assembled an examining board in Singapore. The board was led by a senior captain and was made up of commanders who were all specialists in their examining subjects. The captain was a seaman officer. The midshipmen to be examined all came from ships currently in the Far East and that included those of us based in the Gulf. We were flown out to Singapore on a Thursday on the weekly RAF troop flight. After six months of seeing nothing but brown, sandy and arid deserts of the Persian Gulf, we thought we had landed in 'Shangri La'. Our eyes and senses went into lush green vegetation overload.

We had never seen anything so lush, so green or so wonderful as Singapore. The scents of the plants and trees, the smell of the grass and the colours of the flowers were astounding. We stayed in the wardroom of HMS *Terror*, the RN base in Singapore, a wonderful, rambling, old colonial style building set in large open grounds on the north coast at Woodlands near Sembawang Dockyard. After a couple of days acclimatising and revising, we sat our board on the Monday and Tuesday. We were examined in a series of one-to-one oral exams covering every aspect of an RN officer's profession. In the hot, steamy heat of Singapore, the board was held in the big, high, dark wooden-ceilinged rooms of HMS *Terror* with just the gentle whirring of the ceiling fans and drip of sweat from our furrowed brows, to accompany the persistent barrage of questions that rained down on us from the frowning examining officers. The board probed and teased information from us, made us explain complex seamanship procedures, quizzed us deeply on the Rules of the Road (100 per cent pass required), asked about voltages on main switchboards, steam temperatures in boilers, the procedures for disciplining ratings, how do you order fuel at sea and how do you make a running fix. What does this symbol on a chart mean? And so on and so on. They thoroughly wrung us out until we had no more knowledge left to give. Our task books were examined and we were questioned about what we had done during our midshipman's year. At last on the Tuesday night we were all assembled and told that, somehow, we had all passed and were now free do enjoy Singapore until our flight back to Bahrain on the Friday night.

A group of six eighteen- to twenty-year-olds left free in Singapore for three days and three nights! We had a ball. From the street markets of Nee Soon and China Town to the nighttime sights of Bugis Street and Singapore's exotic nightlife; we enjoyed it all. We even had afternoon tea in the Hilton! After all we were now about to become commissioned officers in the Royal Navy, about to be made acting sub-lieutenants; and no longer mere officers under training. We shopped in the markets for cameras, stereo and silk housecoats with dragons embroidered on the back, We spent our hard-earned money that had few outlets in Bahrain. I even bought a fine, big, one-eyed teddy bear, with a red bow round his neck, from a street stall in Nee Soon village. He was soon given the imaginative name of Edward. In 1971, Singapore was a very different place from the modern city but it had the 'Buzz', the fragrance and the atmosphere of the oriental hot pot that it has always been. Reluctantly, on the Friday, we had to pack up our things and go back to RAF Changi for our flight back to Bahrain to rejoin our ships. My bear even had a seat to himself.

Going Home

In 1971, the British Government decided to pull out its Forces from the Gulf. The minesweeper squadron in Bahrain was disbanded and the ships reallocated to other bases. Some of the ships went to Hong Kong and others to Singapore. HMS

Puncheston and HMS *Wiston* were to be sent back to the UK. Punchy was heading for home and the breaker's yard via South Africa and the Cape. I had been due to leave the ship at the end of my midshipman's time in September but requested to stay on board to help bring the ship home as this would undoubtedly be a voyage to remember. Happily, the Navy agreed. I was promoted to sub-lieutenant the day after we sailed from Bahrain.

We sailed in company with HMS *Wiston* and headed off down the Gulf and into the Arabian Sea. This was in the days before everything that moved had a 'Sat Nav'. Our ocean navigation was done by sextant sights of the stars and the sun. On this leg of the voyage, the biggest problem we had was finding somewhere to refuel as we were only a small ship and so only had small fuel tanks. Most of the way there were suitable ports we could go into but there was a huge stretch from Oman down to Mombasa where there was nowhere we could go. It was decided that we would replenish at sea from a Royal Fleet Auxiliary (RFA) somewhere off Socotra Island near the entrance to the Red Sea. On the appointed day of the rendezvous we were all up early looking for the RFA. She was not there. Had our Astro Navigation let us down? Were we lost? We saw one huge oil tanker on the horizon but discounted it as it was obliviously a VLCC on its way to the Gulf and far too big for us to refuel from. Then she started to flash us by lamp. We were wrong, this was our refueller, the RFA *Dewdale,*. She was a 67,000-ton tanker, in those days that was a very large ship. Initially, the RFA had difficulty finding a small enough diameter hose that would fit our refueling cock. Once they had found one somewhere, we tried to do a conventional under way RAS where both ships steam alongside each other and a hose is passed across the gap. The difference in our ship sizes made this nonsense. Our bridge top was just about level with the deck of the *Dewdale* and we were bouncing about on her wake and being sucked into her hull. It was then decided that it would be far easier if the *Dewdale* just stopped and we came alongside her lee side. They then just handed the hose to us over the rail. Who said naval initiative was dead? They even gave us a tray of fresh bread rolls from their galley. We rose up and down about 10 feet on the Indian Ocean swell while the *Dewdale* appeared to remain absolutely static throughout. *Wiston* and *Puncheston* both took their fuel in this way and soon we were left on our own again as *Dewdale* steamed away over the horizon like a moving island on her way to Singapore and we rattled and rolled our way down towards Mombasa.

Our first stop was Mombasa, where the Kenyan Navy kindly invited us to a fine lunch in their beautiful base wardroom, which was built on a bluff overlooking the tight twisty entrance to Mombasa Harbor and had fabulous views of the harbor and the reef beyond. We were berthed in a small creek just off the main harbor. Berthed across the creek from us on a small jetty was a clean, well-maintained coaster which looked to be about 1,000 tons. The skipper, who was British, came across to say hello and stayed for lunch. He invited us back on board for lunch the next day. It turned out that he owned the ship and it served as permanent home for himself, his wife and their child as they tramp traded through the Indian Ocean, between the Seychelles, Mauritius and the East African coast. What a life! They

Above left: RFA *Dewdale* seen from the bridge of HMS *Puncheston* with HMS Wiston already alongside.

Above right: HMS *Wiston* goes alongside the now-stopped RFA *Dewdale* to refuel in the middle of the Indian Ocean.

had had the main accommodation area altered to make it into a family apartment. What a fabulous job they had done. It was more like a luxury penthouse than a ship's cabin. Unfortunately, he did not need any more watch keepers or I would have deserted the RN there and then.

In Durban we were again well looked after with offers of days out and invitations to parties. On the serious side it had been arranged that we were to scatter the ashes of a local ex-pat who had been in the RN and whose wish had been to be buried at sea. This was to take place as we sailed from Durban. Sod's law applied and, after two glorious days in port, sailing day was filthy with a strong gale blowing onto the shore. The funeral party came on board and as soon as we had cast off from the jetty we felt the effect of the big seas that were running outside the harbour. We continued out and the ship immediately started to bounce around. Normally, for a burial or a committal of ashes, which this was, the ship would stop, or at least slow right down, to allow for a dignified ceremony for scattering the ashes from the stern. In this case slowing down was not an option as the seas were pushing us all over the place, spray was flying all over the ship and we had to hang on just to stay upright. The family and the vicar sheltered in the small wardroom but started to get anxious and became less confident about life as the ship plunged and bucked her way out into the Indian Ocean. Instead of steaming a few miles well out to sea and into the peaceful and remote part of Indian Ocean, this poor fellow had his ashes scattered a few hundred yards off the harbour in a hurried service with the mourners hanging onto whatever they could hold as the ashes were whipped away by the wind. The ashes were last seen being blown straight for the Durban beaches. The family was then hastily dropped off back at the jetty. It is amazing how fast mourners can move at times. We then turned round and set off straight into the gale again for our next port of call, which was Simonstown. In fact, the gale died down soon afterwards and by late afternoon we were enjoying a warm sunny day and had a lovely sail down the coast, with miles and miles of beautiful deserted dunes and beaches to admire, in the spring sunshine.

We were royally looked after by the South African Navy in Simonstown. RSA was an ally and a lot of ex-RN personnel had joined the South African Navy. We berthed in the naval base and the South African Navy gave us their full support and patched up the ships and overhauled what they could to get the ships ready for their long run up the Atlantic. While the South African Navy worked away on board, we spent the time enjoying the place. We saw and envied the lifestyle they were able to enjoy in the South African climate. Everyone on board was invited to some shore function or another. We had lunches in Clifton, the 'Posh' area of Capetown, a day at the races, beach buggy days, trips to Cape Point and up Table Mountain on the cable car as well as enjoying some super meals in Capetown itself. The sailors also discovered the delights of Capetown's night clubs. After almost a year in the Gulf and for some of the sailors, a good while longer, this was heaven on earth.

One afternoon the ship's phone rang and the OOD took down a message that two local ex-Navy gents were inviting two officers out to join them for dinner at a smart hotel in Capetown. Dave; a lieutenant who had come out just for the trip to assist in watch keeping and I were free so decided to go along. This sort of 'blind date' was common for visiting RN ships, especially if the hosts were ex-RN themselves. Normally, the invitation was in return for cocktail parties held on board. We assumed that this was also a follow up to our party of a few nights earlier. We arrived at the named restaurant and met the two hosts. One look at the pink jacket was enough, our suspicions were aroused. 'I'm sorry did we meet you at our Cocktail Party?' 'No, we weren't there but we heard that there were two ships in. No, we are not in the South African Navy.' Alarm bells were already ringing loudly as Dave and I looked at each other. Within minutes it was clear what they were after. 'No, we won't have dinner here but we thought it would be much more cosy if we all go back to our place for a little something.' Obviously, no one had told them that certain, um, inclinations, shall we say, were illegal in the RN. Dave and I made our excuses and left rapidly.

On the other hand, one day Graham and I were invited to lunch by a genuine ex-RN Captain and his wife, who had been on board for the cocktail party. They lived in a large, old wooden house in a wood and set on the side of a hill that sloped down towards the sea a few miles out of Simonstown. The house was isolated from the road and other houses and the whole place was like a time warp where everything was moving at half the speed of the world outside. It was fascinating to listen to them as he had left the RN many years earlier and retired to the Cape. They came from an era when the Royal Navy ruled the waves and they still lived their daily lives as they would have done in those days and they fondly thought that the RN was still the same. They remembered it with

Round the Cape of Good Hope. The Cape seen from the sweep deck of HMS *Puncheston* with a minesweeping float in the foreground.

battleships and carriers galore, with ships sailing from port to port, then spending weeks alongside in tropical ports. Their home was full of memorabilia from those bygone days and postings to the old ports of the Empire.

For most of us, this was our first experience of South Africa and apartheid. I have to say; superficially everything seemed to be OK. The trains into Capetown had 'blacks only' and 'whites only' carriages, of course, but this did not seem to cause any problems. We saw no signs of poverty or animosity towards whites. The one thing I clearly recall is that all the coloured people in Capetown appeared to be well dressed and well fed. However, we were nowhere near the black townships or the shanty areas outside Capetown. There was no violence that we saw, even late at night. We were however warned not to go near certain areas of Capetown as whites were not welcome there. Apart from that we carried on and enjoyed the wonders of the Cape.

We finally had to leave and after sailing out of Simonstown we rounded the Cape of Good Hope, a major rounding for any sailor. Our trip home up the Atlantic was blessed with good weather so we enjoyed long sunny days steaming up through the tropics in a gentle Atlantic swell. The rest of the voyage home passed without any major mishap.

We stopped in Monrovia, capital and main port for Liberia. This was a very different place from Simonstown. We were stopped every time we went ashore by the guards on the dockyard gate. We were warned not to go out of the docks alone, ever, and not to go into town, never take a taxi alone and do not even think about walking anywhere. However, the lads will be lads and always enjoy a challenge. They found some dubious and dingy drinking holes near the docks. A few of us went there one night. The area was very run down and the buildings dilapidated. This was not a rich area. The pubs were no more than shacks that served beer. The dark interiors hid almost everything but they did seem to have a very friendly clientele of dark-skinned ladies and were undoubtedly fronts for houses of ill repute. We kept clear of any sort of trouble and after a couple of beers and a polite 'No thank you, but maybe tomorrow' we headed back on board. In any event the beer was OK.

Our final stop was Gibraltar. The plan was to clean up the ship and give her hull a final coat of paint for our final arrival into Portsmouth for paying off and decommissioning. As it was the last port of call it therefore warranted an extra effort to have a good time. Gibraltar was still a major naval base then and its bars and clubs had a reputation fleet wide. I enjoyed an evening in the casino with Graham and blew a whole £5 on the roulette wheel within five minutes flat!

We set off from Gibraltar up the Portuguese coast and into the Bay of Biscay to be met by the full force of a November gale and heavy seas. We slowed right down to protect the ship from a severe battering. During the night we received word that a yacht had sent out an SOS and so we then had to get moving to try and find her. After twelve to fifteen hours of searching the area we were told that it had turned up safely and we could continue to Portsmouth. The storm had died down by now but it had caused some damage to the ship and especially the paintwork. Everything was coated in salt and most of the fresh paint that was put on in Gibraltar had been stripped off the hull to leave bare wood in places. We were now going to be over twenty-four hours late into Portsmouth but the RN staff there did a superb job of contacting all the families who were planning to come down and postponed the whole arrival by a day.

HMS *Puncheston* dropped her anchor for the last time in the Spithead while the ship was cleared by customs. Then we were cleared to enter Portsmouth and make our way into the MCM Centre of HMS *Vernon*. Ships paying off from RN Commissions fly a decommissioning pennant whose length reflects the number of years of the commission. As Punchy had been in commission in the Gulf for years and years ours was almost as long as the ship. We had decided to fly it from a small bracket on the mast, which was clear of the other signal halyards and duly hoisted it as we picked up the anchor. As we were entering Portsmouth Harbour, past the ramparts of Old Portsmouth, there was an ominously loud crack from the top of the mast. On the bridge we all looked at each other, 'paying off pennant!' said Graham. I dashed out to see what had happened. There, fluttering on the deck and draped around the funnel and rigging was the paying off pennant. The metal bracket itself had snapped clean off the mast with the weight of the pennant. It was impossible to stop the ship now as we were in the narrow entrance to Portsmouth Harbour, so a signalman and I climbed up the mast and hastily rigged a temporary rope lashing to hold it up and we hoped no one would notice.

As we came alongside in Vernon Creek, by the old HMS *Vernon*, a Royal Marine Band was playing and there were all the families waiting and waving on the dockside. The skipper tried hard to mess up his final coming alongside, much to Graham's and my amusement, but eventually he got it right, the ship was secured and for the last time the engines stopped. The families and friends all came on board and we all enjoyed the drinks and small eats that had been laid out in the biggest seamen's mess.

As both the gunnery officer and the correspondence officer I spent three more weeks in Vernon to assist in paying off Punchy, removing ammunition and finalising all the official records, and the mustering and accounting for all the ship's reference books, returning stores, etc. The captain was rarely seen and the first lieutenant, coxswain, chief engineer and I did it. Most of the lads already had their next drafts and had gone off on long leave as soon as we arrived. It was now late in the year and most people were thinking of Christmas. We finally completed the form filling and I said my goodbyes a few days before Christmas and left Punchy to her fate at the breaker's yard. I had also received my orders to report back to HMS *Vernon* in the New Year for a full minehunting control officer training course before going to join HMS *Nurton*, a minehunter based in Scotland, as the minehunting control officer.

Oh yes, Rebel, the ships dog, came home with us too. He was taken on by his main keeper on board, one of the electrical ratings, and after six months quarantine in Scotland, Rebs was last heard of enjoying life chasing Scottish rabbits.

CHAPTER 7

HMS *Nurton* –
Back to Scotland Again

HMS *Nurton* was in Faslane, the nuclear submarine base on the Clyde. The train journey from London to join her, on a Sunday in February, had been a cold, depressing and interminably long one. It was during the power cuts and the three-day week of the early 1970s and the latter part of the journey was through a very dark countryside. As seemed usual at the time the train heating system was not working and the buffet car was 'regrettably not available on this service'. I finally arrived in a very dark and wet Glasgow and then, after another train journey out to Helensburgh and a bus ride to the base, I was confronted with the MOD Police. Apparently I did not have any of the normal security passes that someone based in Faslane would need to get into the base. I also needed another pass to get onto the jetty where *Nurton* was berthed. After a series of phone calls to the ship and MOD in London and checks on my appointment letter the MOD Police finally believed that I was who I said I was and I was allowed to go on board *Nurton* under escort.

HMS *Nurton*, named after a village in Staffordshire, instantly struck me as a friendly ship. The CO was a Lt Cdr John Perryman who was trained as an Observer in the Fleet Air Aim and came to *Nurton* from a Buccaneer fast jet in HMS *Ark Royal*. That meant that he was an expert in avionics and navigation. I quickly realised that he was also a really good man. He was big, self-assured and jolly with a relaxed open manner that inspired confidence, but he also ran a tight ship and would not tolerate any slackness or bad behavior. He was the best CO I had in my time in the Navy. We got on fine and never had any troubles when working together in the ops room or on the bridge. *Nurton* also soon had a new First Lieutenant, Hamish Loudon who was another 'good man'. He was a shortish, bearded Scot from Fort William with a fine 'heiland' accent to match. Hamish was always cheery and had a highly developed appreciation of pretty girls. He was also the Mine Clearance Diving Officer (MCDO) on board and ran the ship's specialist mine clearance diving team. Like all divers, he was highly enthusiastic about his vocation. Most non-divers in the Navy regard the diving community in general, and the mine clearance divers in particular, as people who have somehow 'got lost' in life and are to be treated with great care and tenderness. Well, how else should you treat people who think it is fun to swim about, nearly 200 feet

HMS *Nurton*. (Photo by kind permission of Mr Brian Fisher)

under the freezing seas, in winter, at night, in zero visibility and pitch blackness, feeling for mines with their frozen hands?

Although identical to *Puncheston* in her construction, *Nurton* was a minehunter and not a minesweeper. The difference being that a minehunter is fitted with a powerful sonar system that allows the ship to search ahead for different types of mines, both buoyant moored mines and ground mines, i.e. ones lying on the seabed. With the sonar the ship will hopefully find them before it sails over the top of them. Once found, the mines are detonated using explosive charges. A Minesweeper can only sweep behind the ship for moored mines hoping to cut the mooring cables with wire sweeps which have cutters attached to them and then trying to detonate them with gun fire when they float to the surface. They also use acoustic and magnetic systems that are also towed astern of the ship to try to detonate acoustic and magnetic mines; but again have no way of knowing whether there are mines there or not until they have detonated them.

Although we did a lot of work and exercises in the Forth and on the east coast, most of our time was spent steaming round the top of Scotland from our base in HMS *Lochinvar*, in South Queensferry near Edinburgh, to the Clyde and the Faslane submarine base, where we did a number of exercises and also to northern Ireland for anti-gun-running patrols during the 'Troubles'. A major part of our role was to ensure that we could keep the Clyde and its approaches clear of any mines so that the submarines could sail freely in and out.

Nuclear Hunters

One of the aspects of working in the Clyde was that when we were alongside in Faslane we were able to eat and drink in the big base wardroom. The wardroom, not surprisingly, was full of submariners. It soon became obvious to us that once the submariners realised that we were actually from a surface ship, or 'Targets' as they referred to them; and just a little diesel powered minehunter at that; they rapidly lost interest in us. They would wander off muttering darkly about their 'Time under the ice', or 'Need to Know' security clearances, their 'nuclear credentials', or 'going critical' and other scary phrases. After some weeks of this we decided to show them our nuclear credentials. The next time that we arrived off Faslane the funnel of our little diesel powered minehunter displayed, instead of our usual squadron badge, a big yellow and black nuclear radiation badge. The shipwright had made it and we exchanged badges the night before we went in. The submariners took it well and while the CO was told smartly by the Commodore to remove it 'chop chop', when word got round the submariners they all saw the joke and we made a name for ourselves as 'You lot off the nuclear hunter'.

Fishing Vessel in Distress

We were exercising at the southern end of the Firth of Clyde one winter's evening. The wind was beginning to rise and the sea was just starting to pick up; when suddenly the peace on the bridge was shattered by 'Mayday, Mayday, Mayday' on the VHF radio. Someone was in trouble and not too far away. The call was from the *Golden Dawn*, a 60-foot fishing vessel about 10 miles south-west of us and she was in real danger. Her radio message said she had a net round her screw and was drifting in a rising wind towards the rocks. We stopped hunting and left immediately to look for the boat. We quickly found her on radar then saw her visually. She was indeed drifting downwind towards the rocks at the tip of the Mull of Kintyre. At that point she was about 2 miles from the rocks but the wind was increasing and pushing her towards them with increasing force. An hour later we were on the scene and quickly lowered the Gemini. I was sent over with an engineer and a couple of our lads to see what we could do. The mate explained that here had been an accident on board. Somehow, the skipper had been knocked unconscious by a blow to the head from a metal block while they were hauling the net. In the confusion that followed, the net had become very badly wrapped round the propeller. This had caused the engine to stall and the engineers could not re start it with all the netting wrapped and jammed round the propeller. The mate had already organised a helicopter for the skipper and he was now on his way to hospital.

If we could clear the net with help from the divers then they could re start the engine and hopefully they would be OK. All the while the boat was drifting in a strong south-westerly wind towards the rocks. The boat had swung with her stern to the wind due to the sea anchor effect of the stuck net, so the stern was taking the worst of the battering from the rising sea. One of the divers went down to quickly survey the damage. His report was clear. The nets were well and truly tangled in the prop and there was no way that they could clear the nets as modern nets are made of tough plastic and are almost indestructible. Also, in worsening weather the stern was now starting to rise up then slam down into the waves, making it far too dangerous to put the divers into the water under the stern.

By now we had drifted another mile nearer the rocks and suddenly the dark cliffs of Kintyre looked awfully near and threatening. Darkness was falling and the day was turning decidedly nasty. It was clear that unless we did something very soon the trawler would strike the rocks in less than an hour. The only obvious answer was to tow the fishing boat to safety. We called up *Nurton* which was standing off about half a mile away. Three of us went up onto the fo'c'sle as *Nurton* came alongside and fired a thin line across the bows of the trawler to which they attached a thicker towrope. We hauled it in and secured this to the bits on the fo'c'sle. Slowly at first, *Nurton* took the strain on the towrope, and we took shelter on the main deck. The towrope stretched out coming clear of the water, then the strain came on and the water was squeezed out of the rope. There was a fear that the now violent motion of the trawler would cause the towline to part and no one was going to be on the fo'c'sle if that happened! *Nurton* let out more rope so that the dip in the rope was in the sea and acted as a shock absorber in case of any severe jolts. Slowly the line took the strain and, once moving forward, the trawler obediently followed *Nurton* round and away from the rocks. The immediate danger was over. We still had to find somewhere sheltered to tow her. It was decided that Fairlie, near Largs, up in the shelter of the Clyde, was the best place. In decreasing weather and at night this was a long slow tow that took over six hours. The boarding party stayed on board the fishing vessel and we took turns to stay out on deck near the fo'c'sle to keep a check on the tow rope as we did not want it to part, especially as night had now fallen. Those not on deck during the tow were well looked after by the mate and the crew and treated to some good Scottish hospitality. We berthed at Fairlie late that night and the next day assisted in getting the net clear of the prop. The skipper recovered in hospital and all was well.

VIP Lunch

Our new navigator, Tony, arrived and shared the cabin with me. He was a larger than life guy, full of fun and keen for anything. He was physically large too; about 6 foot 4 inches and 15-stone plus. He had just completed his sub-lieutenant's' courses and a navigation course so was busting a gut to put it all into practice. He also owned a lovely old Sunbeam Alpine, a convertible sports tourer, which was his pride and joy.

After a few weeks on board he said that he had invited his parents on board for Sunday lunch when we were next in our home base of HMS *Lochinvar*. He properly asked the CO's permission and as I was to be Officer of the Day on that Sunday I would be there too. Apart from that all the other officers would be ashore for the weekend. About two days before the event it somehow emerged that Tony's father was actually an RN Admiral who had just retired from the Navy. No one knew. The skipper nearly had a baby. He could just imagine

coming back on board on Monday morning to be told by the base commander
that an Admiral had lunched on board *Nurton* and he would not even have
known! Strictly speaking, for a formal or official visit there were all sorts of local
protocols that we needed to do from telling the base commander, MOD police,
and the squadron commander that an RN VIP was to be in the base and on board
Nurton. There was ship protocol too, of piping the side, the duty crew being in
No. 1 uniforms, etc., and Tony had not said a word. No one on board even knew
that Tony's father was in the RN let alone an Admiral. Tony insisted it was to be a
totally informal family visit in civilian clothes and his father absolutely refused to
have any special protocols applied. On the day all went very well and his parents
were super people. The four of us had as good a meal as could be expected while
enjoying some of the wine that we had bought in France on a recent trip. Tony
had made a point in his early naval career of not letting on who his father was
as he saw that it could only cause problems. Tony handled it all brilliantly and it
certainly did not harm him as he went on to be a distinguished helicopter pilot
and to command a major naval air station. He retired from the Navy as a flag
officer himself.

Russian Lights

During the summer the squadron was sent on a visit to the Baltic. We were led
by HMS *Abdiel*, which was a 1,000-ton minelayer, our main support ship and
captained by the squadron CO. We enjoyed a relaxing, sunny three-day visit to
the port of Visby in Gotland, which is a large island off the south-east coast of
Sweden. It is a wonderful, old, medieval, walled town, very much unchanged
over the years with its narrow winding streets tucked in under the protection
of the town walls. Tony and I were invited for dinner by the Swedish Navy on
one of their small patrol boats that was berthed near *Nurton*. The patrol boat
was about a quarter of the size of *Nurton* and Tony and I felt like 'Big Ship'
men when we went on board. In a tiny wardroom that four of us could just
about squeeze into they provided a fantastic meal. We started with smoked
fish, followed by venison with potatoes and strawberries to finish. They also
introduced us to Swedish punch, a strong liqueur that just about finished
us off.

It was always interesting going into the Baltic as the Russian Navy always
sent out a frigate or corvette to constantly shadow any NATO warships that
may be visiting. When they did this the Russian ship would normally sit about a
mile off our starboard quarter day and night. We had this while we were there
in HMS *Tenby* but this trip, so some reason, we had been left alone. Maybe the
cold war was cooling, or perhaps they thought minehunters were not worth
bothering with.

We sailed from Visby in a relaxed frame of mind and headed south-west
towards the southern tip of Sweden. We were sailing in line ahead and *Nurton*

was the last ship in the line. That night, as we headed for the southern tip of Sweden, I was on watch and I noticed a radar contact about 10 miles away slowly catching us up from the north. When I studied its movement it was clear that it was on a converging course with our group. This was not unexpected as the shipping lanes in that area meant that most of the south-bound shipping had to go through a traffic lane and so converged in this area. I studied this ship though the binoculars from the bridge wing but it was a dark night with no moon and I could not see anything of note apart from her normal navigation lights; two white masthead steaming lights and the red, port navigation light. She appeared to be a normal Baltic freighter, probably about 2,000 to 3,000 tons. However, there was something about it that bothered me but I could not figure out what. Then I realised that the radar response seemed to be of a bigger ship than the lights being shown indicated. As she got closer I studied her more. Then I realised what had initially troubled me. I could not see any cabin or deck lights on this ship. All merchant ships normally have some lights on deck just for the safety of those on board, as well as cabin and saloon lights, but this one did not. There were no lights anywhere apart from her navigation lights. I kept a watch on her. As she got to about 4 miles, I went out to the wing and looked again and suddenly I could make out her silhouette in the darkness. There was instantly no doubt at all as to what she was. The hairs on the back of my neck rose, literally. A glimpse of a bow wave a long way ahead of where I thought her bows were gave her away. I could now make out the dark hull from the darkness, it stretched way beyond the navigation lights, and I could now see the dark, brooding, superstructure and bridge; and then to confirm my fears I could make out the silhouettes of two large gun turrets on the bow. This was a Russian 'Sverdlov' Class Cruiser. A big warship of about 15,000 tons, capable of over 30 knots and carrying twelve 6-inch guns as her main armament. Her navigation lights were placed well aft and low down to disguise her and make her look like a small coaster and they bore no relation to where her lights should have been on a cruiser-sized ship. I immediately radioed HMS *Abdiel*. 'The contact bearing north at range 4 miles is a Russian cruiser and she is on a converging course'. *Abdiel*, as senior and lead ship, had to decide what action we as a squadron should now take. I then gave our captain heart failure by calling him up from a deep sleep to tell him. 'Captain Sir, officer of the watch. I have a Russian cruiser at range 4 miles and on a converging course.' I did not have time to finish the full report before he fled his cabin. He was on the bridge in a flash. *Abdiel* immediately signaled us all to alter course away in a formation turn. We made a full 360 turn and came up on our original course but now we were astern of the Russian who must have been annoyed that his disguise and shadowing tactics had been tumbled. He had no option but to carry on and we followed happily along behind. The CO, John, left the bridge with the words, 'Gordon, don't ever do that to me again!' As if I had somehow arranged it with Russian Naval HQ.

Crew Training

Our CO, John, left *Nurton* and went back to the world of aircraft carriers and noisy jets. His replacement was another aviator Lieutenant Commander, David Goodenough Bayly. David was a helicopter pilot doing his first ship command job. He was, like John, a good man, friendly and open and he went out of his way get to know everyone on board as quickly as possible. He had an aviator's sense of professionalism and expected others to have it too. He worked hard to keep and develop the strong bonds that existed between everyone on board that had grown under John's command.

One of the many good things he did on board was to improve the officer's ship-handling skills. Periodically he would set aside half a day for man overboard exercises. These he ran as a competition. The officer who had the best aggregate times over three runs would win a bottle of champagne which was paid for by the rest. This not only improved our drills but engendered some good friendly competition and rivalry between us all. He also allowed us to bring the ship alongside the pier at our home base in the Forth and to unberth her. To my knowledge none of the other skippers did this. Again he would set aside a half day so we could all have two or three runs at both berthing and unberthing. This allowed us to see and learn from each other's mistakes. It was all done in a good training atmosphere and not something to be used as a reason to berate you if you got it wrong. At Dartmouth we had been taught the fundamentals of ship handling and practiced them on the river Dart in small, twin-screw launches, but it is a totally different proposition in a minehunter with not only the ship's company but also the rest of the squadron's officers watching carefully to make sure you don't hit them on the way in or out. This level of ship handling was rare for junior officers and something that you would never get to do in a bigger ship. We all benefitted from this and our confidence grew immeasurably.

David extended this training to the whole ship and we would have a half day when he would sit in the bridge then call on any one, or any team, in the ship to go and do someone else's job on board. For example he would make a PA; 'Chief engineer to get a diving suit and tanks ready for a dive. The navigator and MHCO (me) to stream the minesweeping gear. The chief to prepare the port anchor for letting go. Leading Seaman Blogs report to the bridge to chart a course to south Queensferry. The first lieutenant to start the main engines' and so on with everyone knowing what was being asked of others so that things could be properly monitored for safety. The cross training worked too, because when a flu epidemic hit the squadron during one Christmas leave period, *Nurton* was able to sail on a reduced crew but with everyone helping out doing other's jobs.

The Buoy

Unfortunately, the exercises did not always work out as planned. We had been working in the Clyde and had spent the previous night, which was Burn's Night, at anchor in Lamlash Bay, a small sheltered spot off Arran. We sailed in the morning after a very good wardroom Burn's Night supper and a bit of Scottish hospitality in the senior rates mess. Our first task was to recover some marker buoys that we had been using the previous day. As we steamed towards the first buoy, the CO, David, was on the con and peering at the buoy and then the compass. I could see that David was clearly not happy and was obviously feeling decidedly rough. He was struggling to focus and looked dreadful, an ashen green colour. I did not feel too good either but was enjoying the boss's discomfort as he tried to judge the wind and tide and balance the ships speed and course for the final approach to the first buoy. When we got to about a quarter of a mile away he suddenly turned to me and said 'Gordon, you take it' and walked out onto the bridge wing. 'Oh bother' I thought. I did what I thought was a good approach and put both engines astern as we got up close to the buoy. Now, these buoys were big, they were shaped like a hemisphere, about 4 foot across and made of white polystyrene with a bright orange plastic coating so they were easily visible, light and easy to handle. Unfortunately, I had misjudged the ship's approach speed a tad and was a bit too close to the buoy. As we went astern on the engines the ship was still moving forward a tiny bit faster than I would have liked. The buoy passed down the port side of the ship and was swept under it. For a few moments it disappeared from view under the stern and Hamish and his sweep deck crew, who were waiting to recover it over the stern, all craned over the side to see where it had gone. 'Stop both engines' I called to try and prevent any damage to the buoy from the screws. Too late. From the bridge we then saw this explosion of snowflakes from the sea. A white plume rose up about twenty feet into the air then gently fell all over the sweep deck, showering everyone in white polystyrene snowflakes. The buoy had been exploded by the propellers. The lads all thought this was hilarious and I must admit that, in spite of getting a ticking off for making a lousy approach by the CO, I thought it was too. Hamish came marching up to the bridge still with white polystyrene flakes sticking to his jersey 'And which of you two officers will be paying for that?', he demanded in his highland brogue. 'It was on my slop chit and is NOT a disposable item!' I think David saw the funny side later; but not until after his hangover had receded.

Newcastle

Once a year we had to take part in a major NATO exercise and this year *Nurton* was given a large area off the mouth of the Tyne to survey and clear of any exercise mines that we found. The weather was bad on the first day and we were having difficulty keeping the sonar properly directed due to the pitching of the ship. We had literally just started minehunting when after a couple of hours the minehunting sonar broke down. The engineers tried for a few hours to sort out the problem while we wallowed about in the choppy North Sea. 'It's one of the gyros Sir', the chief reported to me. 'We will need to get alongside where the ship is stable so we can change it.' This was not a repair that could be done at sea as the ship had to be absolutely still so that the gyro can be installed, lined up and tested.

We went into North Shields and berthed on the Fish Quay but, after trying there, it was decided that there was too much movement due to passing ships and swell from the harbor mouth so we retreated right up the Tyne to the Town Quay, almost right underneath the Tyne Bridge. It turned out to be a more serious fault than we thought and we had to get a couple of specialist artificers down from HMS *Lochinvar* to help. For four days the engineers worked away, eventually rebuilding or replacing all the gyros then checking that the whole system worked properly.

While we were there we had to amuse ourselves somehow and found a very select nightclub called 'Grey's Club' where the manager, one David Macbeth, made us very welcome. That week they had a female singer called Diane Chandler. After two or three nights there we all got talking and invited them both on board for a drink. The next night, which was our last in Newcastle, David, the manager told us that he wanted us to stick around after the cabaret as he was getting the local press in for a drink and to take some photos of Diane. We duly obliged, but by this time it was about 0200 and only the skipper and I were left. The press arrived, we all had another drink and they took their photos of Diane and chatted to us. Then they asked Diane to sit between David and myself for a couple of final photos. A few minutes later the photos were taken; we all said goodnight, went back on board and forgot all about it. We sailed the next day back out into the exercise.

About a week or two later I received a letter from my mother. My mother thought I was miles out in the North Sea on the NATO exercise. As I opened the letter a newspaper cutting fell out. There was nothing odd in this as she often sent me bits from the local paper about people we knew. I picked up the cutting and opened it. The heading was 'The Navy's In' or something like that. Here was a large photo of a smiling Diane in her long sequined gown with a thigh length slit; lying across the David and I on a settee and a paragraph below talking about how 'We naval officers have seen cabaret singers all over the world and Diane is the best by far!' Needless to say the stupid grins on our faces made us look like smirking, school boys rather than naval officers. It turned out that unknown to me; my parents had been driving up to Scotland that weekend and had stopped at an aunt's house near Newcastle. While there my mother picked up the aunt's local paper, *The Newcastle Journal*, and there was her son beaming out at her from page three. My mother's only comment was 'So this is what you mean by 'Being at Sea'. And the morale of this story is? 'The truth will ALWAYS find you out.'

One other event from that week in Newcastle sticks in my mind too. A few weeks earlier I had spotted a very pretty, blue eyed, auburn-haired Wren in the pay office at HMS *Lochinvar*. I had noticed her some time before but had not plucked up the courage to ask her out. I discovered she was called Doreen and she had a lovely lilting Scottish accent. One lunchtime I plucked up all my courage and walked up to the pay office. I peeped through the window to see whether she was there and was delighted and terrified to see that she was and that there was no one else there either. I walked up the length of the office towards her desk, conscious that she was watching me every step of the way. I said hello and asked her if she would like to go out to dinner with me. Without a moment's hesitation she said 'No, Sir. I am working for my promotion exams and do not have any spare time.' I left deflated and forlorn. However, a few days later I contrived to get her to get me some stationery items from the storeroom along the corridor and, while she was up a step ladder searching for pads of A4 paper and I was appreciating a shapely pair of calves, I asked her again. This time she said 'Yes!'

I had only been out with her once at that point and we had been at sea for six weeks since then and I was keen to get back and see if she would go out with me again. One of the artificers who came to help us with the sonar was a young Chief Petty Officer called Keith. Keith was about my age, he was well known to us and was a popular chief who was often on board when we were alongside in Lochinvar. On the Friday morning he came to me. 'Sir, as I have been down here this week I have missed pay parade. As the ship's pay officer, can you advance me a sub for the week end please?' 'Haven't you got any other money chief?', I asked. 'Well yes, but I have a date on Saturday night and need a bit extra.' 'Oh, OK then.' I gave him a sub of £50.00 and entered the papers and wished him good luck. As we were due back out to sea again to catch up on the exercise there would be no weekend for us!

Some months later when Doreen and I knew each other better she told me the story of how Keith had come back up from *Nurton* to take her to a dinner dance that she had known about for ages, with money I had advanced to him. I am happy to say that Keith did not last long. Doreen and I got engaged six months later and have now been happily married for over thirty-six years.

My Brush with a Hero

We were alongside in HMS *Lochinvar* when we received a call telling us that we were to host a group of Royal Naval Reserve (RNR) officers from Portsmouth for a day who were undergoing a minehunting course and needed to be shown exactly how it was done on board one. This was my area. As the minehunting control officer I ran the minehunting operations in the ops room. The team of about six RNR Officers arrived on board from Portsmouth and were met in the wardroom by the CO. He then brought them up to the ops room, where I was getting the systems ready to present and demonstrate the system. They all squeezed into the dark, tiny ops room and leaned over the electronic plotting and radar table. The idea behind the table was that lights shone up onto the underside of the glass top and showed through a paper chart on the top to indicate the position of the ship and the sonar beam and any objects that we detected on the sonar. I welcomed the team and began my planned lecture on minehunting. I looked up after a second or two to find myself staring into the steely eyes of one of my schoolboy heroes. Robin Knox Johnston, Lt Cdr RNR Officer, was about 2 feet from the end of my nose! Here was the first man ever to sail single-handed and non-stop around the world listening to me in my ops room! Robin had sailed non-stop around the world in 1968/69 in his own yacht *Suhaili*. *Suhaili* was a small 32-foot, teak-hulled cruising ketch that Robin had built in India when he was there in the merchant navy. He had sailed her home from India himself. I had read his books and watched documentaries on his extraordinary voyage and now here he was listening to me. I lost my thought thread for a second or two but regained composure, I think. Robin was a very polite listener.

Northern Ireland

We sailed for our first Northern Ireland patrol on a foggy winter's morning. Being based in Scotland we had our share of bad weather however on this occasion we sailed for the Irish Sea from HMS *Lochinvar* in a real pea-souper of a fog. We could not see the Forth Road Bridge from the harbour, even though it is only 200 yards away. As we sailed slowly down the river we could not even see the bottom of either the road or the Forth Railway Bridge as we passed under them! It was quite eerie to hear the traffic rumbling overhead but not be able to see anything.

Fog was often the least of our worries, as the north of Scotland is renowned for bad weather especially in winter. And we sailed round it lots! On one of our early trips we met a westerly gale as we neared Cape Wrath as we were heading for the Minch. We knew the gale was coming across the Atlantic but had hoped to beat it to Cape Wrath. We lost. After going off watch I collapsed into my sleeping bag and was asleep in seconds. The next thing I knew was that I was very wide awake and I instantly realised that there was no bunk underneath me! I lay floating in mid air for what seemed like an age. Then, I felt my body falling through space until it finally caught up with the bunk as the ship stopped at the bottom of a wave. I crashed back onto the bunk, with a force that knocked the wind out of me. Then it happened again, and again.

Once the ship is bouncing about that much it is time to forget sleep as the next time the sea will throw you out of the bunk altogether. Not much fun from the top bunk. At that point, as you obviously cannot walk about the ship, the only safe and sensible thing to do is to stay in your bunk and wedge yourself in by jamming your knees against the bunk boards and your back against the back of the bunk and just hold on for the ride. After an hour or so we rounded Cape Wrath, and were soon in the shelter of the Outer Hebrides so things improved.

When we got on patrol off Northern Ireland our job was to stop and search all shipping in Northern Ireland territorial waters and look for guns and munitions being smuggled in to the IRA. It was known that they were getting their arms brought in by sea but not exactly where the arms were being landed. I was the boarding officer and had a team of six men. We went over to the ships we stopped in the Gemini and climbed on board. We would have to check the voyage and registration details of the ships and check the cargo manifest and crew lists and their passports so that we were certain that they were who they said they were. We stopped everything we saw, twenty-four hours a day. With the numerous possible hiding places for small items, like guns and ammunition, on the bigger merchant ships; the chances of finding any seriously hidden arms cache were slight. However, we never knew what we would find when we got on board or what the reaction of the skipper and crew would be until we were on board. Our crew was well trained and knew where to start poking around on board most types of ship and to watch and see if anyone got restless or obstructive. Any serious prevarication or obstruction would result in the ship being arrested and taken into port where the army would take the ship apart in slow time. We searched fishing vessels and their fish rooms, family yachts, neat coasters from the Continent and some lovely old British colliers loaded with coal that used to ply the Irish Sea. Some skippers were formal and non communicative, others were friendly and helpful, while others even offered me a beer and a seat in their day cabin while the searches went on. We even took divers on these boardings as there was talk that the IRA were bolting boxes of guns to the underside of ships' hulls so that we would not find them. While we searched the ship the divers did a quick bottom search. Again the word went out and the rumours died down. One day, a small coaster, which was heading for Portrush; a delightful small holiday town with a fabulous golf course on the north coast, failed to stop when we called her up. We followed her into the harbour in the Gemini while *Nurton* stayed outside the harbour. We quickly landed on the quay and were waiting by the time the coaster had tied up and we boarded her there. After clearing her, we were ordered to take a walk through the town and report anything suspicious. What we reported was that all the people came out of their houses and hotels to look at the Navy boys with their guns. 'What are they doing in Portrush?' It was clear that we were the first military that anyone in Portrush had seen. One of the local senior citizens walked straight up to me and said 'Why are you here? Is there any trouble?' I said 'No, no trouble, it seems a nice place and a nice day', which it was. We all wanted to stay and have an ice cream but were ordered to return to the ship.

We lost track of the ships we searched but we learned from the army people that the IRA knew all about our patrols so were not tempted to bring arms directly into Northern Ireland by sea.

One afternoon, on an unusually quiet day during one our first patrols when John was still the CO, we were off the mouth of Belfast Lough when an unusual looking ship was sighted coming out of Belfast. It looked like a small tanker of some kind and definitely an old one. The captain called on the ship to stop and the boarding Party went away in the Gemini. I got on board and went up to the bridge. The ship's skipper told me the ship was owned by the Belfast Corporation and was on a regular run out to the deep water. I asked if I could see his cargo. His colleagues on the bridge fell about laughing. 'I wouldn't advise that, Sir', he said. 'Why not?', I asked, 'Because we are the

Belfast Corporation's Sewage Disposal Barge.' I saw the joke and after confirming that she was what her captain said, we left. I did not tell our CO why we abandoned the search over the radio but waited until I was back on the bridge in *Nurton*. 'What was she carrying?' asked the skipper; '350 tons of best Irish S***, Sir.' I said.

On a sadder note, we were patrolling the entrance to Belfast Lough on a hot, calm and gloriously sunny day. We had the army's military radio switched on in the bridge as usual. This normally carried a general chatter between army patrols, but on this afternoon we suddenly became aware that the whole tone of the exchanges had changed and there was clearly something serious going on ashore. Heavy explosions could be heard. It was the first IRA attack on an army post using rockets and we were listening to them exploding as soldiers were being murdered and we were tanning ourselves within sight of Belfast city. It was very eerie as there was nothing we could do at all but carry on with our particular role.

Hamish

Every seven days we had a 24-hour 'Off' period from the patrol. This 24-hour period started the moment we left Northern Ireland's waters and not when we got to somewhere nice. The two nearest ports were Peel, in the Isle of Man, and Campbeltown, in Kintyre. On this occasion, we were going to Peel; a lovely fishing and seaside town in a lovely island. We approached the harbour as normal and sailed past the end of the pier.

The normal routine, when docking the ship was for the captain to con the ship into the berth and for the First Lieutenant, Hamish, to take charge of getting the mooring lines out, the ship secured and the gangway out. My job, as officer of the watch, was to do everything else.

As we rounded the end of Peel Pier, Hamish spotted a very attractive, young lady standing on the end of the pier watching us come in. He looked at the girl, caught her eye and then, without talking his eyes off her, he handed the microphone to me and said over his shoulder, 'You take over', and with that he vanished down the ladder towards the deck. I was occupied getting the ship secured, but before I had finished and well before we had got as far as getting the gangway out, I caught sight of Hamish stepping back onto the ship and helping the young lady across the gap between the pier and the ship and clambering over the guard rails with her to get back on board. When we had finally secured the ship and got the gangway out I went down to the wardroom. There was Hamish already in full flow and chattering away to this girl; each of them with a drink in their hands. 'The gangway is now secured if you would like to bring your guest on board, Sir', I reported. 'Oh, I see you already have.' Hamish is the only naval officer I know of who had brought a lady guest on board and given her a drink before the brow was out. 'BZ' or, 'Well Done, Hamish'.

In time, I was promoted to lieutenant. A big day for me as two gold stripes looked an awful lot better than just one. On the day I was made up I went on board in my new uniform with two gold stripes feeling very self-conscious and a little bit pleased with myself. To celebrate, I invited my fellow officers up to drink at lunchtime up in the main wardroom on the base. We were all there enjoying a drink and, after the second drink, the CO, David, asked in all seriousness 'This is all very nice of you, Gordon, but what are we celebrating?' Even when I waved my arm at him he still did not understand. Tony had to say 'Gordon got made up today Sir', before the penny dropped. Talk about a waste of a drink!

David had one of those accidents in *Nurton* that makes you wince when you hear about it. He was standing in the narrow, main passageway talking to Hamish when someone wanted to go past. David stepped back to let the guy through but failed to notice an open hatch behind him. He went straight down but even more unfortunately caught his leg on the main deck and so landed, straddling the steel hatch coaming that stands about six inches proud of the deck round the side of the hatch and landed on a vital piece of his anatomy. Poor guy was in agony for days, probably weeks. He got a small, inflated inner tube from a wheelbarrow wheel that he always carried with him so he could actually sit down, slowly.

Mine Pinching

During one exercise off the Clyde we had been hunting for exercise mines down near to the south of Arran when the weather quickly deteriorated. We struggled on but once the ships movement was such that the sonar performance was badly impaired, we packed up and headed back towards Faslane. At the same time, other minehunters further up the Clyde were heading back in too.

By the time we got back up to the Cumbraes the wind had eased and there was much more shelter so the seas were calmer than where we had been; but the mine-hunter that had been allocated this section had already gone back in. The CO and I discussed it and with a grin and we decided that we would start hunting again in the other ship's patch as the sea was calm here and it was still only midday. We spent three hours there and found two exercise mines. There was some muttering at the exercise debrief about 'poaching' and 'Mine Pinching' but the force commander appreciated our initiative and as the exercise was still on and the other ship had left her allocated area we were clear to go in and hunt. We came out as the top minehunter of the exercise by two mines.

After over two years of happy times in *Nurton* it was time for me to move on and the Navy decided that I was now due for a frigate job as a lieutenant. I was sad to leave Scotland as I had had a good time in *Nurton*. Doreen and I were now engaged, so it was all a bit of a wrench. However, onwards and upwards!

The Navy have always taken a dim view of officers fraternising with Wren ratings. Doreen and I were no exception. While we did not advertise our growing relationship, we did not attempt to hide it either. Doreen's senior officers discovered that she was going out with an officer and within weeks she had been drafted to HMS *President* in London. This posting however, proved not to be a barrier to true love!

CHAPTER 8

HMS *Rhyl*

To equip me to be a junior lieutenant in HMS *Rhyl*, a frigate, I was sent on various specialist courses. One was a Flight Deck Officers Course, which was great fun, and I spent an enjoyable few weeks, with other trainee flight deck officers, at the Royal Naval air station at Portland learning about helicopters and their operation and how to marshal them over a pitching deck and bring them down safely. A lot of this course involved spending sunny days out on a barge that had been converted into a dummy frigate's flight deck and was anchored out in the middle of Portland harbour. An endless series of helicopters then flew out and practiced landing on the barge under our inexpert guidance as each of us took turns to wave ping-pong-bat-shaped batons at the helicopters trying to get them to do what we wanted them to do and trying to talk to them on the radio.

I also attended the divisional officer's course. In the Royal Navy, an officer will have a number of senior and junior ratings in his 'Division'. The DO is responsible for giving the rating regular formal appraisals and writing his official report when he or the DO leave the ship. He also ensures that the ratings are put forward for the appropriate training courses so they get the right qualifications and experience to go before promotion boards. Equally important, the DO is the rating's point of contact for getting help or advice of any kind; be it professional or personal. As a lot of ratings are newly married with very young families, the separation that being at sea brings can cause tensions and problems both at home and at sea. The DO is there to help the rating and his family when these and other problems occur. For a young, single officer this brings its own challenges as to how to understand and handle some of the marital problems that can arise! The DO also represents the rating if he gets into trouble and is responsible for knowing each rating well enough to be able to speak on his behalf at the captain's disciplinary hearings on board or indeed at civil courts ashore if need be.

Joining HMS *Rhyl*

To join HMS *Rhyl* I was flown out by the RAF in a VC10 to Singapore, where the ship was undergoing a short maintenance period during a Far East deployment.

HMS *Rhyl*, a Rothesay-Class type 12 ASW frigate shown here before her refit in 1972 when a hangar and flight deck were added. (J&C McCutcheon Collection)

HMS *Rhyl*'s new Flight Commander, Tim, and I went out together to join the ship. Oddly enough, both our fiancées were Wrens and both were serving in the Admiralty in London and knew each other. The two-day flight out was a long one as we went via Cyprus, Bahrain, and Gan, a tiny coral island Indian Ocean. Gan is a British RAF base on a tiny island and a few even smaller islands. The runway is short. When you are landing you think you will touch down in the sea but, just when you are reaching for your life jacket, the wheels thump down hard onto the tarmac and immediately starts to brake hard. When the plane has stopped it's very rapid braking and turns slowly round at the other end of the runway you are again looking straight down into the blue waters of the Indian Ocean, but on the other side of the island. It has been a staging post for flights going out to the Far East for many years but is always an interesting landing for passengers. We were allowed off the aircraft and went into a pleasant transit lounge for a while as they refueled the aircraft. Our short stop in Gan reminded me of a story that I had heard about Admiral Le Fanu when he was First Sea Lord in the 1960s. He was one of the most popular Admirals of his day and had the 'Nelson Touch' in terms of how well he treated others. He came to speak to us at Dartmouth and started his talk by telling us. 'I have a carved wooden sign on my desk in Whitehall that reads "There they go and I must follow them for I am their leader".' He said it reminded him to keep up with what we were all doing out in the real Navy.

A story is told that on one occasion he had an urgent need to get out to the Far East quickly and sought the help of the Fleet Air Arm. They happened to be about to fly two Buccaneer aircraft out to Singapore so the Admiral, as an aviator, 'cadged a lift' flying in the observer's rear seat of one of the aircraft. On arrival in Gan, the flight was met by the base CO who took the two pilots off to the officer's mess and instructed a flight sergeant to take care of the No. 2s. In the RAF, the observer would normally be a flight sergeant rather than an officer, let alone a full Admiral. Admiral Lefanu, all done up in his flying overalls and with no real badges or rank epaulettes showing, was taken to the Sergeant's mess for a cup of tea. A few hours later they were told that the aircraft were ready so went back out and flew on to Singapore. A week or so later, the CO of RAF Gan received a letter thanking him for the hospitality of his sergeant's mess during the stop over and signed by the First Sea Lord. Oh, to have seen his face!

We finally arrived in Singapore about mid-morning on a hot and steamy Singapore day and went on board HMS *Rhyl*, We were hot, tired, grubby, jet-lagged and dispirited after the marathon flight. As we got to the top of the gangway, a lieutenant commander in tropical white shorts was standing by the rail talking to a chief petty officer. He was a large man but had a friendly open face and from the way he was watching everything that was going on I thought he must be the first lieutenant. He watched Tim and I struggle up the gangway with our bags and came over and introduced himself to us. 'I am Mike, the first lieutenant', he said, extending his hand. 'You two must be our new joining officers?' We put down our bags and shook his hand. 'The bad news, I am afraid, is that, as part of the maintenance work, the ship's water main is down today so there is no air conditioning and no water in the ship today. The good news is the engineers hope to have it back on tonight. That's why I am up here in the tropical sun as it is cooler than being inside the ship. Welcome to *Rhyl*!' 'Thanks', was all either of us could say! The ship was like a sauna inside and it was certainly hotter than the outside air but we just had to bear it and sweat it out until late in the evening when normal water and air conditioning were resumed. Having flown out together and both of us with Wrens as fiancées, as well as both being 'New Boys' on board; Tim and I became good pals.

HMS *Rhyl* was an anti-submarine frigate of the Rothesay Class; commonly called the Type 12. She was 370 feet long and weighed about 2,500 tons. A twin-screw ship with a top speed of 30 knot, she had a long, thin hull that sliced beautifully through the water. She carried a crew of 235 including about sixteen officers. HMS *Rhyl* had been built in the Naval Dockyard at Portsmouth and launched in 1959. She was equipped with ASW Mortars, a twin 4.5-inch gun and an ASW Wasp helicopter. She lived a long life before finally being sunk as a torpedo target ship in 1985. The Type 12 was replaced by the highly successful and, in my view, one of the most attractive ships the Navy ever built, the Leander-class frigate.

The CO was Commander John Hall. He was an aviator, in fact an observer as had been the CO in HMS *Nurton*. On first meeting him he struck me as a slightly shy man but he tried to be friendly. However, as most of his welcoming words were what he did not expect his officers to do, I decided that he was a bit of a stickler for things being done his way and this proved to be the case over the coming months (I suppose that as he was the captain this was to be expected). After the formal introduction and his pep talk, he told me what my responsibilities would be on board. 'Now Gordon, you are one of my sixteen officers on board

HMS *Rhyl* post 1972 refit. She now carries a Wasp helicopter. She was decommissioned in 1985 and sadly sunk as a torpedo target.

and I expect the best. As you know, you will be one of my bridge officers of the watch at sea as well as an officer of the day in port. You have passed your FDO Course so you will be an FDO. I also want you to be the "Top Part of Ship" officer and the boats officer'. The Top part of ship was the main midships section of the ship's upper deck and it was here that the boats were stowed. This meant that all upper-deck maintenance and painting schedules were my responsibility along with the top part of ship petty officer. HMS *Rhyl* had two boats, both wooden motorboats, which were expected to be ready to be launched at any time and whose maintenance and appearance was now in my hands. 'In addition you will be the divisional officer for all the operations room senior and junior ratings and I want you to be the wardroom mess treasurer'. This last task involved keeping a check on all the officers' food and bar bills, laundry bills and other expenses that they built up each month and issuing them with their mess bills, collecting their money and keeping the books straight. 'Any questions?' 'Err, No, Sir', I managed. 'Good. Carry on.' I left his cabin thinking 'Where the hell do I start with this lot?'

As I left the captain's cabin, my head spinning, a voice called out 'Hi Gord! Hows' tricks?' It was Dave Askham. He was also one of the other lieutenants on board and we had been at Dartmouth together. He had been here for a few months already and was the 'Baby Guns' or Deputy gunnery officer, to give him his proper title. 'I think need a drink' I said. 'No problem, it's on me.' 'Thanks Dave.' After a large horse's neck (brandy and ginger ale) in the wardroom to recover I tried to remember what I had been told.

Hong Kong

About a week later the last dockyard worker left the ship and our Maintenance period was over. We cast off and sailed for Hong Kong and a deployment that would mean endless days at sea on defence watches, doing six hours on, six hours off on the bridge or the flight deck. I soon found my way around and got into the routine of life on a 'big' ship. In between the continual two- and three-week-long exercises we had just two or three days break in various ports around the region.

We were working with HMS *Tiger*, a helicopter cruiser, and HMS *Dreadnought*, the RN's first nuclear-powered submarine as well as other RN frigates in the region and an RFA that kept us fuelled and fed. Mostly, we carried out anti-submarine exercises, but there were replenishments at sea (RAS) every other day, OOW exercises and damage control exercises. No one was ever going to be bored in *Rhyl*.

We arrived in Hong Kong and berthed at the RN Base, HMS *Tamar*, right in the middle of the harbour front on Hong Kong Island. Hong Kong, with all the bustle of the harbour, the junks and sampans, lighters loading cargoes into the moored freighters out in the harbour; was exactly as I had imagined it to be. The Star Ferries constantly thrashed their way across the harbour to Kowloon. In fact, there are only two places in the world that were exactly as I had imagined them before I went there. One was Hong Kong and the other was New York.

On the first day that I was clear to go ashore, Peter, the navigator, and I went over to Kowloon one Saturday morning. Peter had been here before. 'If you have never been here then you have to go on the Star Ferry!', he said. We travelled First Class, on the upper deck, for 20 cents and watched as the harbour carried on its daily business around us and the green and white double ended ferry *Evening Star* ploughed its way between the tugs and barges over to Kowloon. In Kowloon, the main street, Nathan Road, led all the way to the border with Communist China but, at its Kowloon end, its fascinating side streets were a series of Aladdin's caves crammed full of electronics, stereos, cameras, clothing and watches. 'Buy here Jonny, I give you good price!' 'Heh, Mister! You want watch!' 'No mister you come back here, I give another 20 per cent discount!' It was a fantastic place. Peter and I explored as much as we could but after a while, the noise, the dust, the heat and the humidity pressed down on us until we had to get out of it all. Peter led the way. Just off Nathan Road, on Canton Road, we entered the Hong Kong Hotel through heavy glass doors. The air conditioning hit us like a cooling shower. Its lobby was a haven of peace, civilization and culture, instantly shutting out the noisy chaos and heat of the street. I followed Peter straight into The Gun Bar, just off the lobby, which offered chilled, draught San Miguel beer and soft easy chairs. 'Two pints of San Miguel please'. 'Yes Sir,' replied the immaculately smart barman, his red jacket matching the red décor. The soft, cool atmosphere of the bar wrapped us in its luxury. He returned with two brimming, pint-glass tankards of chilled beer sitting on a white-napkin-covered tray. We salivated while he carefully laid out the paper coasters, then the beer, the condensation already forming on the glass. Finally, he moved away with a genuine 'Enjoy your beers Sirs'. We did. Oh the joy as the iced liquid slid over our dry throats and cooled us as it went down.

We were berthed near the Wanchai area, so in the late evenings we used to make our way down to the world of Susie Wong. Wanchai covered a few blocks of narrow streets by the waterfront, but here were streets full of food stalls, bars, restaurants and local food shops. Just above our heads, hundreds of dazzling, coloured, neon signs were directing us down to see bigger, better, barer girls in the dim, dark, girlie bars. 'Heh, Gringo, you want lady? I fix for you lady, very good price!' 'I am not a gringo!' I growled back. The noise of people filled the air, stall owners chanting their wares, club hostesses calling to sailors, cyclist ringing their bells and pop music blaring our from some of the street-front bars. There always seemed to be wall to wall people; mostly they seemed to be those who lived and worked here, carrying boxes or pushing loaded hand carts, but also American sailors on R&R from Vietnam and some, just like us, tourists. We drank in the heady atmosphere of the place and its non-stop vibrancy. Exploring the bars, (a San Mig' beer here, a San Mig' beer there) and then sitting at the food stalls eating all sorts and watching the local ladies was something new and exciting for most of us. The tourist sights could wait until tomorrow!

Before we docked in Hong Kong, Tim flew the helicopter ashore to the RAF station at Kai Tak as he could not fly it off from the ship when the ship was alongside the main naval base at HMS *Tamar*. One day at breakfast Tim took me aside. 'Can you get off for today? I am taking the helicopter up for a training flight over the harbour and up into the New Territories. Do you want to come for the ride?' 'You bet I do.' I quickly cleared it with the first lieutenant and we flew from Kai Tak out low over Hong Kong Harbour, past the ship berthed at *Tamar* and we hovered over the wreck of the old Cunard liner, RMS *Queen Elizabeth*. She had been sold by Cunard to CY Tung, a famous Hong Kong ship-owner who had nearly finished converting her into a floating university, to be called *Seawise University*. Unfortunately a fire broke out on board and she was destroyed. She was lying on her starboard side with half of her rusted and blackened hull and superstructure sticking out of the water and looking anything but the fine ocean liner that she had been. She was a really sad sight. She was eventually broken up where she lay, which was close to the main channel into the container berths. We carried on our flight almost up to the Chinese border, then back to Kai Tak.

During our second stop in Hong Kong a couple of months later there was a Typhoon warning and we were ordered to sail at once and head to the south to avoid the projected route of the typhoon which took it right over Hong Kong. Thirty-six hours later, the typhoon had passed and had missed Hong Kong so we were told we could return to port. We were planning to arrive at the entrance to the main harbour at 7 a.m. I was on the midnight to 4 a.m. watch (or 'The Middle') that night when a signal arrived from Hong Kong HQ telling us to re-plan our ETA for 0730. I handed over the message to the navigator when he came on watch at 0400. I was asleep in my cabin after my watch when at a quarter to seven the captain called me to the bridge. 'Why did you not call me when this signal came in?' 'Well, Sir, it was only a thirty minute delay and I did not think it was important enough to call you. I gave the signal to the navigator when he came on watch at 0400.' The captain disagreed. 'I will be told of all signals concerning our programme when they come in. Your shore leave is stopped for the next three days. Now, carry on.' 'Yes Sir.' Three days stoppage of leave over the last three days in Hong Kong before we headed for home. 'Great! No chance to buy any presents now!' I muttered to myself and vowed to return one day.

In the course of the next few months, as breaks between these exercises, we visited some super tropical places such as Rabaul and Manaus, both down in jungles of New Guinea; Guam: and the huge American base at Subic Bay in the Philippines, where the American insisted on buying us whisky whether or not we drank it, as well as Mauritius and Simonstown in South Africa.

South African Waters

South Africa was as lovely as I remembered it from our stay there in *Puncheston*. Unfortunately, we were not able to stay as long this time and after a couple of days we were off again, back out to chase submarines. During our time in South African waters we did a number of exercises with the South African Navy. During one of these two things occurred that helped to convince me that I was probably not cut out to be an Admiral. As a bridge watch-keeping officer in the RN you are totally responsible for the safety of the ship and her crew. While you are always under the captain's orders, the actual handling of the ship and collision avoidance and safe navigation during your watch are your responsibility. As a young twenty-two- or twenty-three-year-old this is a massive responsibility as you have, in HMS *Rhyl* for example, over 200 officers and men sleeping below decks in a ship with a wafer thin hull, who are totally dependent upon you for their safety. The following two events reflect the seriousness of the job and show how easy it is for major mistakes to take place.

Near Misses

Collision avoidance is probably the most important aspect of the bridge watch-keeping and 100 per cent pass mark is demanded in all exams during training.

This covers all the different lights, shapes and sounds that every type of ship undertaking every possible activity will display or make at different times and from different angles, day and night and in fog. It is therefore something that becomes second nature as you spend at least eight hours a day on the bridge. However, there are times when things go awry.

On the first occasion one of my fellow watch keepers and pal from Dartmouth days, Dave, came down to the wardroom from the bridge at midnight where he had been officer of the watch since eight o'clock. I was having a late coffee when he came in. He was white and shaking. I asked him what was wrong. When he had got a brandy in his hand he told me. There was yet another submarine exercise going on and *Rhyl* was working with two South African frigates to try and locate and 'catch' the submarine. Dave explained that he had been concerned during the watch that the captain and ops officer down in the ops room were not totally aware of where the other ships were in relation to ours as we had all been maneuvering at high speed all over the place and a certain amount of competitiveness between ships of different nations creeps into these exercises. However, there was nothing he could do but drive *Rhyl* exactly where the CO ordered him to via the intercom. Quite often this was at speeds of up to 28 knots. During these exercises all the participating warships were in a state of 'Darkened Ship'. This meant that they had all their navigation and upper deck lights switched off and all the deadlights down over the scuttles to prevent visual detection from the submarine's periscope. The only exceptions were the helicopters, which always had all their lights on including their flashing orange strobe lights. Dave had been driving the ship all over the ocean with big and frequent course and speed changes all night. When suddenly, a dim, round, light, low down near the sea level, appeared out of the night and moved rapidly down the starboard side of our ship and very close to us. So close, in fact that Dave lost sight of it as it passed below the level of the bridge window. After a second he realised that it had been a single scuttle of another ship. He called the ops room to report it and mayhem broke out as they had no idea that we were anywhere near another ship. In fact, it was one of the South African frigates, also darkened down. Someone had forgotten to drop the deadlight on a single scuttle near the stern. We had passed her within 50 feet at about 25 knots and had not even known there was a ship nearby. If we had hit her, both ships could have ended up in half.

A few nights later, on another similar exercise, on a dark and cloudy night, a similar thing happened to me but in a different way. Again, all ships were darkened, except the helicopters. I was OOW and spent the watch holding the ops room/bridge intercom microphone in one hand and listening to and responding to orders from the CO in the ops room; and the wheelhouse intercom microphone in the other hand to pass on those orders to the wheelhouse team. At the same time I was hanging onto the compass stand, or pelorus, by my arm as the ship heeled over during another tight turn. In this exercise HMS *Tiger* was the ship we were protecting and we had been deployed as a screen to detect submarines out in front of her. During these exercises it is accepted that the OOW never has time to go to the back of the bridge to check the bridge radar screen or to go to the bridge wings for a visual check outside as the orders come up in a constant flow from the ops room below and you have to remain fixed to the conning position. As the ops room had all the relevant radar and sonar information they knew where all the other ships in the exercise were. During this exercise, the ops room team was desperately trying to keep track of a submarine contact on the sonar

As we were altering course at 24 knots and steadying up on a new course I looked out ahead and was glad to see that there were no merchant ship's lights down the course we were now on. Then, dead ahead, out in the blackness, a red light came on. It was one small, steady, red light. In the dark it was impossible to gauge its distance from us but as it was quite high up it must be quite close or, something very big. However, it still looked like a small light and not really like a ship's red port light, which have a faded glow about them; this was a sharp crisp light. I stared at it hard through the bridge window to try and work out what I was looking at. 'Ops bridge, can you identify any contacts dead ahead. I have a single red light on our current heading?' I never got a response. My brain was racing. Was it a red flare of some sort? This one red light could not be a merchantman as there were no other masthead lights or deck lights. It was most unlikely to be one of the warships in the exercise as they were all fully darkened and the light was too high up to be from any of the ships with which we were working. In the absence of any guidance or information from the ops room and, as we were doing 24 knots directly towards this light, which was now getting ever nearer; I decided that I needed to act. 'Starboard 20, Revolution 120', at the same time I switched on all our navigation lights. We came round 40 degrees off our original course and reduced speed to 15 knots. I put the lights on so that whatever this red light was, it would be able to see us while I worked out what was going on.

'What the hell are you doing officer of the watch? You have messed up the attack on the submarine!' The CO had appeared behind me in a wild rage having rushed up from the ops room one deck below. 'Sir, can you tell me what that single red light is? I asked him. 'What light? The light was now out on the port beam but still there. I pointed it out to him. He looked at it, said nothing then dashed off below to the ops room to try and find out what it was.

In a couple of minutes it became clear what it was. HMS *Tiger* had a very high flight deck, about twice as high as other warships. One of her Sea King helicopters had started to switch on its engines as I steadied onto a collision course with her. Apparently, when Sea King helicopters start to switch on their engines the first thing that comes on in the start sequence is their navigation lights. This happens before the normal yellow strobe lights. We therefore had been steaming at 24 knots directly towards a ship about four times bigger than us and apparently no one in our ops room knew she was even there. If the helo had not started up at that moment we would probably have hit *Tiger* full on. I always had an impression that the submarine was actually hiding underneath *Tiger* hence our attack course directly at *Tiger*! However, I was not impressed by the CO's reaction as my sole responsibility as OOW was ship's safety. For doing my job I got a bollocking as his game of chasing a submarine had been spoiled.

Unfortunately, later, during the same series of exercises, two South African Hawker Hunter jets collided in mid-air while flying together in thick cloud over the sea and we had to search for wreckage and the bodies of the two dead pilots for two days until they were found.

We finally made it back to Plymouth and half the ship's company were sent off on early Christmas leave. I volunteered to stay on board until Christmas Eve and take the later leave period. I got back home at about five o'clock on Christmas Eve and Doreen was there to meet me on the station. We hugged for several seconds. I had last seen her nearly ten months ago at Brize Norton and I can still remember how good that hug felt.

North Again

It was a cold, still, clear January night off the north Cape of Norway. We were steaming north at a gentle 12 knots and I was on watch on the bridge for the middle watch (midnight to 4 a.m.). We have been sent north on Arctic fishery protection duty. I was working on the chart table when I was suddenly aware that there was a bright light coming into the bridge from outside. I turned round to find that the night had turned into day. The northern sky had a bright, milky white curtain spread across it with an arm of light stretching up into the heavens. This spread, slowly at first, then more quickly until it formed a giant arch, like a very bright Milky Way, up across the sky and over our heads and beyond. It flickered and grew, then slowly shrunk and faded. Then, a few minutes later it started again, this time more strongly with green washes of colour in the milky whites and in a wider arc with definite shapes and folds. I hurried out onto the bridge wing with the duty rating and we stood open-mouthed staring up at the skies. It looked as if the Viking gods were gently shaking successive rows of giant, sheer silk curtains of shimmering light as they drifted across the sky. We could see the stars through these curtains and the trawlers that were around us all lay illuminated by the bright Aurora light. As the lights danced so they changed colour, the milky whites had now given way totally to pale greens, then to stronger, brighter greens and then to bright emerald greens as the bottoms of the shot silk curtains rippled and shimmered over our heads in a cosmic breeze. Sometimes, showers of colour seemed to fall from the curtains as if shaken loose while the lights continued to move and dance. We felt dwarfed by the magnitude and magnificence of this spectacle as it enveloped us totally. It continued to ebb and flow over many minutes. As it reached its peak, soft pinks and deep reds fused into the edges of the greens and whites and the lights stretched almost completely across the whole dome of the sky. Only the southern and eastern skies were unaffected. As suddenly as it came it began to fade and shrink back to the northern skies, back to pale greens, then to milky whites then just a white glow in the north. It went completely and darkness returned. I do not know how long it lasted but well over twenty minutes. Later in the watch smaller displays revealed themselves but by four o'clock it was all over. It was the most fantastic display of the Aurora Borealis (Northern Lights) that I have ever seen.

Perisher

In the spring we were sent to the Clyde to take part in the 'Perisher Course'. This is the final course for submarine officers to qualify for command of a submarine. All of the candidates, or students, are experienced submarine officers and have been selected to come on the course. It is referred to as 'The Perisher' because if the officer fails he will 'perish' as a submariner. If at any point the examiner, or 'teacher' as he is known, decides that a candidate does not have what it takes to be a submarine CO he is put ashore that night and is never appointed to submarines again. The teacher is always a senior and experienced submarine CO who is always very well respected by the 'students'. The final two weeks of the course consists of the candidates taking turns at various manoeuvres and attacks while the surface ships do what is requested by the teacher to provide a good examination. As the course progresses these become more involved with two and finally three frigates acting as targets. For the submariner these are fraught times. They are listening to sonar reports, looking through the periscope when they have to so they can look at the frigates to calculate the rates of bearing change, the courses and speeds of the different frigates and then trying to get the submarine into a torpedo firing position and at the same time not getting hit themselves. It requires, cool, mental agility and at least three stopwatches to be able to do all the mental calculations in a career threatening practical exam situation with the examiner standing right behind you. By the end of the course the frigate officer of the watch has instructions from his CO that when he sees a periscope ahead, he is to charge it at top speed. This is great fun if you are the OOW of the frigate. It is not so much fun if you are the submariner candidate and have not seen the frigate coming. On a number of occasions I stood on the bridge steering for the periscope and willing it to go down as I lost sight of it under the bows of the ship. We never did hit one, though a few must have been very near misses. We were assured that 'teacher' always had things under control and could always 'Flood Q' if he had to. Q was the biggest ballast tank in the submarine that when flooded, it filled so fast that the submarine went down like a lift. Every evening, after the exercises were complete, the submarine would go into Arran and one or more failed submariners would be put ashore.

I am afraid to say that on those runs we often went far too close to some of the local fishing boats, which were trying to earn an honest living. We must have scared them half to death as a 3,000-ton frigate rocketed past a 50-ton fishing boat about 50 feet away at 28 knots.

After our time in the Clyde we went into Liverpool for an official visit. I was the quarterdeck officer at this stage and responsible for managing the crew working at the very stern of the ship as we docked. As we approached the lock entrance, a tug was positioning itself at the stern and waiting for a line to be thrown to it. For some reason the lads were not at their best and three heaving lines all fell well short of the tug. All the time the ship was moving slowly towards the Lock entrance. 'Come on lads, concentrate and get the throw right', I shouted. Another two lines fell short, then one landed on the tug but bounced off. I was getting exasperated but there was little I could do. Throwing a heaving line needs to be done properly and cannot be hurried so hounding the lads was counterproductive. The ship's PA from the bridge then burst into life and the first lieutenant's voice boomed out over the deck. 'Quarterdeck Officer! How much longer are you going be getting a line on the tug?'

In my frustration at the lads, and at the stupid question that had just been asked, I picked up the microphone and replied in as calm a voice as I could muster 'One minute, seventeen seconds, Sir'. There was silence, apart from the lads on the quarterdeck giggling. Ian, the WEO, who was on the bridge at the time said the place fell apart with laughter, even the captain smiled! The first lieutenant never mentioned it again. Well, it was a stupid question.

After such exciting games, my naval career drew to an end as I had done my time as a short service officer. The Navy had offered me a full-time career, but they could not offer me any Arctic fishery protection ships, or a job as a specialist Torpedo and Anti-Submarine Officer (TASO) a subject in which I had become quite interested. I tried to see if I stood any chance of serving in the ice patrol ship, HMS *Endurance*. My appointer informed me he could not put a short service officer forward to serve in HMS *Endurance* as, ideally, I needed to be a career officer, probably a specialist hydrographer and a preferably a 'high flyer' as well. I was certainly not a hydrographer and I had the feeling that 'high flyer' was not a term that the Navy applied to me; so that solved that problem.

The Navy could however, offer me a career that entailed another twelve years of continuous sea jobs in the ops room as a warfare/operations officer before I could expect a job ashore. I did not really fancy that for twelve years so I decided to move on, said thank you very much and a little sadly, left the RN. While the Navy was not to be my career I am still extremely proud of the RN and my short time serving in it. The naval training and discipline undoubtedly did me some good and stood me in good stead for my future. The experiences and responsibility I had, even as a junior officer, were beyond the comprehension of many of my school pals who had gone on to university. When you join the Navy you become suspicious of the intensity of the training and the dogmatic manner in which it is carried out. There is a tendency to see it as brain washing. While you are in the Navy you do not see, or really appreciate, the benefits and the quality of the training you have had. Not just technical and academic training but the need for honesty, integrity, self discipline, self pride in your appearance and team work. When you are living and working day and night in very close proximity with your shipmates, you have to get on with people and ensure you do not antagonise them. In the close environment of a warship any personal failings such as dishonesty or laziness are very soon found out. Giving 'Service' for others quickly becomes second nature and runs deep in the naval blood. It was only when I left the Navy and witnessed the attitudes and lack of professionalism of some people in the civilian and commercial worlds that I realised how lucky I had been to have had the training and experience I had in the Navy. Again, there is a Navy truism for it – 'Once Navy, Always Navy'.

1. *Kingston Onyx* hauling her nets. She is shown in her Hellyer Bros colours. Originally she was owned by the Kingston Steam Trawling Co., before Hellyers took over Kingstons. *Photographic note:* Taken with a hand-held 400-mm telephoto lens from the deck of HMS *Keppel*.

2. *Silvana* loaded high with timber waits to exit the locks of the Kiel Canal. The *Baltrover* is berthed just ahead of her on the other side of the lock.

Above: **3.** MT *Portia* in Isafjord in north-west Iceland. Isafjord was the scene of a double tragedy in the winter of 1967/68 when two Hull trawlers were lost in the same week due to heavy icing.

Left: **4.** A lone Gentoo penguin on a stroll in the sun at Port Lockroy.

Right: **5.** Midshipman Gray taken by a shivering Graeme aboard HMS *Keppel* off Iceland in the winter of 1970.

Below: **6.** A Hull trawler fishing off Iceland. Decks and railings icing up as she rolls in the swell. Believed to be *St Gerontius*, owned by T. Hamlings. *Photographic note:* Taken with a hand-held 400-mm telephoto lens from the deck of HMS *Keppel*.

7. Icebreaker *Kapitan Dranitsyn* run by the Murmansk Shipping Company where she is based. Note the polar bear emblem on the funnel.

8. After a good walk and steep climb we found the nest of a light-mantled sooty albatross above Grytviken.

Top left: 9. A zodiac motors past a grounded iceberg near Ymer Oy (island).

Top right: 10. A small berg, 'like a white pearl sitting on black velvet'.

Bottom left: 11. Doreen enjoying the air in the Greenland Sea on board *Professor Mulchanov*.

Bottom right: 12. Deep in Kaiser Frans Josef Fjord.

Above: **13.** The bear retrieves his lunch from the ice edge and heads off.

Left: **14.** Polar bear. (Photo by kind permission of Carina Svensson of Polar Quest)

Opposite, above: **15.** Disturbed by the ships the walruses stare at us in a totally disinterested way.

Opposite, below left: **16.** An early-morning kill. Polar bears find their breakfast.

Opposite, below right: **17.** Two puffins swim alongside the zodiac.

18. Iceberg in the evening sun just off the village of Scoresbysund.

19. The 14th July Glacier in Krossfjord, Spitsbergen.

20. A walrus eyes us cautiously.

PART 3

Fish Dock and
Polar Trips

CHAPTER 9

Wardroom to Fish Dock

'You will never get a job ashore. All you're qualified to do is stand on the bridge'. Such was the encouragement from Kevin, the bumptious Deputy Weapons Electrical Officer (DWEO) on *Rhyl*. 'Maybe, but we will see'. I said in bravado, but quietly thinking 'Well, he has a point!'

A few weeks later, in a large wood-panelled office overlooking the Hull Fish Dock, Mr Hellyer looked over his specs at me and said 'Well, the job is yours if you want it. Just let me know in a few days.' For about six months before the end of my time in the Royal Navy I had been looking for a job outside the Service and, at the same time, Doreen and I were planning to get married. For work I had targeted the fishing industry due to my previous interest in it and love of trawlers. One of the companies that I wrote to was Hellyer Bros of Hull who had taken me to sea as a sixteen-year-old on the *Lord Lovat*. Hellyer Bros were now part of a huge trawling company called British Untied Trawlers (BUT), which was the biggest trawling company in Europe at the time. Graham Hellyer was the managing Director and offered me the job of Electronics Manager for BUT at a meeting in his office during my Easter leave period. It was Graham himself who had agreed to let me sail in the *Lord Lovat* those years before. He was a tall, slim gentleman, fairly quiet and probably shy, unless angered. He drove a beautiful, old, grey Bentley, always seemed to wear soft green tweed suits and I always found him to be polite and interested in what I had to say, a complete gentleman. But then I was never in the same position as one of his skippers after a poor trip.

Doreen and I got married in her local church in Stirlingshire and set up home in Beverley, a wonderful Yorkshire market town a few miles north of Hull.

So here I was working on 'fish dock.' I had gone from life in an RN wardroom to ''Ull Fish Dock'. This really was 'From the Sublime to the Cor' Blimey'. At the time, the trawling industry was going through an electronics revolution; new types of echo sounders, sonars, net monitors and fish finders were coming into the industry, as well as new radio technology such as single side-band radios and new navigation systems such as Loran C and even satellite navigation were appearing; so the trawler companies needed to be able to keep up to speed on these issues so they fitted the right and best equipment to their ships. The plan was that this was to be my role.

Hellyer Bros was now part of British United Trawlers, or BUT, and Graham Hellyer was its MD. He was a legend in Hull. His grandfather had started the company, Hellyers Bros, in the south-west of England with his brother in the nineteenth century and the family had moved up to Hull when the North Sea herring were discovered in the 'Silver Pits.' After his father retired, Graham and his brother Mark ran the business, continuing to expand and grow the fleet and to send trawlers to the Arctic and return with a profit. They ruled with rods of iron. Hellyers', by the early 1960s, had become the biggest trawler company in Hull and probably the country at that time. Any skipper was only ever as good as his last trip and a couple of bad trips could see him out of a ship and a job for a long time.

The formation of BUT created the biggest deep-sea trawling company in Europe. It now included many of the old trawling companies that had grown up independently over the years. The BUT group operated trawlers out of five UK ports, Hull, Grimsby, Fleetwood, Aberdeen and Granton. In total, BUT owned and operated over 130 side trawlers (freshers) and a fleet of about fourteen of the latest and most sophisticated factory freezer stern trawlers (freezers) in the world, each of about 1,000 to 1,500 tons.

The Job

In spite of the fine title of electronic manager and an office overlooking the dock, as the new boy on the dock I still had to learn the ropes and I started each day at seven o'clock on the fish market. The catches from the ships that had docked the day before were all laid out overnight and sorted by fish type and date of catching ready for the market. The market was a wet and noisy place; water from melting ice was always running everywhere, the rattling aluminium kits of fish being slid across the wet concrete market, the yelling of fish merchants making their bids and the constant calls of salesman running the auction. The filleters, who worked for the fish merchants, were setting up their stands to start their day's work of standing out in all weathers, filleting ice cold fish in ice cold water. Added to all this was all the other apparent chaos of people milling round the fish on an often cold, wet and windy market.

For all matters concerning the fresh fish side trawlers and the morning side trawler inspections at the market, I reported to Fresh Fish Trawler Manager George Hartley, who had been on the fish dock since he left school. George had a wealth of knowledge and was very highly respected. He was a small bull of a man with a shiny, bald head. He was always smartly dressed and mostly a cheery soul. He was very firm and very fair, always asked the right questions, (especially when you did not want him to) and was someone you would not want to cross. He reported directly to Graham Hellyer, or Mr Graham, as he was known to everyone on the dock.

Every morning I got into my overalls and boots and went aboard all the company trawlers that had landed and checked that all the fishing gear had been properly stowed away, that the ropes, wires and bobbins were all properly stowed, etc. These checks also included making sure that the insides of the cod-liver boilers had been thoroughly cleaned. I also checked the accommodation, the galley, the bathrooms, messes, etc., to ensure that they were all clean and tidy and ready for the next trip, which would probably sail the following night. I always went up to the bridge and radio room to read any notes left for me and the radio repair companies by the RO. I then reported back to George that all was well, or not. In general, however, the ships were always clean, safe and tidy.

What made these early morning starts more pleasurable was that after the market had finished (normally by about half past eight or nine o'clock) those of us from the office that had been on the market changed out of our market overalls and into our office suits, then sat down to a proper Yorkshire breakfast of eggs and bacon, toast and marmalade and tea in the directors' dining room, which overlooked the Humber and often, a warming sunrise coming up over the river. Breakfast in the directors' dining room was a welcome time to recoup after the fun of the market and before the day's real work began and to catch up on dockside gossip.

By about eleven o' clock 'the Trip was in'. This meant that the office had worked out the total sales from the catches and deducted the running costs of the ships for the trip and then calculated the pay for each crewman on board. So, by eleven, the MD knew exactly how much money each trip had made. It was a very neat commercial exercise.

Ship to Shore Communications

When I joined BUT the system used for the daily radio position reports from the fleet was under severe scrutiny following the loss of the BUT freezer trawler *Gaul* in early 1974. She had disappeared with all hands in the Barents Sea in atrocious weather. There was astonishment in Hull that a new ship equipped with the latest communications systems could just disappear. The Official board of Trade Enquiry into the loss of the *Gaul* opened in Hull on the same day that I started work for the Company. Late that same afternoon Graham Hellyer returned from the inquiry and called me down to his office. It had emerged at the Inquiry that it was over forty-eight hours after the ship was last seen before anyone in the Hull office realised that something was wrong.

He ordered me to investigate, as a matter of urgency, the whole radio reporting system and the procedures currently used and to devise a better and more foolproof method of monitoring the ships when they were at sea. Every trawler in the company was supposed to make contact with the office, either directly or indirectly, at least once every twenty-four hours. The old Morse radio systems on board the older ships did not always make this easy and quite often trawlers simply could not make contact with the UK shore radio stations. This could be due to lack of transmitter power, atmospherics, bad weather, or just the sheer distance from the UK. I had to sort this out and create a foolproof, disciplined system that would ensure every trawler at sea was accounted for by the office at least twice a day. To achieve this I would need the help of the radio operators and to spend time at sea in the Arctic seeing first-hand what went on.

In the winter of 1974 there had been a large number of trawlers that had missed their scheduled office calls, or 'Skeds' as they were known; for all sorts of reasons and had then called in a day or so later saying all was well. It was this element of doubt that had to be removed so that the duty manager in the office could be confident that all was well, or if not, start a full search at the earliest opportunity. After a few weeks work, and after trips to sea and many discussions with the ROs, I put forward a new system that overlaid the existing system so that if a ship did not respond to a timed sked call a procedure was set in place to find her. One of the trawlers on the ground had to take on the role of control ship and was responsible for all the skeds of the other company ships while it was the control ship. When it left the grounds another ship would take over control. The new system was documented and published in a little red book that was inspected and approved for use by the Trawler's Mutual Insurance Company. Every skipper and every RO was issued with a copy. The books were accompanied by a note from Mr Graham telling the ships to use it – or else! On fish dock an 'or else' from Graham Hellyer meant 'Do it if it kills you because if it doesn't, I will.' In the following winter of 1975, with the new procedures in force, there were no incidents of any trawlers missing their skeds so the new system seemed to work.

Cassio – Trip to the Barents Sea

To properly understand the needs and issues of the radio operators and resolve the daily reporting issues I needed to spend time at sea on board the ships and see how what daily life as a trawler RO was all about. My first trip away nearly started out as a fiasco. I was due to sail on the *Cassio*, a freezer trawler bound for the Barents Sea. The RO was 'Jesse' James. Jesse was a great guy who took his job seriously and we had had many chats in the office where he was happy to explain to me about the issues he and other ROs had in terms of keeping the 'Skeds', contacting shore stations and repairing equipment.

The *Cassio* was due to sail on a Saturday morning. 'What time do you want me down on the dock tomorrow?', I asked Ben, the Ship's Husband. 'Ten o'clock', he said. At ten to ten, Doreen drove me onto the dock. 'Oh look,' I said, 'one of the other freezers is sailing too', as I saw the white superstructure moving slowly above the other trawlers, out through the lock and into the river. Then it hit me. I had missed the ship! It was the *Cassio*! The ship's husband had meant that the ship would sail from the dock at ten (or even earlier), not for me to arrive at ten. I was immediately terrified of the idea of going into the office on Monday morning and having to say I missed the ship. I thought rapidly 'How can I catch up with her?' 'Doreen, quick, drive me down to Corporation Pier.' Doreen drove me down to the Corporation Pier, which was a mile or so downstream from the fish dock,

The stern trawler *Cassio* in Hull Fish Dock. Like many Hellyer Bros trawlers, she was named after a Shakespearean character. Her handsome superstructure is a prominent feature. (Photo with approval from and thanks to the *Hull Daily Mail*)

where a duty Pilot Boat was often berthed. My luck was in and a pilot cutter was alongside the Pier. I rushed down the pontoon and onto the cutter. 'Look, I am sorry but I have missed the *Cassio* in the dock, Can you please take me out to her as she goes past?' 'Oh yeah, and who the 'ell are you?' was the friendly response! I explained. My luck held and they smiled at each other and agreed. We could already see the *Cassio* as she moved out into the main stream and started to pick up speed. She came down the river towards us and her dove grey hull towered over the pilot boat as she approached. The pilot had called the skipper over the VHF radio 'We have got late crewman trying to join the ship. Can you please stop the ship skipper?' *Cassio* slowed, a rope ladder was dropped down the side and I scrambled on board. I made my way sheepishly up to the bridge for a roasting from the skipper for holding up his ship and messing everyone about. However, I was met by a beaming face of the skipper Alfie Myers, and Jesse, who both thought the whole thing was a big joke with lots of comments about 'Management time keeping', and 'Managers always have a long lie-in on Saturdays'. All was well and the trip had finally got off to a good start.

Cassio was built by Yarrows on the Clyde in 1966. She was 224-feet long with a tonnage of 1,500 tons. She had a very handsome superstructure with a graceful, gently curved front; she even had a small promenade deck. From the bows she could have been mistaken for a passenger liner.

I was given the spare cabin on board *Cassio*, which was grandly called the 'Owner's Cabin'. It was a good-sized and comfortable cabin with a porthole looking forward up the fo'c'sle so it was away from the noise of the trawl deck during fishing. It even had a small area of verandah deck outside the door for 'promenading'. I looked about the cabin for a parasol. But, there was not one there!

We sailed up the Norway coast in perfect weather with the crew working in shirt sleeves on the trawl deck getting the gear ready for fishing. I spent a lot of time with Jesse in the radio room learning about the operation of the radio skeds and the other work that the ROs got involved in. Their days were full; from the early morning calls to other freezers through to late night skeds and, in between, those the RO was calling up shore stations to collect messages from the company, sending and receiving crew messages to families for birthdays, anniversaries, etc. They also handled the other skeds between all company vessels on the grounds and, of course, the all important position skeds back to the company office once every twenty-four hours. When they weren't doing that they would probably be trying to fix faulty electronics.

In those days, all longer-range radio calls were sent and received in Morse code. It was fascinating to see the RO tapping away for hours on the Morse key and compiling the positions and catches of the ships. All the ROs were able to recognise each other by the way they used the Morse key. Every operator had a unique rhythm and firmness to their keying action so they always knew which ship was calling them before the ship identified herself. In between handling all of these calls, the RO was expected to keep all the radios and bridge electronics in top operational condition and to at least try and repair any piece of electronics that went wrong or broke down. If he could not fix it then he had to call me in the office with the details and I would contact the main service companies in UK. We would discuss the fault and get the necessary parts sent out to the ship so the RO could fix it or get a local electronics agent ashore to assist. This covered everything from the radios and radars to the warp tension meters on the trawl deck to the TVs and the film projector in the crew mess rooms.

During the run up the coast, I spent some time on deck with the mate, Des. He was a friendly, chatty Welshman from Tiger Bay in Cardiff. He had sailed with the skipper for ages and explained what was happening on deck. I liked Des a lot and we got on well. He was also the spitting image of the singer Kenny Lynch. Thankfully though, he did not sing.

Life on a freezer trawler was altogether much more comfortable than on the side trawlers. The ships were bigger, the accommodation was more comfortable, all the officers, the factory manager and the cook, all had their own cabins and the crew shared four-man cabins, all with port holes, rather than the six-, eight- or even twelve-man cabins on some of the older side trawlers. As the ships would be away for much longer, the freezers were fitted with better recreation facilities and they all had TVs and film projectors with a supply of films put on board for each trip. The atmosphere also seemed a bit more relaxed. I cannot recall any time on

Lord Lovat when the crew sat together other that for a quick pot of tea while waiting to haul the gear.

Once on the fishing grounds off the North Cape, we received reports of good fishing further east, along the coast towards Russia. *Cassio* had several good days of calm weather and good catches and the mood on board was cheery and relaxed. Skipper Alfie always seemed to be in a happy mood and this spread through the crew. After a few days fishing, we moved back to the grounds off North Cape where a number of other BUT ships were fishing. By this time, Jesse and I had gone through all the issues of the daily sked routines on *Cassio* and it was time to change ships. The closest BUT ship to us was the *Pict*, fishing about 5 miles away. It was agreed that I would be transferred across by Zodiac boat later that day after both ships had completed their next hauls.

Pict was one of the top freezer trawlers at the time. She was a newer ship than *Cassio*, built in 1973 by Brooke Marine. The RO was Dave Poole, who I also knew fairly well as Dave was always happy to spend time in the office when he was ashore and discuss the different aspects of his job. The warm weather and clear days continued off the North Cape of Norway and the fishing, while not fantastic, was good enough to keep the skippers relatively happy. The *Pict* was a happy ship and had the same cheery atmosphere on board as I had found in *Cassio*. This seemed to flow down from the skipper, Jo Russel. The freezer trawler skippers were highly experienced and successful fishermen who had all spent many years as skippers in side trawlers before moving to the freezer fleet. They were well respected in the industry and had loyal crews who would sail with the same skipper for as long as they could. Obviously, the skipper wanted to keep the good workers in his crew and this developed tight knit and successful crews. This trust and professionalism engendered the happy relaxed atmospheres that I found on *Cassio* and *Pict*. The food was good and there was always something new to learn.

The radio operators were not employed by the trawling companies but by the radio companies themselves. In those days, there were two main radio companies operating on the dock, Marconi and Redifon. The ROs were appointed by the radio company to the ships that had that company's radio stations fitted as they had obviously been trained to operate and maintain that make and type of equipment. *Cassio* had a Marconi radio fit so Jesse was a 'Marconi Man'. The *Pict*, however, had a Redifon fit and Dave was a 'Redifon Man'.

After a few days in *Pict* spent discussing the issues of skeds and daily reports with Dave and comparing notes with what I had learnt from Jesse, I needed to start to head for home as the office expected me only to be away at sea for just two weeks or so. The skipper started to ask around the other ships in the area to see if any ships were due to head home in the next few days. None were, but the *Arab* was due to go into a Norwegian port for bunkers in a few days. She was fishing nearby, so it was agreed that I would transfer over to her by rubber boat. I would then go ashore in Honningsvaag when she went in for fuel. The ship's agent would be asked to arrange my onward flights back to the UK.

The *Pict* in BUT colours. (Photo with thanks to Walter Fussey of Hull, photographers)

The *Arab*, sister ship to the Gaul and both built originally for Ranger Fishing Co. of North Shields. (Photo with thanks to Walter Fussey photographers, Hull)

As I went across in the boat, the *Arab* loomed up beyond the waves. She was a big, but squat looking ship with a BUT mid blue hull. There was no mistaking the workmanlike air about her, No nicely curved superstructures with promenade decks here. This instantly looked like a hard-working ship. She was also an identical sister ship to the ill-fated *Gaul*.

The *Gaul*

'Factory Trawler lost with all hands' screamed the headlines. We were now fishing in the area in which the *Gaul* had been lost. She disappeared without trace, with all hands, a crew of thirty-six, on 8 February 1974, while 'dodging' in severe weather on North Cape Bank off the North Cape of Norway. The wreck was subsequently discovered some years later in position 72 degrees 5 minutes north and 25 degrees 6 minutes east.

The *Gaul* was built for the Ranger Fishing Company in 1971 as the *Ranger Castor* by Brooke Marine in Lowestoft. She was a big trawler, over 200-feet-long and with a gross tonnage of 1,100 tons. When she was built, she was the latest word in deep-sea factory trawlers. She was bought by BUT two years later in 1973, along with a number of her sister ships, which were also renamed using the names of ancient tribes or peoples (*Kurd*, *Kelt*, *Arab*, etc.). The loss of such a new and modern ship, well-designed and crewed by experienced trawler men, was met with disbelief in the Hull fishing community.

As often happens when no wreck is immediately found, rumors and fanciful explanations start to emerge as to what has happened. The *Gaul*, sadly, was no exception and in Hull the relatives and friends of those missing were treated to the full range of the media's fanciful imaginations in all their glory. One national TV channel even produced a TV documentary that included such nonsense as saying that the Gaul had been boarded and captured by the Russian Navy as she was a 'Spy Ship' and had been taken to a remote Russian Fjord. They even claimed that the crew was all OK and captive in Russia. The TV offered no explanation as to how the Russians might get aboard a high-sided stern trawler in a Force 9 Gale! They claimed that she could have been sunk by a submarine that had surfaced directly underneath her and holed her. None of this nonsense helped anyone and rather than get caught up debating such nonsense with the media the Company adopted a sensible 'say nothing' approach until a proper enquiry could take place.

Others, who knew what fishing in an Arctic winter really was like, and who were wiser, followed the more logical possibilities. All the TV talk of Russian submarines capturing the *Gaul* was totally disregarded by the men who sailed in her sister ships.

At the time of her loss she had been 'dodging' in very bad weather. Trawlers 'dodge' the weather when it is too bad to fish and the skipper wants to stay in the same area. When the weather gets too bad, all fishing is stopped and the factory

The *Gaul*, lost with all hands on 8 February 1974 off northern Norway. (Photo with thanks to Walter Fussey of Hull, photographers)

deck is shut down. The crew, apart from those on watch, will use the time to turn in and catch up on sleep. The ship goes slowly into the wind and weather and then turns and runs down wind to the other end of the grounds and then turns and goes back into wind so that she remains in the same area. As winter gales in the Arctic can last for days, steaming in one direction all the time would result in the ship ending up miles away from the grounds, so they 'Dodge'. The weather on the day the *Gaul* was lost, as reported by other trawlers in the area, started off with rough seas that had been built up by easterly winds of Gale Force 8, and which increased through the morning to Force 9 or even 10. The seas also got bigger. They had built up across the long fetch of the Barents Sea and at the time of her disappearance, three exceptionally large waves were reported by a number of other trawlers in the area. These waves crashed across the front of the trawlers, which were steaming into the wind, and caused considerable damage to bridge windows and other parts.

The official report at the time concluded that the *Gaul* had capsized as a result of excess water flooding up onto her trawl deck from astern as she ran down wind and down sea. I asked the skipper of the *Arab*, Peter Abbey, about his thoughts on the loss of the *Gaul*. He was clear in his mind that she had been broached; i.e. hit by a big sea from the side as she was trying to turn back across the wind to head back up into the wind. He felt that perhaps the ship had been caught halfway round the turn by an exceptionally large wave and rolled over downwind. Once over, the power would probably have tripped off automatically and there would be nothing that anyone could do as they would all have been thrown off their feet in a moment. His view and the view of his colleagues was that this was the likeliest cause. He also felt that there must also have been some other factors involved, such as large amounts of water swilling about on the factory deck, which is directly below the open trawl deck. Such amounts of water swilling about a ship's deck is called 'free surface' and is extremely dangerous as it makes ships very unstable very quickly. This might have occurred if the pumps that drain the factory deck had been turned off or if the drains had become clogged after the factory had been shut down when they stopped fishing. Another contributory factor was the possibility that a door on the trawl deck near the stern ramp, which faced aft and which was not visible from the bridge, may have been left open and this would allow water to flood down into the ship if she was overwhelmed by a big sea. In that case, and, if the ship was in the middle of turning back into wind and was broadside on when one of the larger waves struck her, and if she had free surface water on the factory deck, then there would be nothing anyone could do.

Subsequent experiments carried out by the National Maritime Institute using a large detailed scale model of the *Gaul* concluded that water on the trawl deck alone could not have caused her to capsize and that this could only be a contributory factor. Their conclusion was that the factory deck below must have had excessive flooding as well. The wreck was found in 1997 and an underwater survey was carried out in 1998. What they found was that she had not been captured by Russians or holed by a submarine. The hull was intact and the door at the aft end of the trawl deck was indeed open as were some engine room ventilators in the ship. Some offal discharge chutes were also found to be in an open position but as these were free swinging flap doors then nothing conclusive could be proved. Certainly once the ship had been rolled over and was under water then these chute doors could possibly end up in an open position allowing more rapid flooding; but that in no way proves that they were a cause of the disaster as some have tried to make out. In all other respects, she appeared to be as one would be expect a trawler dodging in bad weather to be.

The *Arab*

As the *Arab* was a sister ship of the *Gaul*, I was excited at the prospect of seeing how this class of ship compared with stern trawlers such as *Pict* and *Cassio*. *Arab* was built in 1971 by Brooke Marine and was identical to the *Gaul*. Unlike the *Cassio* and *Pict*, however, she was a 'filleter'. This meant that she was able to fillet the fish she caught before it was frozen. All the skin and fish heads were reduced to fishmeal and bagged up on board. Because two frozen fillets from one fish take up roughly a third of the freezer space that a single, whole, frozen fish would, this means that it takes about three times as long to fill her hold as a block fish freezer, which merely gut the fish then freeze the whole body including the head and skin, etc. In turn, this meant that the filleter trawlers took two to three times as long to catch the same tonnage of finished product so tended to be at sea much longer. Whereas a block freezer would expect to be at sea for anything from forty to sixty days, a filleter would expect to be out for sixty to a hundred days.

Arab looked a solid and workmanlike ship and her design appeared to be well thought out with good accommodation and she seemed to be more spacious than the *Cassio*. She was also a fine sea ship. During the first twenty-four hours on board, the weather changed for the worse and I was able to experience a Force 8 gale in the *Arab*. It did not bother the ship at all. She ran down sea in this Force 8 and I watched from the bridge for ages but the seas never even threatened to run up the ramp onto the trawl deck. She did not stop fishing and there was nothing to indicate to me that this was anything other than a fine sea ship.

The one thing I noticed almost immediately however, was the mood of the ship. What a difference in ship's mood from *Pict* and *Cassio*. *Arab* was gloomy and the whole buzz that existed in *Pict* and *Cassio* was not there. Everyone seemed sullen and withdrawn. The skipper continued fishing the North Cape Bank catching only medium hauls of fish. The RO, a Redifon man, was uncommunicative and did not seem to be interested in helping me understand his job. He and the skipper hardly said a word to each other, again not the norm as these two people spent a lot of time together at sea and were often good friends. He chose to leave the industry soon afterwards. Meals were eaten in a gloomy silence and I tended to pass the time reading. At the time I was reading that super book *The World of Suzie Wong* by Richard Mason. Having spent time in Hong Kong and having visited Wanchai where the book was set, I was transported back to the sticky heat of a lively, bustling Hong Kong and the street markets and nightlife of Wanchai while I was sitting on a freezer trawler on a grey and gloomy Arctic Ocean.

By the Monday morning, the *Arab*'s skipper decided that it was now time to refuel and we went into Honningsvaag, a small town at the northern tip of Norway and the closest town to the North Cape itself. I went ashore with the ship's agent and I watched *Arab* as we drove round the bay to the town: her blue hull and white superstructure dominating the small port. The agent put me onto a bus to Lakselv, the nearest town with an airport, about two-hours' drive away. From there I flew back to Oslo, then home via London.

Scottish Boats

We were always looking at new electronics equipment that was coming onto the market and I had to try and evaluate whether or not it had any benefits for the fleet. This covered navigation as well as fish-finding equipment. The best way to do that was to go to sea in boats that had already had the new equipment fitted and talk to the skippers about whether it actually improved their catches or not. As they say in fishing 'If it does not catch you any more fish then it is a waste of money', as all the money needed by the company to run itself has to come 'Out of the Cod End'. I therefore spent time visiting Scottish boats and meeting their skippers and going to sea with a few of them. These included Skipper Buchan in *Lunar Bow*, a newly-built purse-seiner fishing for herring in the Atlantic to the west of the Orkneys Islands. She had a brand-new sonar that was creating a lot of interest in the industry.

Chris, a friendly salesman from Kelvin Hughes in Hull (who had sold the new sonar), and I arrived on the quayside at Fraserburgh on a wet and windy Sunday night. Some of the boats were starting up their engines and deck lights were coming on around the harbour. Crewmembers arrived in taxis, some were dropped off by their wives. Some were carrying boxes of groceries for the trip, others just a holdall. Other boats lay dark and silent, their crews safely tucked up in bed at home. Chris and I were warmly welcomed by the skipper as he arrived and we were taken on board. We were given a mattress each on the deck of the main crew cabin. We sailed just after midnight, as Scottish boats traditionally do not set sail on Sundays. Once we had cleared the harbour I settled down in my sleeping bag for the rest of the night.

We headed north and, as we cleared the Pentland Firth and sailed out into the Atlantic, a strong gale quickly developed from the west. It soon became too bad for any attempt at fishing so the skipper sought shelter in the lee of the Orkney Islands. Seasickness had set in again for both Chris and I so I was glad when we ran for the shelter of the islands. We got inside and anchored while the gale blew itself through. Eventually, after a few hours, the gale and the seasickness had passed by and we set off again.

The new sonar had a screen like a radar display and it gave a 360 degree view of the surrounding waters as the beam was transmitted out in all directions at once and we started looking for herring. There were other boats in the area now also looking for herring. The sun came out and it turned into a beautiful clear day with a big blue Atlantic swell rolling under us and a fresh breeze was blowing. In the clear light we could see, low on the southern horizon, the cliffs of Caithness in sharp detail.

The aim of purse-seining is to catch mid-water, or pelagic, fish by laying out the net around the shoal. The boat encircles the fish by going round the shoal to the end of the net that was first put in the water and hauling it in. The net hangs like a giant curtain down into the sea and around the fish caught inside it. When the other end of the net has been picked up, a rope that runs through the bottom of this curtain is hauled in until the bottom of the net forms a big bag, or purse. The top of the net is then drawn in as the boat lies alongside it and the fish are brought on board by big pumps or by brailing them in using small crane nets.

The skipper found a big herring shoal with the sonar and after carefully working out the wind direction, the direction the shoal was moving in and being aware of the other boats working in the area; he positioned his boat ready to slip the net. The crew were already on deck and with one yell of 'Let Go' out of the wheelhouse window, a big, red, rubber buoy was thrown over the stern. This was attached to the net and the net then ran freely out of its stowage area in the stern. The *Lunar Bow* steamed to starboard round the shoal and, with the aid of the sonar, the skipper was able to keep the shoal and boat in the right positions. Without another word from the skipper the boat came up to the buoy and the purse was hauled in. The ends were drawn up and the catch of herring was brailed up and into the fish tanks in the boat. The whole operation was done with just two words of command.

The fishing continued for three or four days until the skipper felt he had his quota of fish and we headed for home. However, it was realised that we had more herring than we were officially allowed to land under EEC rules. Therefore, to avoid paying a hefty fine for exceeding his quotas, the skipper had no choice but to dump a quantity of fish back into the sea. This fish dumping is something brought on by the EEC and the Common Fisheries Policy and is regarded by all as a total nonsense, if not a crime.

Picket Busting

On the fish dock you had to turn your hand to anything to get the job done. I discovered what this involved during a strike by shore workers on the fish dock. I cannot even recall what the strike was about but I know that the pickets at the entrance to the docks prevented many of the electronic service company vans driving onto the dock. Therefore, to keep the trawlers running and ready for sea we had to find another way to repair faulty equipment. When we had a fault on equipment, such as a radar set or an echo sounder; I would take the report from the RO and go and talk to the service engineers in their workshops. They would show me on a similar set in the workshop what the problem might be and what the broken part looked like and how it fitted into the equipment. I would then go back on board the ship and try and identify the bit with the fault. As this was in the days before mobile phones so, if I had any queries I had to go all the way back up to the office and call from there. Once I had found the right printed board or module I had to dismantle the set, take it out and, without being seen by the pickets, get it round to the electronic company's workshop for repair. The next day, after it had been repaired, I did the same thing in reverse. As the pickets roamed the dock during the day we did some of this work at night, by torchlight if necessary. Of course, if I got the wrong bit then we had to do it all again!

Deep Sea Trawling and The Common Market

Britain had always had the best fishing grounds in Europe and had controlled her own stocks and managed her own quotas. After we joined the EEC or Common Market, Britain had to fall into line with the requirements and wishes of all the other fishing nations of Europe. This meant that we had to share our traditional UK grounds and that meant smaller quotas in our own waters while foreign boats from Spain, France and elsewhere could come and happily fish alongside our boats. Many traditional British near-water fishing grounds all around the UK were opened up to our European brothers who eagerly came in large numbers. A number of grounds ended up being fatally overfished. There were no other viable European fishing grounds that we could have access to that would balance this out.

The EEC Common Fisheries Policy has always been a very sore point in the whole fishing industry and I am not expert enough to try to explain it other than to say it was well known within the industry, before we joined the EEC in 1975, that the Common Fishery Policy was not going to help the UK fishermen in any way and that it would spell the end of the UK fishing industry. That came to pass.

The distant water industry, based mainly in Hull and Grimsby, was decimated by a combination of factors, of which the Common Market's Common Fishery Policy was one. Other factors included the fact that older freshers or side winders, built in the boom years of the 1950s and early 1960s, now required replacement, or at least expensive hull surveys and refits, to comply with modern insurance rules; the ever increasing cost of fuel oil; the extended fishery limits out to 200 miles in Iceland and Norway: the reduced fish quotas where they could fish as well as the new EEC CFP. Since the 1970s, we have witnessed the total disappearance of the deep-sea fleets from both the Humber ports, the over-fishing of traditional UK grounds by other countries, the continued reduction in catch quotas, the decline in the number of boats and the decline of the once flourishing boat-building industry, particularly in Scotland. On top of that, we have seen the introduction of the insane EU laws that force skippers to dump tons of good, but dead, fish back into the sea if they caught more than their quota allowance.

Time to Move On

As the Industry started to collapse in Hull, more and more trawlers were laid up and then sent to the breaker's yards. My work then became focused on de-equipping ships of their electronics and saying goodbye to ROs. The end was in sight and so I and many others bade farewell to fish dock, a sad end to a great industry and a fantastic community, that was brimming with fine people who understood what tragedy and hardship at work really meant but came out of it as kind, good people who always had time to help you. However, nothing lasts forever and we had to move on.

The prospects for work in Hull were poor. The decline of the trawling industry affected the economic climate of the town. To find work in the marine industry, I needed to move away from the area and I was lucky to find work in London working for one of the major Marine Electronics companies as a sales and marketing manager. This effectively ended my career in terms of working directly with ships and we moved south to start a new life in the suburbs, commuting into London and a nine to five world far removed from the sea and seven o'clock starts on the market. However, I was now working for a major international supplier of marine electronics to the shipping industry and so spent a lot of time talking to shipping companies and demonstrating new equipments on board ships and getting to know the world of the merchant marine.

From now on, major trips to sea would be as a passenger and so offered a new perspective. Whereas, before, any places I visited were because that was where the ship went, now I could choose the places I wanted to visit and select a ship to take me there.

CHAPTER 10

MV *Marco Polo* – The Antarctic

After the excitement of Hull Fish Dock, Doreen and I were working at building our new lives and careers in the 'Wicked South', well, London anyway. For me, the international marine electronics industry, and for Doreen, as an Air Stewardess for Sir Freddie Laker.

However, the tug of the Polar Regions does not go away and after a few years of dreaming and many months of gentle persuasion I convinced Doreen that we really should try and visit Antarctica. She was naturally nervous about some of the reports we had read of small basic ships and the Roaring Forties but eventually we found a trip that met both our needs. We both got such a thrill going to the Antarctic and being in the Southern Ocean, that we later did some trips to the Arctic on different ships and to different areas.

'South'

When I was about eight or nine my grandfather and I were chatting and I told him that I wanted to see icebergs. He went to his bookcase and handed me a brown-coloured book. 'Here you are, you might enjoy this.' The book was called *South* by someone called Ernest Shackleton. I had no idea what it was about and I thought it must be about the south of England. However, as he had said that he thought I would enjoy it, I read it. It was of course Shackleton's story of his 1914 Imperial Trans-Antarctic Expedition. Shackleton became my hero and I have since read it many times and all the other books covering the different aspects of that incredible expedition.

Shackleton and twenty-seven men sailed in his ship *Endurance* from Grytviken, in South Georgia on 5 December 1914 and headed south. The aim of Shackleton's expedition was to try and cross Antarctica, but the *Endurance* was trapped by the ice in the Weddell Sea before the party were even able to get ashore. After wintering in the ship, trapped by the ice, the ice finally crushed and sunk *Endurance* on 21 November 1915; nearly a year after leaving South Georgia. They were then forced to live on the ice and drifted round the Weddell Sea in the ice pack for months until they finally arrived back at the ice edge near the tip of the Antarctic Peninsula. Here they launched the three boats that they had salvaged from the *Endurance* and kept with them on the ice. After struggling for days with gales and fog, sailing by day, sleeping on ice floes by night, if they could; they managed to reach a totally uninhabited and desolate rock called Elephant Island. They arrived here on 14 April 1916; dry land after fifteen months at sea and on the ice. There, they made a camp and Shackleton then set about going for help. He and five companions then sailed over 1,200 miles, in winter, in an open boat, the *James Caird*, from Elephant Island and made a desperate landing on the west coast of South Georgia on 8 May 1916. Shackleton, Capt. Frank Worsley and Tom Crean then became the first people to cross the unmapped, 3,000-metre high Allardyce Range as they had to get from where they had landed on the uninhabited west coast to the inhabited east coast to get to the whaling stations and help. Finally, almost eighteen months after the *Endurance* had sailed from South Georgia; Shackleton got back to the safety of the whaling stations and was able to take charge of the rescue of the remaining twenty-two men on Elephant Island. After three attempts to reach the Island, it was not until 30 August 1916 that Shackleton finally got through the pack in a Chilean tug, *Yelcho*. After five months on the Island, all twenty-two men were rescued safe and well. Ever since I read that book I have been in awe of Shackleton's achievement and have wanted to visit the Antarctic. However, in the 1950s and 1960s the only ships that went down to the Antarctic were the whale factory ships and the RN Ice Patrol ship, HMS *Endurance*. Expedition trips and soft adventure tourist ships had not even been thought of then. If I really wanted to go then I needed to become a whaler.

In the 1960s, Salvesen of Leith operated an annual whaling expedition to the Antarctic. It was mostly crewed by Norwegians but they collected a number of British sailors from the Orkney Islands and Scottish ports on their way. In those days, they took all sorts of people who would do the many basic, manual tasks on board the factory ship and the catchers. The key jobs on the whale catchers and most of the jobs in the factory ship were skilled or specialised and given to those with appropriate experience. In 1968, I wrote to Christian Salvesen in Leith asking if I could join their annual whaling expeditions to the Antarctic. I received a letter back from Salvesen saying that they were sorry but the previous year's expedition, the 1967 Norwegian expedition, had been the last one and they were no longer involved in Antarctic whaling. I was one year too late.

The Voyage

A few years after I left the Navy, I started to read stories in the press about expedition trips to Antarctica. The idea of expedition voyages had been started by Lars-Eric Lindblad, He was a Swedish explorer, who felt so strongly that people should have the chance to visit Antarctica that he set up his own company to run

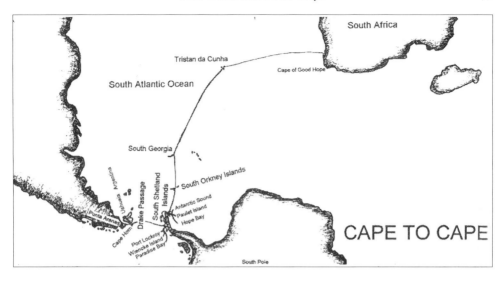

Sketch map showing the route of *Marco Polo* from Cape of Good Hope to Cape Horn via Antarctica.

Marco Polo, originally the *Alexander Pushkin*, at anchor off Grytviken, South Georgia.

expeditions himself. He bought a ship and converted it for expedition work. He called the ship *Lindblad Explorer* and began trips from South America. I then read of a new company called Orient Lines, which had bought and refitted the old Russian passenger ship *Alexander Pushkin* and renamed her *Marco Polo*. In 1993, she was to make her first trip to Antarctica on a voyage billed as 'From Cape to Cape'. The ship was to sail from Cape Town in South Africa down to Antarctica and then land her passengers in Ushuaia in Chile, having sailed past both the Cape of Good Hope and Cape Horn. The expedition leader was to be Lars-Eric Lindblad.

The *Marco Polo* was built in East Germany for the Russians in 1966 and she and her sister ship, the *Mikhail Lermantov*, were managed by the Baltic Shipping Company running a regular transatlantic service between Leningrad (now St Petersburg) and Montreal. Both ships were of 24,000 tons and built for the North Atlantic. She began cruising in the Far East in 1975 and in 1992 was sold to Orient Lines and underwent a major refit in Italy. Her first cruise as the *Marco Polo* was down through the Suez Canal to South Africa which is where we joined her for her second trip. This was to be Lars-Eric Lindblad's largest and most ambitious expedition to Antarctica and on the biggest ship ever to go down there. Passenger capacity was reduced to half, to just 400, for safety reasons and to satisfy the demands for minimising the impact of tourism on the Antarctic continent.

The stab and dull ache of a dodgy tooth woke me in the night. We need to leave for the airport at lunchtime but I dash to the dentist in the morning before we set off. Nothing is found and I am given some tablets to take if it gets worse. We are due to fly from Heathrow to Paris and connect to an Air France night flight down to Cape Town. My tooth is still playing up and I spend our time in Charles de Gaulle Airport, a grey and most depressing place, looking for and failing to find, a shop that sells painkillers.

We arrive at the ship the following day and boarded her, by what must have been one of the longest and highest gangways in the world! It stretched out from near the top of the ship, like a giant feeler, touching the dockside some 30 yards from the ship. As we climbed up and up the gangway and into the ship, it seemed to go on and up forever. The ship towered above us while her new, blue painted hull and white super structure gleamed and shone in the warm South African sun. Thankfully, the tooth seems to have settled down. The ship is gleaming after its refit and we wander through the new public rooms, all clean new and decorated in soft, relaxing colours. Our inside cabin is comfortable, very roomy and with plenty of storage space. By the evening I am feeling fairly ropey again with my tooth and decide to go to bed early in the hope my tooth, helped by painkillers, will settle down. The ship is not due to sail until the following afternoon so that will give us the morning for some sightseeing in Cape Town.

I wake in the night feeling rough and feverish. I sleep fitfully until, at about five o'clock, I realise that my face has swollen to the size of a melon, or so it feels. I tell

Doreen that I am feeling bad but she adopts her Florence Nightingale voice and says sympathetically 'Look, you are not having a heart attack so go back to sleep as there will be no one around at this hour anyway'. How I love her! She promptly goes back to sleep. I spend the rest of the night thinking 'Here I am about to go to the Antarctic for over three weeks with freezing temperatures and icy winds, and a bad tooth, a face the size of a melon and no dentist! Great!'

At 7.30 am I am first in the queue for the sickbay. The doctor looks at me. 'Oh! We don't have a dentist here.' Is that his remedy? However, we do find the ship's agent, who arranges for me to be taken to a local dentist in his van. Dr Van de Merve is a good man. He identifies the offending tooth, which has abscessed and drains it without any fuss. The relief as his drill cuts through the tooth to relieve the pressure of the poison is wonderful. He asks me where the ship is going and when I tell him he says 'Oh dear!' in a doom-laden tone. I panic as I think he is about to ban me from travelling but he decides that he needs to work harder to clear out the remaining poison and he sets too again squeezing my face and gums a lot harder with his fingers and thumbs of both hands. With that all done, he stuffs cotton wool into my bad tooth, gives me a big packet of penicillin tablets and sends me back to the ship. We sail an hour later. That night after dinner, Doreen and I stand together at the stern rail and watch the lights of Cape Town get smaller as we head off past Cape Point, the Cape of Good Hope on our 'Cape to Cape' voyage via Antarctica.

On our first day at sea the weather deteriorates and it is deemed too rough to hold lifeboat drill. I spend the day taking life easy, trying to read and eating penicillin tablets. During the day I realise that I have left my camera somewhere out on deck during the day. I report it to the Purser. I assume that I must have left it out on deck when I came back from the dentist and as I was not totally 'with it', and forgot to pick it up. It never turned up but we at least had Doreen's Olympus Trip as a back-up.

After a few days the weather improves and my face returns to its normal size. I begin to feel a bit more human and have a full American breakfast to celebrate. It is a nice sunny day and we see our first albatross, a yellow-nosed albatross, which spends most of the afternoon wheeling around the stern of the ship. Our first call is at Tristan da Cunha where we are to go ashore for the morning. Ships normally lie off in an open roadstead near the settlement of Edinburgh and all stores and people are transferred by small, open boat as there is no sheltered anchorage and certainly no harbour. However, today, there is a big swell running into the settlement and the ship is rolling heavily as she stops off the coast. The local boats come out and try to come alongside but the heavy swell makes it difficult for them to approach the ship. The captain correctly deems it too dangerous to transfer passengers to small open boats with the 10 to 12 foot swell running. The trip ashore is therefore cancelled. Even so, there were passengers who thought they knew better and complained bitterly to ship's staff that the brochure had said they would go ashore at Tristan da Cunha!

Southern Ocean

South Georgia is 1,400 miles away from Tristan da Cunha and way down in the Southern Ocean, deep in the Roaring Forties; home to endless gales and huge seas. The Southern Ocean is a vast, mystical place, a place of mariner's tales and empty loneliness. It is an ocean where only albatrosses and the strongest and best-sailed ships can survive. The ocean begins to live up to its reputation. During the next day, the sea gradually gets up as the wind increases from the south-west. A large, low pressure area is moving towards us and we are told to expect heavy weather. As the morning goes on, the ship starts to pitch and broken seas wash across the fo'c'sle as the ship slides down into the troughs between the growing waves. Her bows throw masses of white water aside as she pushes her 24,000 tons down and forward into the next wave. In spite of the howling wind, it is a sunny day with blue skies and scudding white clouds. A few albatrosses still circle the ship as well as some Cape petrels and prions. The albatrosses, on their long thin wings, wheel round the waves with one wing tip millimetres from the water but never ever touching it. Then they swing up to catch more wind and without any apparent movement at all they wheel round in a wide circle and start again. They glide motionless for hours, skimming across the wild, roaring ocean and the breaking seas.

The clouds cast hard, dark shadows onto the waves as they fly across the sky in a headlong race with the waves towards the east. It is a rough night, with shudders, bangs and crashes echoing through the ship as doors slam and loose items finally let go of their hold and crash across the cabins. In the morning, we go up on deck to find that the wind is now up to about 40 knots, a full gale and howling out of a clear blue sky. It is spectacular. The seas have built up and some of the waves are about 40 to 50 feet high. The ship has slowed down and is still pitching as she tries to hold her course. If we have an engine failure now the seas and wind would knock the ship down and capsize her in seconds. From the open deck, the waves appear like moving mountains ranges of water as they come sweeping towards the ship with a threatening, hypnotic effect. You cannot take your eyes away from them. The ship reaches the bottom of the trough and the wave mountains rear up high above us. As we climb our way up the slopes the rest of the range comes into view and the wind howls louder as we reach the exposed higher slopes. We can again see the vast expanse of range upon range of waves, with their tops blown off leaving white tails streaming from them. The decks tilt forward as the ship begins her slide down the far side and into the next deep valley, the wind drops and it gets quieter down in the shelter of the next mountain of water as it appears ahead and begins to towers above us. So it goes on, hour after hour.

We are now truly in the Roaring Forties and can absorb the atmosphere of the place, the biting wind that races round the planet and the great, white-crested waves that rear up menacingly and then ignore us as they remorselessly march towards to the east. I have never seen seas like this, the white crested waves and the deep, dark troughs between them stretch out in lines like dark, snow-flecked hills, out into the vast emptiness as far as the eye can see and then further, much further. The sense of emptiness and loneliness of this ocean is awe-inspiring. The albatrosses wheeling round astern of the ship only add to the extreme isolation of the place. If there is another ship or a yacht out there then we will never see it in the vastness of this chaotic spray-coated ocean.

It is now definitely getting colder too with a real bite in the air. During the afternoon we are told that we are at the half way point to South Georgia and I see the first 'sooty' albatross, or Grey Mantled sooty albatross to be correct.

By the evening the wind is at last dropping and the motion of the ship is a little easier. The waiters set the dining room for dinner. We hope that we are now past the centre of the low pressure system and things will improve. At its peak, it was a full Force 9, gusting to 10. The following day dawns sunny and much calmer; the sea is down to state 4 and wind down to about Force 4 or 5. We have a clear, crisp horizon and a sharper edge to the wind. Aerobic classes start again up in the gym and the restaurant is definitely busier too.

South Georgia

The cold, wet, clammy fog wraps itself around the ship. Ten days after leaving the UK, we excitedly go on deck to see the mountains of South Georgia as we make our approach to the island, but we are met by this all-enveloping fog. It swirls around the ship and most passengers stay inside, but we decide to go on deck and tuck ourselves in behind a metal screen, out of the wind. Then, there is a cry from forward. 'It's clearing!' We look out from behind our shelter and in a matter of seconds the fog starts to thin as the ship passes through the entrance to Cumberland Bay. We move out to the bow as we sail out of the solid fog bank and enter a calm, sun-filled, blue and white world. There before us is the most beautiful sight: the open expanse of Cumberland Bay, its blue peaceful waters extend away to left and right. Directly ahead, across the bay, the white, jagged mountain peaks of the Allardyce Range are bathed in sunshine and stretch away north and south with vast sweeps of drifted snow covering their sides. Glistening, silent glaciers come from the mountains down into the bay. Looking astern, we can see the fog bank lying like a solid grey wall on the sea and our wake emerging from it. The huge Nordenskjold Glacier emerges at the southern end of the bay. Cumberland Bay is more like an inland sea than a bay, as the land closes right round to the entrance. It is a calm and serene scene, with the sun warming the green shore line, white clouds gently drift along the tops of the mountains and then clear from Mount Sugartop, above Grytviken, to allow it to look down at the newcomers. A little further to the south, the highest mountain on the Island, Mt Paget, remains aloof and hidden in the clouds

South Georgia was officially discovered by Captain cook, who landed here and claimed it for Britain in 1775. He named it 'Isle de Georgia' in honour of King George III. The *Marco Polo* anchors off King Edward's Point but not without a little difficulty, as the windlass seems to be playing up as they veer out the cable.

The old, Norwegian whaling base of Grytviken lies at the head of a small bay just beyond the point. As we leave the ship by boat the storm damage is evident and the blue paint on the bows and hull has been sucked and stripped off by the seas, leaving a rust red finish that does not really enhance the ship's looks.

Once ashore at King Edward's Point we feel the gentle warmth of a summer's day as we pass the time with a group of young elephant seals who have decided that the main track is a good place to bed down for the afternoon. Some small penguins waddle by on their way to the beach. We had been told by Lars-Eric that under no circumstances must we get closer than 15 feet to any animal. The only problem was no one had told the penguins or seals that. We walk round the bay and arrive at Grytviken.

Whaling was first started here in 1904 by the Norwegian Carl Larsen. He identified the area as a good spot for shore whaling stations when he was Captain of the *Antarctica*, the ship carrying the Swedish Antarctic Expedition in 1902 under the Swedish explorer Nordenskjold. Larsen returned here and built Grytviken, which was the site of an earlier base for seal hunters. Their blackened blubber boiling pots were still lying along the shore when Larsen arrived. The name Grytviken means 'Pot Cove' in Norwegian. By 1912, there were seven whaling stations on the east coast of the Island run mostly by the Norwegians and the British but some were run by Argentineans and the South Africans. However, by 1964, all whaling had ceased as it was no longer economically viable and the stations were left to fall into ruin. Three of the old whale catchers that never left, the *Dias*, the *albatross* and the *Petrel*, are still here, aground and half submerged in the shallows beside the rotting flensing plan. The *Dias* and the *albatross* lie together derelict, silent, rusting and forlorn while further round the bay the *Petrel* sits in a similar state, untouched, since the last whalers left in 1964. At its peak, nearly 300 men lived and worked here including the crews of the whale catcher boats. There is a small museum in what was the station manager's house, run by a couple who live on their yacht, which is berthed at the jetty. They look after the base and are most helpful and show us the way round.

There is wreckage all around as a lot of the old station has been dismantled and the hazardous materials cleaned or removed; but a lot of the iron and steel and the remains of the heavy machinery is still lying around. In addition to the huge wooden flensing plan, where the dead whales were hauled up, the blubber cookers, and the storerooms are exactly as they were left. The most notably building is the beautiful, little, white-painted Norwegian chapel. It was built in Norway and sent out to Grytviken in kit form by Carl Larsen, where it was rebuilt, including two bells. It is as clean and lovely as it must have been in the days when the whalers used it on Sundays. The chapel sits just apart from, but incongruously close to, the main factory area where the massive slaughter of huge whales, the noises of winches and saws, the yells of men, the screams of cutting tools and the smell and steam of boiling whale blubber would fill the air all season long. In the store rooms by the jetty there are still large coils of the whale line that was attached to the harpoons.

The highlight of the trip ashore is the visit to Sir Ernest Shackleton's grave. He died here of a heart attack in 1922 after arriving on the *Quest* for another expedition. His grave is in the whaler's small graveyard on a hillside just along the beach from the whaling station. The graveyard has a smart, white-painted, palisade fence around it to keep the seals out. Shackleton's grave has a stone surround with gravel top and a plain, rough-hewn granite tombstone. It says simply:

To the dear memory of
Ernest Henry Shackleton
Explorer
Born 5th Feb 1874
Entered life eternal
Died 5th Jan 1922

Above left: Sir Ernest Shackleton. (Library of Congress)

Above right: The grave of Sir Ernest Shackleton in the Whaler's graveyard in Grytviken.

Shackleton's *Nimrod* leaves Cowes in 1908 for the Antarctic. (J&C McCutcheon Collection)

A further memorial to Sir Ernest Shackleton lies round the bay at Hope Point on a small hill overlooking the whole of Cumberland Bay. It is a stone cairn with a white cross on it and was erected by the men of the *Quest*.

I wake up and lie still, listening for the throb of the engines. There is no noise. We should have sailed late last night to go to the Bay of Islands but there is no indication that we are at sea at all. I go on deck and find we are still at anchor in Cumberland Bay. It turns out that the windlass motor, which we had noticed had not been too happy when letting out the anchor, has decided that it certainly won't be hauling it in. For the present we are stuck. If we cannot get the anchor in then we cannot sail away! They could of course break the cable, put a buoy on it and leave it on the seabed and try to recover it later; but that would be a last resort. The engineers set to work to change the motor from the starboard windlass for the dead one on the port windlass. Once they have done this and heave in the anchor, we can sail but now with only one working windlass. The work will take all day and so gives us an extra day to explore the area. Some of us go with one of the ornithologists to look for the nest site of a sooty albatross. To our delight, not only do we find it, but there is a sooty sitting on the nest. They are big and beautiful birds but they are not as big as the wandering albatross. Their heads and body plumage is a soft charcoal grey that looks like velvet. Their delicate eye markings give them an inquisitive, but nervous look. This one, however, remains firmly on its nest and allows us up to our 15-foot limit. Its nest is on a cliff face and, by carefully climbing down to a nearby grass ledge, we are able to spend ten minutes or so watching the albatross and enjoying the view of the bay from its prime nest site.

The next few days are spent visiting the fantastic wildlife of South Georgia. We visit the colonies of millions of king penguins, small colonies of sea lions and all of their attendant smells. There really is nothing quite like the awful smell that comes from a colony of sea lions. Penguins are bad, but sea lions are worse! At the King Penguin colony we see a curious sight. A leopard seal has come ashore and is lying by the water's edge. Normally, a leopard seal would swim along the beach by the penguin colony and attack any passing penguins. The king penguins in their manner of haughty, but interested gentlemen, waddle up to about 5 feet from the leopard seal and stand for a few minutes staring at it and examining it closely. The seal just lies there unconcerned. Yet once in the water they would have swum as far away from it as they could. We visit a wandering albatross colony; where the nests are actually 2- or 3-feet high mounds of earth and grasses and are scattered over an open tussock grass-covered hilltop where the wind blows continually. The birds must have this wind to help them get airborne. They are huge birds. Close up I would think they are at least twice as big as the sooty albatross. Their heads are about 18 inches long and somehow they manage to fold their huge wings up so they become part of their backs. Like the seals, they are content to let us walk up and take their photos and they just watch us in an 'interested but I don't care' sort of a way.

We leave the magic of South Georgia and head further south towards the South Orkney Islands. We see the first iceberg at 57 degrees south. It is quite an impressive one too; on a grey cloudy day the iceberg is a silver gray colour with sides looking like sliced ice cream, a sculptured mass drifting along on its own in an empty ocean. Now we really are in the Antarctic!

Antarctica

The next morning we reach the South Orkneys, a beautiful string of small islands lying to the north of the Weddell Sea. In spite of a hazy sun the sight is spectacular, all gleaming whites, greys and blacks. The black mountains, grey mists and shadows, white icebergs and floes, and black sea all around us. As the icy sun breaks through gaps in the haze, the scene changes and different parts of the scene are highlighted in the bright sun while others vanish into the haze or behind a drifting berg.

On Coronation Island there is a large colony of Adelie penguins. These are small penguins with cute faces and round, white-ringed eyes. They clamber up and struggle over the big lumps of drift ice at the water's edge. They slip, slide and fall but always bounce up again and clamber back up the ice before they stand at the water's edge and look carefully out to sea for any leopard seals and waiting for one of their braver relatives to jump in first. If he swims away without being attacked by a leopard seal then the others will happily follow. How on earth do they decide who will go first? They are all totally unafraid of humans and walk right up to within a couple of feet of people on the shore peering intently at these new strangers on their beach.

We leave the South Orkneys, heading further south, down into the Weddell Sea and for Paulet Island. The sky clears and the sun comes fully out and we see a spectacle of huge tabular icebergs lying in a flat blue sea. Most of them seem to have grounded as the sea starts to shallow near the islands. These bergs are massive with flat tops and vertical cliff sides. Some are tilted and lie there like a slice of ice cream cake on its side. It is hard to estimate just how big they are but certainly twice as high as the ship and at least half a mile long. They continue below the sea for at least four or five times as far as they do above the sea. The icebergs stretch away as far as we can see. We leave this rare and beautiful scene and turn in as it is now about midnight.

Into the Pack Ice

During the night I become aware of occasional faint scraping noises running through the ship. I listen, ice! We must have reached the edge of the pack ice. By four o'clock in the morning the noise has increased to a juddering and scraping clearly coming from the hull. Then it falls quiet and the engine vibration drops quietly away. I get up and go on deck to find that the ship is stopped in the middle of the pack ice. It is overcast and snowing with the visibility down to about 2 miles. The pack ice extends as far as I can see on all sides. The ship tries to move ahead again, pushing the floes aside with her ice-strengthened bow. There are no visible leads or areas of open water and the floes have closed right up against each other. At six o'clock the ship finally comes to a stop. Silence falls over the ship and the peace and beauty of the pack embraces us. Off to port, a large iceberg with big floes round about it lies trapped in the pack. Some of the floes around the ship are over 10 feet high and the pack has ridges running through it, some extending quite close to the ship. The ship had been trying to follow leads through the ice but these kept closing up, leaving her stuck with nowhere to go. The ship tries to get under way again at about seven o'clock, but with the floes like solid concrete blocks floating at the side of the ship and extending down about 10 or 12 feet into the water, this is impossible.

Lars-Eric comes on the PA. 'As those of you that have looked out can see we are stuck in the pack ice. I have spoken with the captain and we cannot get to Paulet Island so we must go back and find a way out of here. When the pack ice is this dense it is termed 9/10th pack and is impenetrable for anything other than an icebreaker. Also, the wind is from the north and if we stay here we could be in real danger of becoming trapped in the pack and with a large berg to leeward, this is not a good place to be.' Not the most encouraging wake-up call, but true!

The captain tries to manoeuvre the ship round but there is a real danger that one of the ice chunks will damage or even break the propeller. If that happens we could be here for a while. Gradually, by going ahead and astern and trying to turn the ship he eases her round and we start to back track through the ice that we have already passed through. Slowly, we head back to the north. Then, as we get into more broken pack ice, the swell increases telling us that we are now near to the ice edge, so we start to turn to the west.

Iceberg Alley

Paulet Island is a tiny island to the south of Joinville Island and Dundee Island on the north-eastern tip of the Antarctic Peninsula. Our approach from the north-east had failed. So now we make for the northern end of Joinville Island with the hope of passing round its northern and western edges and then south through the Antarctic Sound from the north and reaching Paulet Island and its large Adelie penguin colony that way.

When we arrive at the sound at five the next morning the weather is still poor. It is foggy, snowing and there are icebergs everywhere. The sound is known as 'Iceberg Alley' by those that know. We finally get through but only as far as Hope Bay on the mainland. Here, there is an Argentinean Research station, and as

Just one of many tabular icebergs in the Antarctic Strait, or Iceberg Alley.

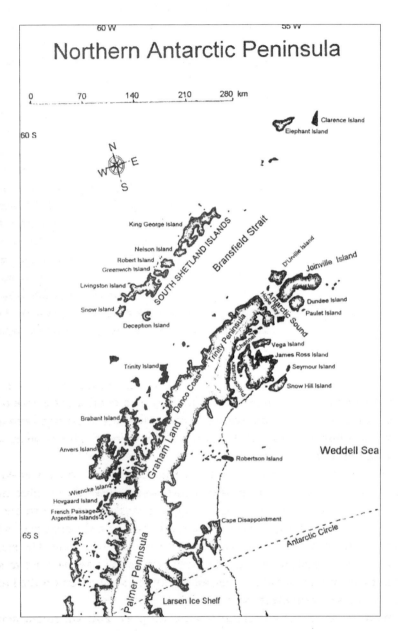

Sketch map showing the Antarctic Peninsula and the places visited.

A cheeky chinstrap penguin takes a close interest in a bright-red coated seal.

the fog clears, there before us is the mainland of Antarctica, a mass of ice, snow and mountains in the sunshine. We are looking at a continent the size of North America with less than a couple of hundred inhabitants, most of whom are only there for the summer anyway. This is the last continent. This is what we have come to see and to set foot on.

Any hope of landing at Hope Bay is now dashed by the wind. A 40-knot gale rises up and the sea is soon a mass of white horses. The wind pushes the loose pack ice against the only shore that it might have been possible to get to in a Zodiac. So, after our voyage to this wonderful continent, the chance of a landing here is taken from us. We must try another place, another time. The ship again slowly turns and we head back up the Antarctic Sound passing close to some of a large number of huge tabular bergs, all of which have broken off the Larsen Ice Shelf, as they always do every year.

The plan to reach Paulet Island is now dropped and we steam across the Brantsfield Strait to Half Moon Island in the South Shetlands group. Half Moon is a small, low, rocky, crescent-shaped island with a sheltered shingle beach. Behind it, the high snow-covered mountains of Livingstone Island provide a magnificent backdrop. Half Moon is home to a small colony of chinstrap penguins, so named because they have a black chinstrap marking running from their black caps under their white chins and beaks. They are small birds and some were struggling up the ice at the back of the beach while others were tobogganing down to the beach.

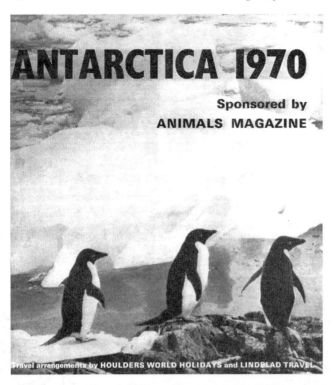

Left: A brochure from *Lindblad Explorer*, the first expedition cruise ship. (J&C McCutcheon Collection)

Below: Marco Polo at Port Lockroy being watched by a gentoo penguin.

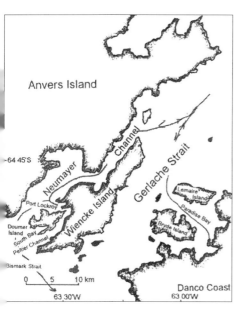

Above: Sketch map of the Neumayer Channel and the route taken.

Right: Sketch map showing the Le Maire Channel and Booth Island.

To watch them from their low level and to be more comfortable I lie down on the beach behind the ice edge and wait. After a minute or so, one of them stops on his way to the sea. He has spotted me. He leaves his pals and sets off towards me in a very businesslike manner. He gets to about 10 feet and then stops; peers at me from top to toe then he moves closer. He gets to about 3 or 4 feet away and stops again. What is he going to do? He peers even harder at me and I am sure that he is going to give me a peck to see if I will do anything. He then obviously decides that I am just a boring, bright-red seal and not of much interest, so he turns on his heel and marches back to his pals with his report.

Marco Polo enters a misty and gloomy Le Maire Channel.

At Last, the Mainland

We sail for Paradise Bay in Graham Land on the Antarctic Peninsula and arrive there at eight o'clock the next morning in the middle of a blizzard. It is supposed to be one of the most beautiful spots on the coast but due to the weather we see nothing of it. We go ashore and at last set foot on the mainland of Antarctica. This is a real thrill. Even in the snow and cloud it is a special and spectacular place as the Antarctic ice cap reaches down to the sea. High, vertical, forbidding white cliffs of ice and snow hang silently above the bay; their tops invisible in the drifting cloud and making them seem even more threatening. Bergy bits and small growlers sit in the waters off the beach and the only movement is from a few Gentoo penguins scuttling about the shoreline. The scene has not changed in thousands and perhaps millions of years; yet like all of Antarctica it is only in the last 100 years that man has known about it and only in the last twenty years that people have been able visit and to marvel at its fantastic isolation and beauty. The ice ridges from the main ice cap come down to the water's edge, leaving only a few feet of tide-cleared shingle beach to walk on. We walk round the small bay as far as we can and paddle in our boots in the crystal clear sea by a large grounded bergy bit.

Our voyage continues down the Neumayer Channel, a narrow channel running between Anvers Island and Wiencke Island, where we spot three large humpback whales swimming south and further down the channel we see some smaller minke whales. Both are baleen whales that feed by draining krill through the baleen strips that hang from the top of their mouths. Both species are endangered but the humpback is more endangered as there are fewer of them than the minke whales. After a scenic sail down the Neumayer Channel, with its ice-clad mountainsides, we arrive off Port Lockroy on Wiencke Island, the site of a former UK base. The scenery in the islands is stunning. White mountains, with the sun playing hide and seek through the swirling clouds, the constantly changing light highlighting a different area of mountain and ice then casting it into grey, blue shadow. It is so still now, there is not a breath of wind and the sea is like a piece of wet, grey slate. Once ashore, the sun breaks through to reveal even more spectacular mountains, many of which have not even been named let alone been climbed.

The following day, we pass through the spectacular Lemaire Channel between Booth Island and the mainland. It is shorter, but narrower, than the Neumayer and often choked with ice so we are lucky that it is clear for us. The black, snow-scattered, near-vertical mountain sides rise straight out of the sea on both sides of the ship and vanish into the mists above. The engine noise of the ship echoes back off the rock walls as we slide slowly through the still, black waters.

Drake's Passage and Cape Horn

We exit the strait and enter the Bellinghausen Sea. After reaching 65 degrees 12 minutes south, we turn north and head for the Drake Passage and Cape Horn 600 miles away. It is Christmas Eve and, as we turn towards the north, the fog descends and Antarctica rapidly vanishes into the mist. After a short while it might not have been there at all. It is easy to understand how early explorers failed to find it for so long. My lasting feelings were that I must go back again and I still plan to one day.

'This bacon is not crispy!' Clearly others on board had other things to worry about! When we went down for lunch we found ourselves sitting near to two middle-aged English ladies who we had seen about the ship. They never seemed to be too happy about life. Today, they were both arguing with the waiter about their club sandwiches. 'It is not properly toasted. The crispy bacon in it was not crisp and there was too little dressing on the salad. This really is not acceptable.' Here we are in Antarctica, at the southern end of the Drake Passage on Christmas Eve with a storm forecast, and their major interest was the bacon in their sandwich.

On Christmas Day, the westerly wind rises again and the sea starts to get up. The ship is due to be off Cape Horn at about four o'clock this afternoon. However, with the wind and weather deteriorating, there is a concern that we will not see the Horn. By early afternoon, a big beam sea is making the ship roll and waves are starting to come over the bow. The spray lashes across the upper

Cape Horn emerges through the
murk, the graveyard of many
ships and sailors.

decks and rattles on the windows. The upper decks are soon put out of bounds.
At about a 3.45 p.m., disregarding the out-of-bounds warning, people start to go
out on deck to try and see if we can see the Horn. Ahead of the ship all we can
see is a grey murk. Suddenly, a woman in a yellow parka points excitedly out to
starboard and we follow her arm. There, off the starboard bow, emerging from
the cloud, is the instantly recognisable dark shape of Cape Horn. A hunched
mass of rock, its sharp, pointed peak and sheer southern face point defiantly to
the south. The wind continues to rise, up to 40 knots with the seas getting up
to 20 or 25 feet high. It is a brilliant sight, to actually be here seeing something
that you have only ever read of in clipper ship histories or lone yachtsmen's
journals. Now we are there seeing it with our own eyes. The sun breaks through
and, in spite of the spray and the howling wind, it shines on the Horn itself. This
legendary lump of rock that has been written about by many but seen by few
is the last piece of land at the tip of South America. So many sailing ships have
been wrecked and sailors' lives lost at its feet and on the islands close by, while
trying to sail round it. Most of them are unrecorded, ships that were just posted
'Missing'. Of those that did get round it, either after the long run from Australia,
or going the other way, to windward, coming from Europe and going up to Chile
and the west coast of America, most never even saw the Horn. Either they were

too far south or the Horn was lost in clouds or darkness. Some of those ships that tried to sail round it to the west spent literally weeks tacking to and fro across the Drake Passage trying to edge past the Horn. Some gave up and turned round then sailed eastwards downwind all the way to the west coast of America via the Indian Ocean and past Australia, just to save the ships from the pounding that the seas off the Horn could give them.

The *Marco Polo* holds her course heading north-west as if she is carrying on into the Pacific Ocean. When she is about 3 or 4 miles west of the Horn she turns to the east, down wind and sea and steams past Cape Horn. We sail 'Round the Horn' on Christmas Day. In the traditional maritime sense of the old wind jammers, we have not sailed 'Round the Horn'. The Horn lies at exactly 56 degrees south and in the days of sail to claim that the ship had sailed 'Round the Horn' she must sail from 50 degrees south in one ocean round to 50 degrees south in the other. However, we have sailed 'past' Cape Horn. Once we are clear and the fearsome Horn falls astern we go below, back into the warmth for some Christmas 'cheer' and a piece of Christmas stollen cake; something that the sailors on the wind jammers would not have been able to do.

Once past Horn Island the ship turns north and heads for Ushuaia at the eastern end of the Beagle Channel. The ship is soon in the lee of the islands that are the last remnants of the southern tips of the Andes as they disappear beneath the Drake Passage before they re-emerge as the Antarctic Peninsula. Once in their lee, the sea calms down considerably and the wind drops away. We even managed a short stroll on deck before the formal Christmas gala dinner. What a day!

Beagle Channel

The final leg of the voyage was up the Beagle Channel and out into the Pacific Ocean then back into the Cockburn Channel before turning into the Straits of Magellan. This whole area is spectacular, with pointed high mountains, glaciers and natural forests. We had a fantastic, calm, sunny day for our trip through the Beagle Channel, which, so we were told, is highly unusual. The guides kept saying 'This weather never happens. It is always cloudy, very windy and wet here.' The Beagle Channel, named by Charles Darwin after his ship, seemed to go on forever, with hundreds of islands and rocks along the way. Navigation must be difficult but thankfully the water is deep. So we found our way into the Cockburn Channel and then into the wide expanse of the Straits of Magellan. The mountains had gone and the landscape was flat and agricultural with just low hills in the distance. The Strait was wide and we could not see the other side.

Throughout the voyage, Lars-Eric Lindblad kept us fully up to the minute with his chats from the bridge, telling us what was, or was not, happening and why we were going to do whatever it was. He was a wonderful man and so enthusiastic

Marco Polo at Punta
Arenas showing off her
lost paint caused by the
storm in the Southern
Ocean.

about everything. His enthusiasm was contagious and his love for and concerns over Antarctica were very evident. He was determined that Antarctica must remain a pristine reserve and must not be damaged in anyway by tourists, industries or others and, equally, he knew that only by taking people to Antarctica will the general public develop strong feelings for the preservation of the continent. He was, I am sure, always trying to get Captain Eric, from Norway, to take the ship into places that the captain would rather not go but between them they made sure that we always did something memorable and exciting, and we did get to most of the places that Lars-Eric had hoped to take us. The lectures on board all carried this message throughout the voyage as well as providing masses of information about this fantastic continent, such as details of its geological history as well as its exploration and its wildlife. Every day we seemed to learn something new about penguins, seals, whales or albatrosses. Lars-Eric was a true champion for the Antarctic with his 'Leave only footprints and take only memories' motto. It is thanks to him that the controls governing visiting ships and how people behave ashore were put into place. Lars-Eric sadly died in 1994.

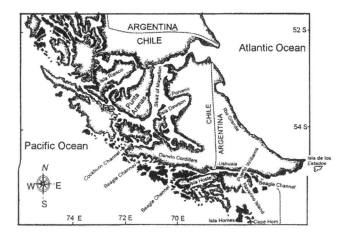

Sketch map of Tierra Del Fuego showing the route of *Marco Polo* to Ushuaia, through the Beagle and Cockburn Channels then into the Straits of Magellan and on to Punt Arenas.

We finally docked at Punta Arenas and left the ship. They wanted us off the ship so they could clean it for the next trip later that day and so we were taken for the afternoon to The Cape Horn Hotel. The ship organised a buffet dinner for us that evening at an out of town eatery before we were taken out to the airport for the overnight charter flight back to Miami, via Santiago. Unfortunately, everyone who ate the chicken dishes at the buffet went down with chronic food poisoning on the flight. The aircraft toilets were blocked off as they were full and it then took over two hours before we could get off the plane in Miami as the US Port Health had to get the sick off to hospital and interview everyone else. Doreen and I had looked at the chicken but decided it looked dodgy anyway so left it alone. Thank goodness we did! We spent twenty-four hours in Miami and finally arrived home exhausted but elated after a real 'trip of a lifetime'.

Of all the places we visited and in spite of the fantastic ice caps, glacier fronts and mountains of Antarctica itself, South Georgia was the place that made the strongest impressions on me with its own climate, its history, the spectacular scenery and incredible wildlife. Now, there is a place I would really love to visit again.

CHAPTER 11

Professor Molchanov –
NE Greenland

Oh Greenland is a dreadful place,
It's a place that's never green
Where there's ice and snow
And the whale fishes blow
And the daylight's seldom seen.

So goes one of the verses of a sea shanty about the Greenland whale fishery sung by whalers in the eighteenth and early nineteenth centuries. It is not a bad summary of Greenland in winter. It is a huge and inaccessible place to visit and parts of it are still virtually unknown to the outside world, in particular the east and north-east coasts.

The Vikings discovered Greenland in about AD 1000 and settled along the green, southern tip and up the west coast, but the northern parts on both coasts remained virtually uninhabited. Apart from a thin coastal strip, Greenland is totally covered in a vast, deep, ice cap. This ice cap is thousands of feet thick and where it breaks through to the coast massive glaciers tumble down into the sea, often at the head of long, deep fjords.

After the Vikings in the tenth century, the first European to venture up the east coast of Greenland was the English mariner Henry Hudson, of Hudson Bay fame. In the 1570s, in his ship the *Hopewell*, he was searching for the north-west Passage. Hudson named the area he was in at 73 degrees north as 'Hold with Hope' and this is the first English recorded place name in the area, although doubtless the earlier Thule and Inuit inhabitants had their own names. Hudson did not find the north-west Passage and on a subsequent trip in 1611, during another search for the north-west Passage, he worked his way up the west coast to the Baffin Bay area. There his crew mutinied and having overcome Hudson and the officers, they cast Hudson, his young son and seven men adrift in a small boat without food or water. They were never seen again.

It was then not until the early 1800s, when Arctic whalers started to sail in the area, that any interest was taken. Among them was a Yorkshire whaler from Whitby, called William Scoresby. In the ships *Baffin* and *Fame* he sailed along the east coast in his search for whales, but in doing so he logged everything he saw. Explorers followed; Douglas Clavering and Edward Sabine separately explored the coast and the place names reflect their work. (Clavering Oy and Sabine Oy, for example). Oy is Inuit for island. The whalers continued to make discoveries and added new names as they went; Jameson Land and Liverpool Land, an area of high, jagged, mountain peaks and fjords that is totally unlike Liverpool and the Mersey estuary. After that, several expeditions under Swedish, French and Danish leaderships charted the north-east coast giving European names to the places as they went. From the west, the American, Robert Peary, spent twenty-three years exploring the north-west coast and, in 1892, got across the ice cap to Kap Bridgeman on the very northern tip of Greenland. It was Peary who proved that Greenland was an island with no connection to any land further north. In 1907, a Danish expedition team, led by Lt Johan Pater Koch, got to Kap Bridgeman from the east, so completing the exploration of the coast round Greenland.

The Greenland ice cap was first crossed by Fridtjof Nansen and five companions in 1888. Since then, a few expeditions have crossed it, notably in 1988, when a multinational expedition which included a Russian glaciologist, Dr Victor Boyarsky, who we were to meet later, crossed the Greenland ice cap with dogs from the southern end to the north-west coast, (the long route) as a training exercise! They did this before they crossed Antarctica with dog teams in the 1989/90.

One of the reasons that I was keen to visit the north-east coast was the fact that, apart from the early explorers and whalers, very few people had ever been there. I wanted to see the seas, mountains and fjords that were familiar to whalers like William Scoresby. Scoresby came from Whitby and was a whaler's son who stowed away on his father's ship when he was ten. He became not only a famous and successful whaling captain but a scientist of note, for his work carried out in the Arctic. On his voyages he recorded all the information he could on the weather, ice, whales and the land. In 1822, a year when the ice on east Greenland receded to leave clear water up to the coast, he explored over 400 miles of coast line charting and recording the features and giving them names including, of course Scoresbysund. It is actually named after his father. Scoresby put all his findings and narratives of whaling into a famous two-volume work called *An Account of the Arctic Regions*. I wanted to visit the seas described so graphically in the whalers log books where they recorded tales of their boats being capsized, whales lost, overwintering in the ice in leaky ships, men falling into the icy seas and all the daily perils of nineteenth-century Arctic whaling.

The Trip

I had read of a trip, the aim of which was to sail west from Spitzbergen across the remotest part of the Arctic Ocean and the Greenland Sea, along the southern edge of the ice pack and then down the north-east coast of Greenland visiting what fjord systems and sites it could dependent upon the ice and weather. The ship was then to cross the Denmark Sraight, head south and land in Iceland. This expedition is based on the Russian expedition ship *Professor Molchanov*, a converted Russian research vessel and able to carry about fifty persons.

To join the ship for this trip we first had to get to Spitzbergen. We arrive in Longyearbyen, the main town in Spitzbergen, late at night after the flight from London via Oslo and Tromso. We are met at the airport by a tall, fair-haired young man, called Peter, who is over-enthusiastic and announces that he is our expedition leader. 'Get your bags quickly! It is late we must hurry!' A few of us look at each other with some concern. After getting our bags from the baggage area, we congregate around the bus and wonder what we are in for. The party are dropped off singly and in pairs at various hotels and hostels around the town. We noted that out leader was not for waiting to see if the customer was able to get into their hotel or not. As soon as they were off the bus with their bags he ordered the driver to drive off. Doreen and I are dropped off at an expedition hostel outside the town. The place is deserted and mostly in darkness apart from a girl in the reception area, who has waited just for us. Once she has given us our key she climbs onto her scooter and leaves for home. Our room is in a different building about 200 yards down the road. We find our way there and discover that

Professor Mulchanov in the still waters at the head of Scorebysund, Greenland. Formerly a research vessel, this Russian ship makes an ideal expedition vessel.

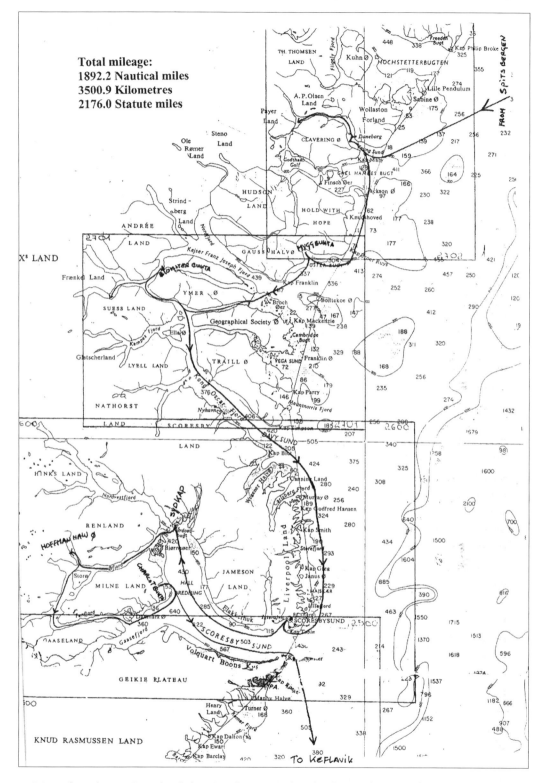

Map of north-east Greenland showing the route taken by the *Professor Mulchanov*.

the room has just one single bed. After a night with both of us crammed into this small single bed, we are up early to look round Longyearbyen before joining the ship.

On the way along the road to the jetty, we talk to a Dutch couple, John and Margarete. John is a retired marine engineer in the merchant marine and has similar interests to myself. Margarete is a friendly and down-to-earth lady who allows nothing to go by without good reason. We discussed our arrival at the airport and the expedition leader's behaviour. We agree it is not a good start. As we walk onto the jetty, having met up with some more of our fellow shipmates, all we can see of the ship is the top half of her white superstructure. The *Professor Molchanov* is not big. She was built in Finland in 1983 for the Russian Government as a polar and oceanic research vessel. She was 72 metres long and 1,753 tons.

As soon as we are all on board we set sail. Our cabin is comfortable, but basic. We have an upper and a lower bunk, a small bench seat by a porthole, a desk and a bathroom with a shower. As we will only be in it for sleeping, it proves ideal, apart from the fact that the bunk is a bit on the short side for a tall fellow like me. The dining room is more 'canteen messing' than 'haute cuisine' but the food is simple but good and well cooked by the Russian cook. A small working deck at the stern, with a hydraulic crane, provides a good stowage and working area for the Zodiac rubber boats. The ship operates an open-bridge policy for passengers, which means that we are able to go on the bridge at any time. The skipper and watch-keeping officers, who were all Russians, are friendly and helpful and in spite of imperfect English they always try hard to answer any questions. We are relieved to learn that 'I am the Expedition Leader' Peter from last night, is not the leader, just the deputy leader. We meet the actual leader at the first briefing. He is a dour Dutchman called Rene.

The trip across to east Greenland is uneventful. The ice edge that we hope to see is reportedly some 100 miles to the north at 81 degrees and it is deemed by Rene, to be too far out of our way to get to even though everyone on board is keen to see the edge of the pack ice. We start to get to know more of our fellow explorers. There are a number of Dutch people and they are good company and we strike up friendships with them. There is Derek and Anne from Salcombe. They are a charming, easy going and friendly couple. Even though Derek walks with a stick, he is an enthusiast for the old Brixham sailing trawlers and spends most summers on board one. We also have a Japanese film actress, who we are told is very famous in Japan, but of whom none of us have heard. She travels with two male companions and everywhere she goes, on board or ashore, she clutches a soft toy polar bear. It turns out to be the only polar bear we see on this trip.

We spend our time on the bridge watching the Greenland Sea go by as we sail across a calm, empty ocean with just the odd small iceberg drifting in the sun. Because the ice edge was well to the north we hope that this means that most of the fjords are free of ice so we can visit parts of the coast normally cut off by the ice even in summer. Greenland is Danish and a large part of north-east Greenland is a vast national park and entry by non-Danish groups is not permitted. We need both a Dane on the trip and the permission from the Danish Government to land there. So, on our team, we have a Danish naturalist who has been asked to join the expedition to enable permission to be granted.

One of the other passengers with whom we strike up a friendship is a Swede, travelling on his own, called Per Magnus. He is a warm and friendly guy who runs his own polar travel business in Sweden called Polar Quest. He is here as some of his clients are on the ship and he is also keen to see how this expedition, run by the Dutch, works out as he is planning to run his own expeditions to similar areas. Per Magnus is calm, sensible and very aware of peoples' different needs and capabilities, and speaks easily and with confidence about running an expedition such as this. He gives us all a feeling of confidence. He naturally takes a very keen interest in the skills of our leaders on this expedition.

Sirius Patrol

Our land fall is Daneborg and we arrive there mid-afternoon on a dull but calm day. This area, even in summer, is very often ice bound. We anchor in an ice-free

Daneborg, home to the Danish Marine's Sirius Patrol and their dogs. The ship lies at anchor just off shore.

Young Sound. Here, low hills by the water quickly rise to high mountains as the fjord winds its way deep into the mountains. There are large patches of snow still lying on some of the hills and the higher mountains still have their white caps on, but the lower slopes and shoreline are all clear of ice. Daneborg is a Danish Marine camp, set up in 1950 and home to the 'Sirius Patrol'. It is the only military dog sledge patrol anywhere in the world. The name Sirius is taken from the brightest star in the constellation of Canis Major and known as the 'Dog Star'. From the station, the Marines carry out military surveillance and policing patrols throughout the year, round the whole of the north and north-east coasts, using dog teams in winter and boats in summer. The patrols are also a key part of keeping a military surveillance eye on what anyone else may be doing in the area. Greenland is on the route from Russia to the USA and in the Cold War there were concerns about what ambitions the Russians might have had for Greenland.

We go ashore there and meet some of the marines and their dogs. They have over a hundred dogs: big, strong Husky dogs, many of them bred at the station. The twelve or so marines live here for about two years at a time in modern, well-equipped huts that make up the camp. Needless to say, the whole camp has an aura of being well organised, as it has to be to survive without any outside contact for most of the year as well as carrying out the patrols and caring for the dogs. Their patrols consist of two-man teams with ten or eleven dogs to each team pulling one large sledge. As the sledges have to carry everything that the whole team is ever likely to need for many weeks at a time, including all the dog food, they can weigh between 300 and 500 kilos each. The patrols can often last up to four months; so the dogs are bred for endurance pulling rather than speed. These are not racing sled dogs but true beasts of burden. They are all highly trained and well cared for and all of them wanted to be petted and told how fine they were. At feeding time they all sit patiently by their bowls in their allocated spaces, with their food already down in front of them. When all the dogs have their bowls put out, then the marine gives a one-word command and the dogs are instantaneously head and shoulders into the bowls, eating furiously.

On their patrols they also check that the emergency huts in the area are properly secure from weather and polar bear damage. If a bear can smell any trace of food it will try to break into the hut and a number have been found totally wrecked by bears. The huts we visit on the coast are all of a similar style and size. They can be used by hunters caught out in bad weather or anyone who needs an emergency shelter. They are small but big enough for two or three people to use in an emergency and equipped with just a stove for heat and cooking and some basic food. They have a stock of firewood and always a box of matches on the table with one projecting out of the box so anyone with frozen fingers can get hold of it easily to light the fire. There is normally a bottle of whisky there too and some blankets or fur pelts for warmth.

Walks

Our trip takes us down the coast with several ventures ashore seeing walrus, white Arctic hare and musk ox on the way. We go on a number of walks into the interior, walking in remote, empty valleys and on hills that few people have even seen let alone walked. At Clavering Oy, once we are ashore, the leader divides us into two small groups. One group is to head for a walk around a hill while the other group could wander along the shoreline or immediate hinterland at their own pace. The hill walk group are a mixed age group with a few who are definitely senior citizens and others who are not that naturally athletic. We all want to see what we comfortably can of the place. The young deputy leader, Peter, is to lead this walk. Some of the party ask him if he knows the route and if it is suitable for us as we are all wearing the wellington boots we needed for the wet shore landings from the Zodiacs and not proper walking boots. He assures us it will be fine. Our enthusiastic young friend then sets off up a 40-foot high scree slope of loose rocks and stones. We scatter for safety as loose rocks slither and fall down the slope, landing and crashing all about us as he races for the top. We yell at him to stop but he is oblivious to us. This is not a good start. This splits up the group as we all have to wait until the loose rocks have stopped sliding and coming down on us before some try to follow him up the scree slope and others look for a better way round the hill. Once we have all got to the top we find that our leader has already set off across open ground, thick with clumps of tussock grass and wet, marshy areas. We let him race on and follow at our own pace enjoying the scenery and views. After a while he stops and, when we have caught up, he leads us up into the higher uplands where we do have fantastic views of the interior. A beautiful, wild, and empty valley seeming to stretch away forever, rushing streams pouring off the hills and musk ox grazing in the far distance by a wide rocky river. Beyond that the mountains loom and behind them the white flecks of the ice cap itself shine in the sunshine.

He leads us on across the moor where progress is naturally slow as there are no animal tracks to follow so we each cautiously make our own way through the tussocks and round the bogs and become spread out right across the hill top. Then we drop down the side of a hill into the main river valley. Peter announces from way ahead that we have to cross the river even though doing so will mean that we will have to find a different beach, for the Zodiacs to collect us, from the sheltered beach we had used to get ashore. The river is rock-strewn and fast running but thankfully today relatively shallow, about 3 feet at the deepest points. It is perhaps 50 or 60 feet wide but the river bed is made up of round, wet and very slippery rocks. In a flash, our young leader splashes across it and then sits resting on the opposite bank, proud of his efforts. The rest of us, however, have to select our own routes across, and while guiding and holding one another, ensure that the more elderly and less agile are able to make their way over without falling in or twisting an ankle. Eventually, we all make it and we head back towards the coast. Here, as we feared, the shoreline is both steep and exposed and the waves are high and crash onto the beach.

As we predicted, we are also now cut off by the river mouth from the other group and the Zodiacs. After a delay and radio mix-ups the Zodiacs find us. However, the waves here are too high for them to come straight onto the beach, but the crewmen try. Twice the Zodiacs are flooded as they try to get onto the beach bows first then finally they come into the beach stern first, which puts the outboard motors at great risk. This also means that we have to wade out further into the waves and time our boarding leap to try and avoid the bigger waves and surf. Two people are knocked over by the waves and need to be manhandled into the boat and end up in wet, crumpled heaps of boots, parkas, cameras and bags on the flooded floor of the Zodiac. Finally, everyone manages to get on board and we go back to the ship, albeit wetter than we had planned. However, the trip has shown us some fantastic scenery and the experience of hill walking in rubber wellies.

In north-east Greenland we are very isolated from the rest of the world. It is easy when you are on a well-run ship, with good food and warm bunks, to feel that nothing can go wrong. After all this is a just 'Soft Adventure' and nothing can happen to you. However, in remote places, such as this, a simple slip or a fall on wet rocks or wet grass can easily lead to broken bones and, if it happens when you are well away from the beach and the ship, this can quickly turn into a major survival exercise. If, when you fall, you are out of sight and hearing of anyone else you may not be immediately missed. If the weather then changes, or a radio fails to work, or a rising wind and heavy surf prevent the Zodiacs getting back inshore, then these factors will conspire against you as they often do in emergencies. A constant awareness of your circumstances is needed all the time. Even if in the event of a serious accident people can get you back to the ship then a hospital and qualified medical help are not available until the ship takes you to one, which may be many hundreds of miles away. Any good leader will always have all these factors under constant review and be aware of the capabilities of the weakest members of the team. It seems that our young leader must have been away from expedition leader course on the day they covered that.

The Fjords and Icebergs

Our first sightings of icebergs is at the entrance to Kaiser Frans Joseph Fjord where the bergs sit, silent and gleaming, in the sun on a mirror calm, blue sea. We sail past them and up Sophia Sound into the narrow Antarctic Sound, where the setting sun is turning the whole landscape a glorious warm, reddish orange colour. The bare red mountains rear up from the fjord and as the sun sinks so a hard black shadow slowly moves across the hillside and replaces the sunlit orange, as we continue deep into the fantastic fjord systems of East Greenland.

The following morning the ship anchors at Ymer Oy, an island deep in the fjord system. There is no wind, we are totally sheltered on all sides by the mountains. After a short walk ashore we set off in the Zodiacs to explore some of the icebergs nearby. Per Magnus takes one of the Zodiacs and invites his clients and a few others, including Doreen and I, to join him for a tour round the icebergs. Unlike our Dutch deputy leader, who proceeds to roar off round the fjord with his passengers hanging on grimly, Per Magnus hardly uses the engine. Now, when we are right alongside the icebergs and looking up at them from sea level we stop, switch off the engine and let the Zodiac drift on the flat, deep, black water. Then we just watch and listen and appreciate their size and beauty even more. The ice itself takes so many different forms. Sometimes it is a solid impenetrable white mass; sometimes it is totally transparent. Sometimes it is like a delicate filigree sculpture and riddled with holes. In some of the icebergs ridges and scratch marks show where they have torn at the seabed or land on their journey into the sea. In others we see straight lines of transparent blue ice running right through an opaque white mass. Most of them have erosion lines made by the sea water and waves washing at their bases and most also show signs that they have toppled over and capsized at some time as the water erosion lines rise up at acute angles from the present waterline. In the sun, the icebergs gleam and glisten with a dazzling whiteness against the black, shadowed sides of the fjords, yet when they are in the shadow they become grey and flat; losing all their angular shapes and lustre. All the time, as the sun shines warmly on them, there is a gentle noise of water dripping off the iceberg into the sea or gurgling as it runs down hidden channels deep inside the ice. Their colours vary with the light, from pure white through greys and vivid blues to pale greens. As we look down into the water, we see that the white colours gently give way to soft greens, then to deeper greens and blues before they vanish into the black of the cold, deep water. The icebergs come in all shapes; some are flat-topped, some are sculptured like giant statues, some have tall pinnacles and some are rounded and smooth, while others are rough and jagged. The icebergs are continually changing, their shapes change with perspective and viewing angles; their colours change with the sun, which throws deep, dark, blue shadows across the shaded sides of the iceberg that contrasts strongly with the bright sunny side. Every iceberg is different; every one of them fascinating in its shapes, its ice forms and its colours. Later, as we watch from the ship, one of the bergs that we had motored round earlier slowly rolls over and settles into a new position. Waves wash out from it as it settles.

We sail on deeper into the Kaiser Frans Joseph Fjord system right to the head of the fjord. This fjord is thousands of feet deep and the sheer-sided mountains along its side are thousands of feet high. This is a real fjord; long, deep, dark, brooding and silent with the mountain cliffs climbing vertically from the black depths up to unseen peaks behind the high shoulders of the cliffs that form the walls of the fjord. Big icebergs sit silent and unmoving in the black shadows of the fjord. As we move slowly through these deep shadows we are sometimes illuminated, as if by a searchlight, as a shaft of sunlight cuts through a gap in the mountains. Occasionally, we see a pure white iceberg sitting in a totally black background as the sun catches it against the deep shadow of the cliffs. It sits like an imperfectly shaped pearl on a cushion of black velvet.

No one speaks as we all stand on deck and try and absorb the sheer splendour of this fjord.

We leave the fjord late in the afternoon and head south down the Kong Oscar Fjord, a beautiful, wide fjord between Traill Oy and the mainland. Gradually, the mountains recede and the land opens out on each side as we head towards the open sea. Later in the night we are given a small show by the Northern Lights. For ten or fifteen minutes, the soft green, silky trails dip and ripple across the sky like a silk curtain, before they fade and leave us alone in a black, empty sea.

Dawn brings us to a white mountainous coast on a clear sunny morning. The ship rolls gently along in a sparkling blue sea. Away to starboard, we can see the jagged, snow-capped mountains of Liverpool Land. The chart reveals the mixed history of this area and the nationalities of those who came here first; with Kap Godfried Hansen followed by Kap Smith; Canning Land followed by Carlsberg Fjord.

Icebergs, one clear and one white, lie at peace in the sunshine.

Scoresbysund

We enter the biggest fjord system in the world, Scoresbysund. It stretches over 300 miles inland and comprises many islands and smaller fjords. Its entrance, between Cape Brewster and Cape Tobin, is relatively narrow at about 15 to 20 miles wide. As we enter we can see the mountains of Cape Brewster shining away to the south. We sail into the massive fjord and head for the main settlement of Ittoqqortoormiit, or Scoresbysund. It was set up in 1925 by settlers from Ammassalik, some 500 miles to the south. The aim was to enable them to develop a community using the traditional hunting skills of their Inuit forefathers. From the sea, the village looks attractive with the coloured wooden houses of red, blue, pastel green, some white, all sitting in a haphazard way on the hillside and with roads leading down to a small, sheltered quay. However, initial appearances can be deceptive. When we get ashore we find that the only road is a wet, muddy track, littered with old and broken sledges, old packing cases and bikes, while loose barking dogs roam the streets. The crew warn us not to pet them as these are not trained sledge dogs, but scavenging strays that wander the town. A small Inuit girl of about four or five years old follows us around at a distance, staring silently at us all the time. She is wearing a fantastic blue-black sealskin coat that reaches her feet and is topped by a fur hood. Wooden racks of drying seal, ox and polar bear skins are scattered around. Alcohol is clearly a problem for some here too; although we were assured that a moratorium on spirits has helped the problem. Of the 500 or so people only about thirty are actually hunters, the remainder that are in work are in social services of some sort and very under-employed. The locals are friendly and happy to let us wander about and look at their town but once we had done the tour the only thing to do was to go back on board. Per Magnus knows someone here and goes off to find him. The man was a hunter who had just returned from a trip up the fjord and reported that there are narwhals in Scoresbysund at the moment.

We sail that evening and head into the fjord but only after circling a large iceberg in the bay which is constantly changing colour as the sun sets in the west while we look at it from all points of the compass. The following day, having steamed up the fjord overnight, we are greeted by a majestic sight of many huge icebergs floating in the still waters of the fjord. The fjord at this point is very wide, more like an inland sea than a fjord. These bergs are all many times larger than the ship and we thread our way through them towards Norosti Bukta and Nordvest Fjord. We go ashore and for a couple of hours we just sit on a rock and watch, entranced as iceberg after iceberg drifts out of Nordvest Fjord into the main fjord. Although they are moving slowly, when we watch them against the background of the mountains they appear to be racing out of the fjord. Nordvest Fjord leads up into a mountain range known as the Staunning Alps and from where we are we could see why it is so called. The sparkling white peaks peep out over the nearer mountains, resembling a Swiss

Left: A towering berg floats out of Nordevest Fjord into Scvoresbysund.

Below: Slow ahead as we weave between the icebergs.

scene. At its head, the fjord is fed by the Greenland ice cap. It is impossible for the ship to find a way up Nordvest Fjord due to the number of bergs and the speed at which they are all moving. This is a one-way street. These icebergs are tens of feet high, some must have been well over 100-feet-high, and our ship is often lost behind them as she manoeuvres in the open water of the main fjord to avoid them. Later that afternoon, as we sail off to the west, we look back. The sun has now moved round and the icebergs have become silhouetted. The sea has become a silver glistening mirror on which sits a monochrome of dozens of black icebergs.

We sail right up to the far end of the fjord system, or at least as far as we can. We stop near the top and a few of us go ashore for a walk up a little beautiful glen by the Rypefjord. Ellie, a spirited and chatty Dutch lady, who must have been in her eighties, led the way. I call it a glen because that is what it reminded me of, a lovely, empty, peaceful, Scottish highland glen. The slightly marshy glen floor is covered in wild flowers and tiny shrubs and berries, all of which seem to be blooming together and the rich colours of rusty reds, corals and yellows form sweeps of carpet across the rocks and the hillside. We have arrived at the height of the short summer and the glen is in full bloom. A small burn runs down the glen and its gurgling is the only sound to be heard. The hills above step up through raised moorland to the red coloured sandstone mountains basking in the sun behind the glen. We sit on a couple of warm rocks and chat to Ellie about the trip and enjoy the warmth of the sun in this beautiful spot.

Later that night we are very lucky to see about forty narwhals in the distance, but due to the ice we cannot follow them. Some hunters, who are camping in the area, come out to the ship that evening and tell us that they had seen a school of about 100 narwhals earlier in the day in the same location.

Our passage round the back of Milne Land is stopped by a field of broken pack ice made up of glacier bergy bits and small icebergs. The ship tries to nudge and push her way through but it proves difficult. That night, as the sun sets, the shadows of the hills to the west fall across the lower hills of Milne Land to the east and turn them black; but as the sun still shines on the snow of the higher hill tops it looks as if they had been set on fire, so brilliant is the sunset. Above the black shadow on the lower slopes, the higher areas are bright flame red then orange as they reach the summits. Here, they soften to yellows and merge with the pure white of the snow on the tops. All these colours are reflected back in the mirror-still waters of the fjord between the floating patches of ice. All too quickly, it fades as the sun sets and the black shadow quickly climbs the hill and puts out the flames, leaving a still scene with the ship surrounded by broken ice and black hills. After a few hours gently feeling our way through, we finally clear the ice and are able to continue down to the south side of the island and then east along the south side of Milne Island.

An iceberg with heavy scouring on its side. A sign that this part had once been at the bottom of the berg.

The Denmark Strait. The *Bismarck* and HMS *Hood*

After three days exploring the inner reaches of Scoresbysund we head out and into the Denmark Strait on a grey, rough and miserable morning. There is now an air of urgency on board as the vibration of the engine throbs through the ship, after days of gentle cruising, as now we are bound for Iceland. Also, a depression is coming up the Denmark Straight from the south and the wind is whipping up the waves into a lumpy and confused sea that makes the ship take on an uncomfortable motion. The clouds close down to the sea and all around us is now grey after days of pure whites.

Professor Mulchanov moves carefully between the huge icebergs in Scoresbysund.

It was through these cold, desolate and grey waters that, in May 1941, the formidable new German battleship *Bismarck*, (50,000-tons) and her escort, the cruiser *Prinz Eugen* (15,000-tons) made their run for the open Atlantic from Germany. They tried to creep down through the Denmark Strait, keeping close to the edge of the pack ice along this coast in the hope that bad weather and the ice would hide them from the Royal Navy. Their aim was to get into the Atlantic and harry the Allied Atlantic convoys. *Bismarck* had to be stopped; and it fell to the Royal Navy's pride, the fast battleship, HMS *Hood* (48,000-tons) with others to try and stop her. *Hood* was classed as a battle cruiser due to her high speed, but as she was the same size and had the same armaments as similar battleships of the time, but was 3 knots faster; she was effectively a 'fast battleship'. HMS *Hood* had been built by John Brown's in Clydebank in 1918 at the end of the First World War and was 'state of the art' in modern warship design and construction at the time. She was, at 48,000 tons, the biggest, longest and fastest warship ever built. She was

Black icebergs. Icebergs silhouetted against a silver sea in Scoresbysund.

armed with 8 x 15-inch guns, which exactly matched those of the new *Bismarck* when they met in 1941. The one weakness she had in 1941 was one that did not exist in 1918 when she was built. Her deck armour was not strong enough to protect her against the new higher trajectory shells used in the Second World War.

The two ships met in battle in the Denmark Strait on 24 May, after the cruisers HMS *Norfolk* and HMS *Suffolk* had located and tracked the *Bismarck* down through the grey murk of the Strait. The engagement did not last long. While closing the *Bismarck*, *Hood* fired her opening salvoes. To the Germans, these looked like great, bright suns in the Arctic sky. The *Bismarck* responded. In an early salvo, a modern, high trajectory shell from the *Bismarck* came straight down onto the *Hood*'s deck, penetrated the relatively thin deck armour and exploded in one of the main magazines. The ship was literally blown to pieces in an instant. Out of 1,419 men, only three survived. There is still conjecture as to whether the German shell penetrated the decks and went directly into the magazine or whether it exploded on the deck near a ready-use ammunition store and it was this explosion that then blew the hole down to the magazine. In any event the result was the same.

What must that battle have been like for the men on both sides in the icy waters of the Denmark Strait? With the grey mist and rain, the bitter wind off the ice to the north and the noise and vibration of the big guns firing, it must have been dreadful. There would be carnage inside the ship as shells hit and exploded in the ship. Flash fires would ripple through the passageways and compartments burning everything and everyone in their path, before anyone can turn out of the way, as the flames exploded into mess decks and gun turrets alike. The screams of dying and trapped men, burning steel shrapnel and white-hot splinters flying around, severing water pipes, steam pipes and electrical cables as well as cutting off power and access for those down below.

The enemy ship would be seen first by the frozen look-outs as a slightly darker grey patch in the patchy grey wall of mist and murk. 'Was that a patch of thicker mist or is there something there?' 'No, just a heavy bank of fog.' The lookout wipes his binocular lenses and looks again. The dark patch is still there but it is getting bigger and darker. It even has a bow wave! Suddenly a ship takes shape and detaches itself from the murk. It is not just a ghostly patch of fog in the far distance, but a solid enemy ship just a couple of miles away! The low, squat, grey hull and the tall superstructures of a modern battleship operating at full speed, its low sharp bows throwing the spray and waves aside as it sliced through the seas with its menacing, deadly main guns pointing straight towards you. It must have been an awesome sight. How the three men from the *Hood* survived is a mystery itself as, after the shock of the explosion,

Sunset on the hills of Milne Land.

Icebergs floating off Milne Land at the West end of Scoresbysund.

the shock of hitting those icy waters would numb and paralyse anyone, never mind any injuries caused by the explosions themselves. Hyperthermia would normally render a man totally helpless in seconds and kill him in minutes. The three survivors were picked up by HMS *Electra* a couple of hours after the explosion.

Bismarck was caught and finally sunk a few days later by swordfish torpedo aircraft from HMS *Ark Royal* and torpedoes from HMS *Dorsetshire*. When she sank, the *Bismarck* suffered an even greater loss of life than the *Hood*. 1,995 died in *Bismarck*, 1,416 died in the *Hood*.

North Cape of Iceland

Our passage through the Denmark Strait is less eventful and later that day the weather improves and we come up to a small school of four or five humpback whales feeding in the rich Icelandic waters off the North Cape. These grounds

A tall berg floats near the entrance to Scoresbysund.

used to be some of the best cod fishing grounds in the Atlantic and always had a number of trawlers from the UK and Europe fishing them. Today, apart from a couple of Icelandic trawlers in the distance, they now seem to be deserted. It was near here, in the Isafjord, that the Hull trawlers *Ross Cleveland* and *Kingston Peridot* were lost in 1968. The whales are escorted by about forty white-beaked dolphins that leap from the waters and swim all around the ship. The big, slow whales just carry on, occasionally rolling slowly over in the water to cast an eye over this new white member of the school and waving a long fin as they glide by. They swim under the ship and they appear placid and relaxed. We stay with the whales for over an hour, transfixed by the serene beauty of these great whales before we reluctantly head for Keflavik, our final destination.

This had been a strange trip in some ways. A polar expedition when we had seen neither sea ice nor polar bears. Yet we had seen some rare and fascinating things and been to places that few have been to before. The Sirius Patrol, the spectacular fjords of north-eastern Greenland, which few people in the world have ever seen and which are just as dramatic as the famed Norwegian fjords: the vastness of the Scoresbysund fjord system and the fantastic icebergs that come from the ice cap into those fjords. Seeing narwhals, even in the distance is a rare event. To me, seeing with my own eyes, things that I have only ever seen pictures of in books and also things that few people have ever seen before is thrilling and satisfying and that makes the experience worthwhile. I recall standing on a small rise on one of the trips into hills and looking down over a crest onto a beautiful river valley, with musk ox grazing way below, the valley framed by hills and backed by great mountains with the ice cap behind it all and thinking 'Has anyone ever looked at this before?'

CHAPTER 12

I/B *Kapitan Dranitsyn* – Franz Joseph Land

From St Petersburg in Russia, take the night train that travels due north and, twenty-eight hours later, you reach the end of the line, Murmansk. Murmansk is the port that was the destination for many of the Arctic convoys in the Second World War and was, until recently, a closed city. It is the naval base for the Soviet Northern Fleet. If you then take a ship and sail due north across the Barents Sea towards the North Pole for two and a half days you reach a group of islands on the edge of the Polar ice cap that are nearer to the North Pole than they are to Murmansk. You will have arrived at Franz Josef Land; a land that, even today, few people have heard of and even fewer have visited.

Franz Joseph Land (FJL) is an archipelago of 191 ice-cap-covered, uninhabitable islands on the northern edge of the Barents Sea. It is about 800 miles due north of Murmansk and 550 miles from the Geographic North Pole. The islands stretch over 100 miles from north to south and about 200 miles from east to west. Franz Josef Land was probably first sighted by Norwegian sealers in about 1765 when they reported sighting land when they were well to the east of Spitzbergen. Then, in 1873, an Austro-Hungarian expedition set sail from Germany in their ship, the *Tegettoff*, to find the north-east Passage. The expedition was led by two men, Julius von Payer and Karl Weyprecht. They never found the north-east Passage. As they sailed eastwards through the Barents Sea, they were suddenly caught by early ice and the ship was trapped. They had no choice but to drift with the ice and pray that one day they would be released. One year later and still frozen in, they looked out over the rail at the endless white fog and ice and then, through a clearing in the fog, they realised that they were looking at two jagged cliffs appearing to the north-west. They named the new land after their Emperor, Arch Duke Franz Josef. They named the cliffs Cape Tegettoff, after their ship. Franz Josef Land was then subsequently claimed by both Norway and Russia until, in 1926, Russia issued a decree stating that it was Russian and imposed a ban on anyone visiting it. It remained closed until 2002 when the Russians allowed one or two small expeditions to visit the islands. Even now it can only be visited during a few brief weeks in high summer due to the ice and, even then, only by a Russian icebreaker.

But why would anyone want to go there? Firstly, because it is reportedly a beautiful area with all the islands having their own ice caps. Secondly, it is a

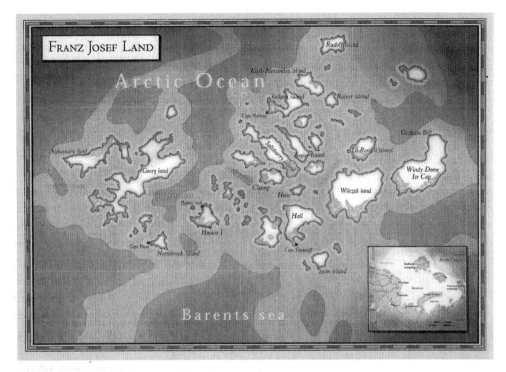

Map showing the islands of Frans Josef Land (inset).

haven for polar wild life – polar bears, walrus, whales as well as birds. Thirdly, it was where Fridtjof Nansen spent the winter of 1895/96 after his attempt to reach the North Pole from his Trans-Polar ship, the *Fram*. He, and his sole companion Johanssen, lived in a hole on a beach on Jackson Island for the whole winter. Having read of Nansen's exploits I want to go there and see the place. And finally, I want to go because it has the most northerly point of land in Europe or Asia, Cape Fligely, on Rudolf Island. Only the most northerly point of Ellesmere Island in Canada is nearer to the North Pole.

I wrote to Per Magnus at Polar Quest in Sweden. We had met him on the Greenland trip and I asked him whether he knew of any plans for expeditions to Franz Josef Land. He wrote back saying that he was in touch with a Russian Expedition Company that was thinking of mounting an icebreaker expedition to FJL the following year. 'If the icebreaker company, the Murmansk Shipping Corporation, committed to the trip, were we interested?' he emailed us. 'Yes, we are!' All went well, forms were filled in, deposits paid, visas sought and travel plans made. All was looking good but then, two months before the departure, the Murmansk Shipping Corporation cancelled the voyage saying there were not enough people wanting to go to make it worthwhile. Maybe they would plan it again the following year, if they got enough people. If not then the chances of anyone organising a trip to FJL were pretty remote and our chance to get there could have gone for good. We really thought that our chance had gone, but we had no choice, we had to just wait and see. Happily for us, the following year, the Russians did set up the trip again and this time enough people were interested, so we were on again.

Murmansk

The *Kapitan Dranitsyn* is a Russian icebreaker, operated by the Murmansk Shipping Corporation and based in Murmansk. She and her sister ships, including a fleet of nuclear-powered icebreakers, keep the northern sea route open throughout the year. To join the ship we have to go to Murmansk and that in itself is very special. Murmansk is the headquarters of the Russian Northern Fleet and a major submarine base. Having been in the Royal Navy during the Cold War and having sailed along the northern coast of Russia in RN warships and UK Trawlers, Murmansk is a place of mystery. You read about it in spy thrillers, or you heard of allied submarines watching the coast 'off Murmansk' but no one I knew had ever actually been there. What sort of place is it really? It is reputedly a desolate and miserable place where sunshine, food and happiness are scarce. You felt that military security ruled the town and all that goes on there and that greatcoat-clad, rifle-touting guards watched every street corner and anyone without the correct papers is a spy. The only people who lived there only did so because the Russian Government had sent them there either as part of the Navy or to support the Navy. Was it really going to be like that?

In Helsinki Airport, we meet up with the others going on the trip and then fly on by a special charter flight to Murmansk to join the ship. Per Magnus, who has arranged the trip for a total of about eight people, has sent one of his senior staff to accompany us. Her name is Carina, she is a slim, no-nonsense, Swedish lady in her early thirties, who tries hard to answer our questions and keep us together as a group. Most of the others on the trip are German with their own German guide.

We fly north, up over Finland and Lapland, before then turning east and descending across the Finnish/Russian border and the fells, birch forests and rivers of the Kola Peninsula to land at Murmansk. The airfield is deserted and there are no other planes in sight anywhere. Ours is the only plane in town. We go through Immigration where our Visas and passports are studied in minute detail. The arrivals hall is empty and we are shepherded straight onto a bus by a uniformed and serious-looking lady and told to wait in the bus. We wait and watch while the rest of the party are cleared and the luggage is taken by porters from the arrivals area and put into two lorries.

The terminal is a big and impressive three-storey, glass-fronted building. The airport car park outside the front of the terminal has about half a dozen cars parked there. No other cars arrive or leave while we wait. There are no signs to the short stay, or long-term car parks and no drop-off-only zones. No taxis, minibuses, no car-hire-courtesy buses, just the two buses for us pulled up in front of the terminal. Grass grows wherever there isn't concrete and the whole area has a sleepy, forgotten atmosphere that we have disturbed by our arrival. Eventually, everyone is on board and we set off towards the town. The scenery on the way is very attractive. The Kola Inlet is a long finger of water and runs deep into the countryside. We can see the wide estuary in the distance with green, wooded hills rolling down to the water's edge. Behind it, the low fells roll away to the west and the Norwegian and Finnish Border. Silver birches grow everywhere. As we get nearer to the town the Russian official tells us that we are not allowed to take any pictures of the town from the bus or even of the ship from the quayside. The buses take us directly to the ship and as the airport is on the south side of the town and the ship has been berthed at the southern end of the docks, we see nothing of the town itself except one roundabout and a few blocks of flats. Some are five or six storeys, made of concrete, while some are wooden, two-storey buildings that have been painted pale blue a very long time ago. The bus drives round the end of a warehouse onto the dockside and the *Kapitan Dranitsyn*'s black hull is suddenly there towering above us. She looks huge. We go on board to be greeted by a friendly, smiling Russian lady offering us cake and salt, a traditional Russian welcome. More staff show us to our cabins and we begin to settle in while we wait for the luggage.

The *Kapitan Dranitsyn* was built in Finland by the Wartsila Shipyard, which is world famous for building icebreakers. She was launched in 1975 but not completed for another five years. She is 12,000 tons, 25,000 hp and has a crew of sixty. She is one of a class of icebreakers designed for the Russian Northern Sea Route round the north coast of Siberia. This sea route is an important route for Russia and the icebreakers keep the seas along route open all the year round. This huge stretch of sea, from the Barents Sea, through the Kara Sea, the Laptev Sea and the East Siberian Sea give access to the main ports of Dikson, Tiksi and Pevek. The icebreakers need to be big and strong. In spite of all the claims about global warming and melting ice, the Northern Sea Route can still get blocked and ships can get stuck, even in summer. The ice is not as bad as in winter and it does retreat northwards in the summer, as it always has. But if the wind blows from the north, then the pack ice comes down to the coast along the north-east Passage.

The nuclear ships are even bigger at 25,000 tons and can generate 75,000 hp. They have a crew of almost 140. All the icebreakers have double hulls, with steel 48 mm thick at the bow. They also have a water-ballasting system between the hulls to enable the ship to be rolled by pumping water from side to side to free it if ice freezes to the hulls. An air bubbling systems forces high pressure air out through holes deep in the hull and prevents ice freezing to the ship. Special polymer coatings are used on the hull to reduce friction. Also, the ships can break ice going forwards or astern. *Kapitan Dranitsyn* is powered by a diesel-electric power system. She has three propellers, port, starboard and a centre line shaft. Her Captain, Sergei Papko, is an experienced icebreaker captain, having spent fifteen years on icebreakers in the northern seas. All her accommodation is within a main seven-deck-high superstructure unit that allows a high degree of noise insulation between it and the hull, so minimising the continual noise of ice breaking. She is well equipped for expedition work, having berths for over a hundred people and with a large dining room, lounges and a bar. She is very comfortable and a nicely decorated ship with comfy chairs and colour photos of Arctic wildlife on the walls. In addition, she has a well-equipped hospital, a gym, a heated indoor pool and a large, very hot sauna. The cabins are very comfortable, with two bunks, one of which folds up and becomes a settee during the day. There is a desk, plenty of storage space and a good bathroom as well as a large window that opens for fresh air.

We sail later in the afternoon. Murmansk is built totally down the east side of the Kola Inlet, between the hills to the east and the water, so it stretches a long way while, on the other bank, there is nothing but green woods and hills. The only bridge lies well south of the town and is the road to Kirkeness in Norway. I am amazed at how big the town is. Murmansk seems to stretch away for miles towards the sea. We pass the fishing vessel berths, where well over a dozen large, modern stern trawlers are tied up. Most look to be in good condition and some are obviously undergoing overhauls and refits, but some look derelict. We sail slowly down the Inlet past the industrial areas of the town, past warehouses, a power station and some large, forbidding, grey buildings that look from a distance like government offices. Along the hills behind the town is a series of tower blocks, which we assume are housing areas. We pass the commercial docks where the tops of freighters rise above the general collection of warehouses and cranes. We pass the ship repair yards where an icebreaker similar to the *Kapitan Dranitsyn* is in a floating dock. The Inlet widens and anchored off the port in the middle of the Inlet is a smart new freighter with a bright red hull and an icebreaker bow. The *Arctic Express* is one of a new class of cargo icebreakers operating along the northern coasts.

Gradually, we leave the last of the town and begin to see the start of the naval area. At the water's edge and out on the other side of the Inlet we can see a number of wrecks of submarines and warships that have sunk. They lie rotting and neglected, sticking out of the water. At one point, the last 30 feet of the stern of a naval patrol boat or corvette sticks vertically out of the water. There are no buoys around it to warn of its presence, so presumably all the local shipping will know it is there. Further down we pass the 'Atomflot', the base for the seven nuclear icebreakers. The nuclear icebreakers look very impressive, squat and workmanlike with their black hulls and rich orange-red superstructures. The first nuclear icebreaker, the *Lenin*, commissioned in 1959, is also berthed here. She is now decommissioned and has been turned into a museum ship. Nearby is the home base for *Kapitan Dranitsyn* and the other conventionally-powered icebreakers. As we pass the base, two sister ships of the *Dranitsyn* lie alongside. We wonder if the *Kapitan Dranitsyn* had been taken to the far end of the port for us to board her so that we would not see anything of the town or the port area from the bus?

High above on the hill stands the 'Alyosha', a giant, 35-metre high memorial, which was erected in 1974. It is a figure of a Russian soldier looking out over the port and it dominates the area. It commemorates all the soldiers who died defending Murmansk from the Nazis in the Second World War. Murmansk was put under heavy siege by the Germans, second only to Stalingrad, but Murmansk never fell and the Germans never captured it or the vital port and railway links.

Further down the Inlet on the eastern side we pass the closed naval city of Severomorsk. This is the headquarters and main naval base for the Russian Northern Fleet. As we pass we can see the base stretching out to the East round into a large bay. In the far distance, across the bay, ships and dockyards line the shore. The scene is dominated by the largest floating dock in Russia, moored near the main channel. The aircraft carrier, *Admiral Kuznetsov*, is in the dock undergoing maintenance, her ski jump ramp jutting out over the water. In addition to Severomorsk, there are six other small naval bases situated to the west of the Inlet hidden along the fjords and bays of the Kola Peninsula. It was from one of these bases, at Ara Bay, that the *Kursk* sailed on her fateful last voyage in 2000. During the Soviet era, there were over 200 submarines of all types based in this area. In addition, there is another large submarine naval base at Severodvinsk, near Arkhangelsk (Archangel) in the White Sea.

As we reach the entrance to the Inlet, the ship is ordered to stop by the Port Control and stay where we are, as a naval exercise is taking place with vessels leaving Severomorsk. We wait for about an hour or so before we are cleared to proceed. We finally come out of the Kola Inlet and reach the Barents Sea. As we head north, a westerly wind is blowing and the sea develops into a chop. The captain takes us well off to the west as we have been ordered to avoid the naval exercise areas just off Murmansk. It is not long before we are made aware of the one failing of icebreakers; they roll. As they cannot have any attachments on the outside of the hull as they do not have stabilisers or bilge keels and hence they roll a lot.

North

For two days we steam due north. During this time we are shown round the ship and meet our expedition leader, Dr Victor Boyarsky, a famous Russian polar expedition leader and the director of the Arctic & Antarctic Museum in St Petersburg. In 1995, he was part of an International Trans-Antarctica Expedition that crossed Antarctica using dog teams. They did so through the previously untravelled and coldest part of the continent, the 'Pole of Inaccessibility', as well as the Geographic South Pole. He has also taken part in many North Pole and Franz Josef Land Expeditions and runs the Russian ice station at 89 north, set up by Russia every year.

During these two days steaming we have time to explore this fascinating ship. At the stern there is a big, open, working-deck area and right at the stern itself is a 'V' shaped notch, about 10 feet wide by 4 feet deep, built into the stern and well covered with heavy, flexible fendering. At the forward end of this deck is the winch room where a powerful towing winch is housed. The ship is equipped as an ocean salvage and rescue vessel so it needs a powerful towing and salvage winch, and a number of special workshops on board. It also accounts for her having so much passenger accommodation. I notice a large, black, pressure cylinder, about 4 feet long and about 2 feet in diameter mounted on the deck, firmly fastened to the deck at its forward end and with a securing eye at the other. It lies on heavy wooden shock pads. Just as I am looking at this thing and trying to work out its purpose, one of the sailors, a thin, middle-aged man, appears from the winch room wiping his hands on a rag. He sees me looking at the cylinder and stops. I point to the black cylinder, 'Can you please tell me what that is for?' He smiles at me but does not speak. He seems to understand what I am asking and after a moment's thought, he kneels down on the deck, and takes out a small pencil from his dungaree pocket and begins drawing on the metal deck and explaining to me in Russian what happens. He is showing me that when they break ships out of the ice, the icebreaker backs the big V at the stern right up to the bow of the stranded ship. The ship is then secured hard and fast into the V at the stern of the icebreaker, hence the heavy wooden fenders. The securing cables are attached to the black cylinder. In the middle of his Russian I hear the English word 'Damper' and it all becomes clear. This cylinder is a form of giant spring designed to take up the sudden jerks and jolts that will undoubtedly occur during such an operation. I thank the sailor and we shake hands. He is delighted that I understood his explanation and I am delighted to have found the answer to my question with only one word of a common language.

Above the winch room is the flight deck where the small red and blue helicopter is lashed. I walk forward and climb the eight decks up to the bridge. It is one of the largest bridges I have been on. It is fully enclosed from wing to wing and with deck-to-deck head windows at the ends. The ship operates an 'open bridge' policy on these expeditions and the rule here is that passengers can use the starboard side, the crew use the port side. The starboard side has a couple of chairs and plenty of ledges to sit on and it even has a slave radar display. Down below, the dining room stretches across the width of the ship. It is bright, decorated in warm pinks and cream colours and always set for the next meal with pristine white table clothes. The bar, one deck below, is a light, warm and cosy area with plenty of easy chairs and a small, but well-stocked, bar in the corner.

The Islands

We arrive off the southern end of Franz Josef Land late in the afternoon. The sea is clear of any ice and as we come on deck to look at the islands, just off to starboard, two humpback whales spout a welcome for us. The islands stretch across our path. One of them, Bell Island, is easily identified by its distinctive steep sides and a bell-shaped silhouette. The islands are all low and flat-topped as all are covered in ice caps and cloud. The sun shines brightly on the ship and, as we get closer, we can make out the cliff faces and glaciers where the ice caps flow down into the sea.

We hope to make a landing at Cape Flora, on the south-west tip of Northbrook Island, but the heavy swell prevents this. It was here that Frederick Jackson set up a base in 1895 and where, in 1896, Nansen and Johanssen were rescued after overwintering nearly 100 miles further north. Maps of the islands did not exist then so they had no real idea exactly where they were. They were kayaking down through the islands hoping to meet a sealing ship or, if not, they planned to try and kayak to Spitzbergen, some 200 miles away across the open Arctic Ocean.

As they paddled along the coast of Northbrook Island they were attacked by walruses that drove their tusks into the kayaks and tore them badly. The two men just managed to get to shore and then spent four days repairing the kayaks with what little gear they had. As they finished the work and were about to set off again, Nansen thought he heard a dog barking in the distance. Johanssen did not hear it but Nansen set off on skis towards the sound. Perhaps he had been mistaken but he was sure he had heard something and so he skied on. Then, he heard it again and skied further and sure enough there, beyond a mound, was a dog and beyond the dog, a man. It was Frederick Jackson of the Jackson-Harmsworth Expedition, which had set up their wooden-hutted base camp at Cape Flora. The meeting was a miracle of chance. The Jackson Harmsworth expedition had left the UK long after Nansen and the *Fram* had been frozen into the polar seas so Nansen had no knowledge that there were any other expeditions there. It was the only one in the 191 islands at the time and had Nansen not been attacked by the walrus at that point or, had they sailed a few minutes before the dog barked they would almost certainly have perished trying to kayak to Spitzbergen. As it was, they went back to Tromso on a supply ship a few weeks later to be greeted as heroes.

I am disappointed that we can not visit the site of this famous rescue but perhaps before we finally leave we may get another chance to try and go ashore there. We sail on, up through the wide British Channel past George Island. The next morning finds us off Hooker Island.

Polar Bears

As we wake up we can tell from the noises that we are now in the ice. We look out and the ship is moving slowly through the pack. Then, right by the ship, we see fresh polar bear paw tracks in the snow-covered pack ice. They are leading away from the ship, off into the snow. The ship has just crossed their track. Later that day we see the bears. They are resting on fast ice in a large bay. They are probably about a mile away from us so the ship moves slowly into the bay, breaking the ice as she goes. When we are about half a mile away we stop in the ice and we wait. Sure enough, curiosity is getting the better of the bears and they come out to see who we are. There are two of them, a mother and a cub. They walk right up to the ship looking hard at it: stopping then peering and stretching and sniffing to examine the new smells and sights that have arrived in their bay. Then they walk a few paces closer. The cub is timid, always carefully keeping its

Polar bears. A mother and cub survey the ice for seals. (Photo by kind permission of Carina Svensson of Polar Quest)

mother between itself and the ship as it peeps out from under her legs. We stand silently and excitedly on the fo'c'sle and watch them; the only sound the clicking of cameras and the sniffing and snorting of the bears. They walk right round the bows looking at both sides of the ship but not venturing further than the bow itself. After a while they become bored and wander off back to their resting spot. As we watch we can also see a number of seals lying on the ice all around the bay. The bears must have eaten recently or they would have been far more interested in the seals than in us.

The Ice Closes In

A shore visit to Tichaja Station, an old Soviet polar station on Hooker Island, showed the speed at which conditions can change. As we arrive off the disused station it is calm and the water is free of ice and we all land by the Zodiacs. On a gloriously sunny afternoon we are enjoying the wild flowers and the scenery and exploring the few wooden buildings that make up the station. I stop and look out to sea and notice that the ice is now moving in towards the shore on the tide. Looking along the coast I can see that a huge area of loose pack is now on the move and coming into the bay. We call to some of the others and head back to the shore. We warn the guys running the Zodiacs that the ice will soon be onto the shore but they seem happy to stay there. Half a dozen of us get a Zodiac back to the ship as it is clear that in a few minutes the shore will be cut off from the ship by the ice. Most of the others choose to stay or they have wandered further along the shore and have not noticed the ice. Already the ice is drifting past the landing point and there is a raft of ice between it and the ship. Driving the Zodiac back is not easy and the driver has a real job to pick a route through the moving ice floes, which by now are moving thick and fast along the shore. The floes are big, about 4 to 6 feet high, so it is difficult to see the route ahead and the Zodiac driver has to stand on the side to get any view of the way through to the ship. We get back, but we were the last Zodiac to make it. After a while it becomes clear that the ice is here to stay so the remaining people ashore have to wait there while the helicopter is made ready and they are then ferried back six at a time in the helicopter. Without the helicopter they would have had a long wait.

Loose pack ice of FJL.

One of the sights of the Islands is Rubini Rock (Red Rock). This large, prominent rock, possibly a volcanic plug, rears straight up out of the water so it has deep water right up to its seaward sides. It is a haven for sea birds with thousands of kittiwakes, guillemots, little auks, and glaucous gulls nesting and screaming on the cliff sides. The captain takes the ship almost to within touching distance of the rock. His ship handling is impressive as the ship is in tidal waters but he keeps the bows close to the rock and just a few feet off, for over an hour. He keeps the centre screw running at slow astern and manoeuvres the ship forwards using just the two outer engines. This means that at any time he can put the outer engines to stop, and the ship will go straight back away from the rock on the centre engine alone. By doing this he is able to 'hover' the ship just a few feet off the rock for as long as he wants.

During the trip the ice conditions vary from clear water to heavy pack. None of it bothers the ship and we proceed as planned. The pack is made up of large flows, some with considerable ridging. The ridges are very jagged and in other places you can see where floes have ridden over one another to throw up peaks and cliffs on the ice. In many places, icebergs are trapped into the pack and drift along with it until they ground on the seabed and leave the pack to float on. All the while the land itself is ice locked. The ice caps meet the sea as sheer ice cliffs

Kapitan Dranitsyn in the ice near Jackson Island. (Photo by kind permission of Carina Svensson of Polar Quest)

Doreen and myself out on the ice and dwarfed by the huge ship. (Photo by kind permission of Carina Svensson of Polar Quest)

many tens of feet high and great smooth sweeps of ice take the eye across the icescape until they fall on another ice cliff edge or the broken area of crevasses where the ice twists round some deeply submerged rock many feet below. For all we can see we are looking at ice islands. In most cases there is no land or rocks to see. Everything is ice, complete islands many miles long and many hundreds of feet high made totally of ice. Watching the ice, either the pack or the land ice, becomes a totally absorbing occupation and we spend many hours just watching the ice crack, split and slide away from the bows as the ship moves relentlessly onwards.

On the western shore of Rudolf Island, high on the black basalt cliffs, sits the remains of the Teplitz Station. This was a Russian weather station that was only closed in 1995. It looks desolate and lonely, the two or three dark buildings black against the ice clad hill behind it. Here, they were quite literally the last people on Earth as beyond Rudolf there is nothing but ice until you reach Alaska.

Polar Ice Pack

There is rarely a week goes by now without some TV commentator telling us that because of global warming the Polar ice caps will have all melted by next Tuesday and actually it's all my fault for driving to the paper shop. This is usually on the basis of a photograph of a polar bear swimming in the sea and the commentator saying 'There I told you so, the ice must have all gone!' During this trip I asked our captain whether he had noticed the effect of global warming on the amount and extent of the ice. He said, without any hesitation, that in the fifteen years that he had worked in the Arctic Ocean, apart from the normal annual differences, he had not seen any definite changes. It is well known, and has been for centuries, that the amount of polar ice varies from year to year. In the summer of 2002 there was very little ice or snow in north-eastern Greenland. In Spitzbergen, in 2008, however, the polar ice was further south in June than anyone could remember. It is interesting too that, in September 2009, the papers and TV were carrying the story that two merchant ships had sailed through the north-east Passage and this was due to global warming melting the ice. What they did not report was that a Swede, Nils Nordenskjold, first did it in a sailing ship in 1878, or that two Royal Marines sailed and rowed through the north-west Passage the same month and reported there was twice as much ice as they had been told to expect by the weather bureaux. They had to drag their boat over the ice to get through. It is hard to know who to believe, the scientists who say that the global temperature changes are a reflection of the sunspot cycles of the sun, a well known and recorded phenomena, or the global warming disciples who believe that because we heat our houses we are guilty of melting the ice caps. As with all these things, there are merits in both sides and the truth probably lies somewhere in between.

Cape Fligely

On a grey, murky day we round Cape Säulen, the north-west point of Rudolf Island, which is dominated by two massive, ice-capped basalt pillars of rock rising high above the sea ice. The Russian explorer Capt Sedov vanished in this area in 1914 and a plaque on the shore commemorates him. We sail out into the Arctic Ocean and into the main pack ice. It lies across the ship's bows and stretches as far as we can see. We are now out of the channels and, as we turn east, we are sailing along the north coast of the northernmost island. We are heading for Cape Fligely, the most northerly point of land in Europe and Asia.

Cape Fligely on Rudolf Island. The most northerly point in Europe and Asia.

Unfortunately, when we get there, the heavy ice means we cannot go ashore by boat and the low cloud, strong winds and constant snow showers mean we cannot go ashore by helicopter either. Doreen and I stand out on the cold, snow-swept deck and watch the Cape. It must be one of the most rarely seen and seldom visited spots on the planet. The number of people who have seen this point can probably be counted in the tens rather than hundreds. The ship moves round through the ice just off the point. We are now just 565 miles from the North Pole. From a mile offshore, the Cape itself is not the grand, high buttress of a headland you would think it should be as the last place on the planet. It is a fairly low point of land and ice that drops gently down towards the sea with only the black rock on the low cliff edges showing us that there is land there, as all as the rest is covered by thick ice. It is almost as if the land is submitting to the sea and ice and bending in submission before the Arctic wastes. The low cloud and snow flurries make the isolation even more total. To the North, the Arctic Ocean stretches away to the North Pole as a pack-ice-covered sea. The white ice merges with the grey cloud as the squalls of snow blow through. As the light plays on the pack ice it also plays tricks with your eyes. It creates effects that show ice-covered cliffs in the far distance. It is easy to see how the early explorers were fooled into reporting that a great continent existed to the north.

We wait for over two hours for the weather to improve but it doesn't. If anything it worsens, so we turn our backs on this memorable spot and head back towards the west. After the chill outside, we decide that a celebratory drink is needed to mark our furthermost north. On the way down to the bar we meet Victor Boyarsky. 'Come', he calls. 'Let us celebrate our furthest north with Vodkas! Large, neat and very chilled Vodkas of course! Nostrovia!'

Man Overboard

We head back through the Islands the way we have come as the sea to the north and east of Franz Josef Land is too dangerous as it has never been surveyed. Later that afternoon we clear the pack ice and reach open water off Jackson Island where, if the weather allows, we hope to make a landing. It is dull and windy but otherwise fine enough for a Zodiac landing. The crew start to get the Zodiacs ready for the shore landing and we are in the cabin getting ready to go ashore when the ship's alarm gives out six short blasts and we hear the running of feet past the door and urgent yells in Russian. From what we could understand later, the ship was stopping as we approached the landing beach. The deck crane lifted the first Zodiac from the deck and the driver was sitting safely on the 'T' bar that hangs from the main cable above the Zodiac itself. The Zodiac was craned over the side and was being lowered, but, as it got near the water the wind swung it round and up so one side dipped lower and was caught by the waves. Due to the speed of the ship, this flipped the Zodiac up in the air and the driver was knocked from his 'T' bar seat. He fell into the Arctic Ocean and was quickly left well astern of the ship.

Immediately, the other seamen on deck somehow clear the flipped Zodiac from the crane wire, and get another Zodiac in the water. We go out on deck, Carina is there and she tells us what has happened. The next Zodiac is already in the water and comes alongside the boarding ladder. Victor is there at the foot of the ladder and he leaps in with one of the seamen and they speed back to look for the man. The seawater temperature is -2 °C. The chances of survival are minimal unless the person is very lucky. The ship has now stopped and, from the ship's deck, we can just see the man in the water but he is drifting away astern in the waves as the rescue Zodiac races towards him. Those on deck are silent and helpless. Soon, the man is invisible to us and lost astern in the waves. However, with help from the bridge by radio, the rescue Zodiac finds him. By that time they reach him, the man is paralysed with cold and can do nothing to help himself. He has been in the water now for at least three or four minutes. Victor and his companion get to him and try to drag the deadweight bulk of a frozen, sodden seaman into the Zodiac as it rocks and tips in the swell. At last, they manage to haul him into the boat and set off back to the ship to get him back on board. We wait at the ladder to help but amazingly the man is able, with help from Victor, to get up the ladder himself. He is taken straight to the sickbay where he soaks in a bath for a while. He is a lucky man; just to have been found was lucky, to survive, very lucky. He was undoubtedly saved by the survival suit that all the Zodiac drivers wear. After a few hours in the sickbay, recovering his body warmth, he was fine. Needless to say, he was not short of offers of vodka in the bar for a couple of days. It was a truly sobering event, but, thankfully, one that turned out well.

Nansen and Johanssen

All this happened at the spot where Fridjtof Nansen and Hjalmar Johanssen spent the winter of 1895. In June 1893, Dr Fridjtof Nansen and a crew of twelve left Norway in the *Fram*, a specially-designed ship, with the objective of testing Nansen's theory that the Arctic ice drifted from east to west across the Pole. They planned to deliberately let the ship be frozen into the ice towards the eastern end of Siberia and letting the ice's supposed westerly drift across the Polar Basin take the ship across the North Pole. This would prove that there was a polar ice drift across the top of the world. The *Fram* was caught by the ice and frozen in mid-way along the Siberian coast in September 1893. This was probably further west than Nansen would have wanted but he had no choice. By February 1895, after seventeen months locked in the ice, the *Fram* had reached 84 degrees north and it was clear from the track that her

Nansen and Johanssen, summer 1895. (J&C McCutcheon Collection)

The west coast of Jackson Island just as Nansen would have seen it, black rock peeping from the white ice cap.

drift, although clearly westward, would not take the ship across the Pole itself. Nansen then decided to make a dash for the Pole on foot. He and Hjalmar Johanssen, a superb international skier, set off for the Pole with two dog teams, sledges and kayaks, The sledges, tents, stoves, and kayaks had all been designed by Nansen. His designs have proven so successful that they are still used as the basis for similar equipments today.

At first they made great progress over good smooth ice, but then conditions worsened and the ice became broken with many ridges. Eventually, on 8 April 1895, Nansen had to admit that they could not get to the Pole and then safely back to Franz Josef Land with the provisions that they had. They had reached a new Farthest north of 86 degrees 13.6 minutes north, just about 240 miles from the Pole. They had always known that they would never be able to get back to the *Fram* as she would have moved many miles in the ice by the time they would arrive back; so they had set off with the plan to go to Franz Josef Land and take their chances of finding a sealer to get them home. If that failed, then they would make for Spitzbergen where they were certain to find human help. They headed back for the islands. During the trip, both their chronometers stopped so their navigation became a bit haphazard, but eventually, after many days, they sighted land. They could see mountains to the east but with open sea between them and the land. The problem was that they had no idea which land

Fridtjof Nansen.

Cape Norwegia (Cape Norway). Nansen was able to get ashore here from his kayak on the only piece of beach in the area.

Above: The desolate narrow beach at Cape Norwegia showing the flat area at the top of the beach and the cliffs behind.

Below: The remains of the hut with the beach and sea beyond. Nansen's daily view for nine winter months.

The remains of Nansen's 'hole' or shelter. This shows the rocks they had to dig out to make walls and the tree trunk they used as a roof beam.

it was, as there were no proper maps. After a number of frustrating days waiting for the drifting and melting floes to carry them closer, they finally shot their last two dogs for food, launched their kayaks and set off by sea. They managed to get ashore on one of the islands in early August 1895, 146 days after leaving the *Fram*. But where were they and were there any sealers still in the area this late in the season? They soon realised that they were alone as the last sealers would have left the area by now as winter was about to arrive. They saw more islands to the south so paddled their kayaks down the sounds, with the sledges tied across the two of them to form a catamaran. On 17 August, a storm blew up. They struggled to get to shore through the heavy seas and drifting ice and managed to land on a lonely beach near a small cape. They landed on the one beach in the area where they could land their kayaks as elsewhere along the coast there had been nothing but sheer ice cliffs. As the weather worsened and the ice came in to the shore, they realised that winter had indeed arrived and they could go no further. They named the area Cape Norvegia (Cape Norway). They then settled down to spend the winter on the beach. The almost vertical cliffs behind the beach and ice blocking the sea meant that they had no choice but to stay there. Some walruses lying in the sea just off the beach were their first meal.

The small narrow strip of land above the beach offered little in the way of building materials so they dug out rocks from the ground to make a 3-foot deep hole and built up a wall of rocks round the edge. They found a piece of driftwood to act as a roof beam across the top. As trees do not grow in Franz Josef Land this itself was a lucky find. That beam is still there. Then they covered the walls and formed a roof with walrus skins. These immediately froze solid. They called it 'the hole' for that is exactly what it was. They lived there in mind-numbingly-low temperatures of anything down to -40 or -50 °C, enduring the screaming storms during the long, dark, polar winter and living on polar bear and walrus meat. For most of their time though, they stayed inside the hole and slept.

Finally in May 1896, after nearly nine months in the hole, the sea ice started to break up and they continued down the coast in their kayaks until 100 miles to the south they had their chance encounter at Cape Flora with the Jackson-Harmsworth expedition and were rescued. After Cape Flora there was nothing but the empty Arctic Ocean. It was the last island on their route.

The *Fram* itself completed her drift and came out of the ice west of Spitzbergen. She arrived back in Norway only a few weeks after Nansen. All the expedition team had survived and Nansen's theories about the Polar ice drift had been confirmed.

Salisbury Island from the north, a land totally covered in ice.

The Hole

As we are getting ready to board the Zodiac at Cape Norvegia, a polar bear is spotted walking along the beach. We watch and wait. If he stays there we may not be able to get ashore after all. It sniffs the air and wanders on then it walks off over a rise so we carried on. From the sea, the Cape seems to be nothing more than a low rocky beach with steep, mountain slopes behind it. Ice and snow-bound crevices cover the cliff face and, above that, the ice cap comes down from the cloud to the very edge of the dark grey cliffs. The wind has got up a bit since we first stopped and the Zodiacs bounce from wave to wave and a few of us get a good dousing as we head into the beach. We land among large, hard and rough lumps of sea ice that clutter the shoreline and move around in the waves. Some walruses are idling in the breakers a few yards along the beach, just as they had when Nansen landed here just over 110 years earlier. They appear to be totally unaware of us. At the top of the narrow shingle beach is a raised and gently sloping area that stretches about 20 or 25 yards back up to the foot of some rough scree at the base of the cliffs. This raised area is made up of rocks and mosses with some grasses struggling to cling to the thin soil. In the middle of this grassy stretch we see an old log, bleached white and about 15 feet long. As we get nearer we can see that it is lying across a small hollow in the ground. The hollow is surrounded by loose rocks and stones. This is Nansen's hole. It was here that Nansen and Johanssen spent the winter of 1895/96. A plaque is mounted on a post some yards away. It commemorates, in Norwegian and Russian, 'Nansen and Johanssen's survival over the winter of 1895/6 at this point'.

I am now looking into the hole. It seems barely big enough for one man to lie in let alone for two men to live in it for a full polar winter. Dried bones of bear and walrus still lie by the hole. Although tiny, low wild flowers bloom in vibrant pinks and greens nearby, it is a desolate and depressing place. This is August; what must it have been like through the dark of the winter night? The view from their front door is across the sound to the low ice covered hills of Salisbury Island in the far distance. It is a humbling experience to stand here where two men, through sheer determination, survived for so long. How tough, mentally and physically, were these men? And to do this after they had pushed themselves to the extreme trying to ski to the North Pole only to be defeated by lack of supplies: then racing back to find land and to try and find a sealer to take them home before finally realising that they had another nine months of winter to survive by living off the land.

Walruses

The three walruses are lying asleep on an ice flow in the middle of the sound. We left Cape Norvegia at about midnight on what is now a still windless night and encounter the walruses about four miles east of Cape Norway. From a distance they are reddy-brown, motionless lumps, like well-rounded sandstone boulders on

Walruses on their flow drifting in the sea near Jackson Island.

the ice. The captain manoeuvres the ship so we drift to a stop alongside the ice
flow. As we draw closer we can see that the boulders are made of leather and are
very fat. The three great masses of very wrinkled, leathery, wobbly walrus slowly
wake up and raise their heads to look up at the ship through small, round eyes
that are both bleary and bloodshot. They each probably weigh well over a ton and
are about 10 or 12 feet long. They all need a shave too with their prickly whiskers
sticking out from their top lips. They belch and snort as the biggest one prods its
neighbour with its tusk. These boys look as though they had a really good party
last night and have only managed to get as far as this ice flow on their way home.
One of them, bored by us already, starts to scratch itself with the ends of its flipper
and then tries to go back to sleep. The other two start to scratch themselves now
they are awake. They manage to avoid each other's tusks as they swing their heads
about and start to move to make themselves more comfortable. Even a small
movement of their head causes a ripple effect across their whole body as the fat
under the thick, dry skin is set in motion. Ripples run out from the flow as they
move about on it. Unlike seals, which look as though they are about to burst out
of their skins, the walrus skins seem to be far too big for them, with masses of
folds, creases and spare material. They look as though they are struggling to move
about inside a great leather sleeping bag. After a while they decide that the ship is
here to stay and as they cannot get back to sleep they will sit up and look at this
strange, huge, black thing beside them. Even though we are no more than 20 feet

Ice floes and ice caps, a typical Frans Josef Land scene.

The edge of the ice cap meets the sea in a cliff of ice well over 50 feet high.

Right: Kapitan Dranitsyn breaks through the ice as she ploughs remorselessly northwards.

Below: Icebergs, glacier and mists. Near Hall Island FJL.

Sunshine and shadows as the mists swirl and roll across the islands.

A small bergy bit off the coast.

from them and tower over them, they just lie on their flow and look quizzically at us without fear. They are totally unafraid and disinterested in us. When they are out of the water and dry like this, their skin is a reddish-brown colour and stands out in the Arctic white. This is unlike any of the other Arctic creatures which all tend to be white. However, when they slide into the water, they turn a glistening black and instantly merge into the black waters. It is such a very peaceful scene, the walrus, the ice floe drifting gently among others in the open waters and the panorama of the ice-covered islands stretching in all directions. We slowly move away leaving them to go back to sleep on their peaceful ice floe.

The next day we stop to go and look at a huge walrus colony. This colony is on the end of a spit of land and as we approach by Zodiac we can see the steam rising from this mass of over 100 walruses. Some of them are swimming about in groups just off the shore and as we approach they start to take an interest in us. About twenty of them swim across to the Zodiac and, when they are about 10 feet away, they stop and sit with their shiny, wet heads and tusks out of the water examining us. They get more agitated and concerned as we go closer to the colony and they start to move closer to the Zodiac. We decide that discretion is the better part of valour and move away. The walruses then chase us off, following the boat to ensure we did not go back. Knowing what we do about their skills at sticking their tusks through kayaks we make sure our rubber Zodiacs are out of their immediate range. We watch them for some time from a distance and it becomes clear that the walruses in the water are acting as guards for the females and young ones on the beach. Once we move away a little they were happy to watch us go. One of the other Zodiacs was not so lucky and a walrus did puncture one of the buoyancy chambers, although luckily not seriously and they were able to get back to the ship.

We leave them to it and motor quietly along a massive ice wall. At this point, the ice cap meets the sea and ends in a sheer wall of ice that is about 40 to 50 feet high and has the appearance of a freshly-cut block of vanilla ice cream. Here, we can see crevasses that run at right angles to the ice face, like knife cuts, running down through the edge of the ice almost to the sea level. Some have snow bridges across their top. Ice caves disappear into the ice and water drips from melt streams deep inside. Trying to imagine the vast quantity of ice that lies behind this half-mile-long ice front and the distance it goes back over the island makes us feel very small indeed.

Bentsen and Bjorvik

A day or so later, after sailing down to the south-east end of the archipelago, we come to Cape Heller on Wilczek Island. The day is very still but with a low cloud cover. The ice floes lie motionless all across the bay. The low cloud deadens any sounds so intensifying the silence of the place. It was here at Cape Heller that two Norwegians, Bentsen and Bjorvik, from the American Wellman Expedition of 1898/99 overwintered in a stone hut. They were an advance party for the spring expeditions and set up their camp in the late autumn. Unfortunately, poor management meant that they were left with insufficient provisions or proper equipment. They managed to build a good, solid, stone hut in which to overwinter but without sufficient materials to properly finish it they were forced to use walrus hides for the roof. The whole surrounding area is covered in loose stones ideal for building and their thick, dry-stone dyke walls still look fairly substantial even today. Tucked up against a small steep slope it was much more substantial in every way than Nansen's hole. Wellman and the main party were meanwhile living in proper wooden huts in the base camp at Cape Tegettoff. Like Nansen, Bentsen and Bjorvik had to live on polar bear and walrus but they did at least have a better-constructed hut than Nansen and Johanssen were able to build. Sadly, Bentsen died during the winter and as it was impossible to dig a grave in the frozen ground. Bjorvik kept his friend's now frozen body in its sleeping bag in the hut with him so it did not get eaten by bears, until he was rescued in the spring. Bentsen's grave lies a few yards away down near the shore. We try and imagine living in it through the long darkness of the winter, without food, proper stores or equipment and with just the dead body of your only colleague for company.

Cape Tegettoff

The south-eastern end of the archipelago is off to starboard, about half a mile away but wrapped in fog, just as it had been on the day that Payer and Weyprecht looked out from their ship only 133 years earlier. We wait for the fog to lift so we can go ashore at this historic point. As the morning goes on the fog does slowly lift and reveals the two tall, rock pillars that had never been seen by man before 1873. The Zodiacs are launched and we go ashore. Wellman set up his base camp here at the foot of the cliffs on a flat area on the spit of land that runs from the cliffs towards the twin pillars. All that remains are a few sections of the base of his wooden hut. It is ironic that there is more remaining of Bentsen and Bjorvik's hand-built stone shelter than the purpose-made, prefabricated base camp. Quickly, the fog descends again and we lose sight of the ship in the fog. We also lose sight of some of the party who have moved away from the shore and up towards the cliffs behind the beach area. Victor is keen to get people back to the ship as he does not think that the fog will lift. The dangers of one or more Zodiacs, each with twelve passengers, getting lost in the fog are very real. Zodiacs do not offer good radar targets so are very difficult to find in fog. Even in summer, the chances of survival here if a boat gets lost in fog are not good. Victor, who, as usual, is totally in charge, is down on the beach and orders the Zodiacs to only go back in pairs and to keep well in sight of one another. Doreen gets away in the Zodiac ahead of the one into which I climb. The Zodiacs find their way back with help from modern technology. Each Zodiac has a hand-held, sat. nav. receiver and can steer towards the sat. nav. position of the ship, this being passed to them by radio.

Even so, malfunctions and errors can occur. The fog is now so thick that we lose sight of the Zodiac ahead and can only follow its wake. The trip back seems to go on forever. Surely, we must have passed the ship by now? Should we not turn round? Everyone in the boat is anxiously looking about to find any sign of the ship in the fog, then anxiously looking at the coxswain for reassurance that all is well. All we see is wet greyness. Shouts and calls come out of the fog but it is impossible to know from which direction. We motor on into seemingly endless fog, locked in our own cocoon of grey. The driver, while looking about all the time does not seem too concerned. Suddenly, a shaft of watery sun breaks through the fog just as a black cliff emerges above us. Where are we? But it is not a cliff, it is the ship and she is shining her powerful search light towards the shore so the zodiacs can follow the beam back to the ship for the last few yards. We have made it. It is with a sense of relief that we all make it back to the safety of the ship.

Belugas

It is our last day in the Islands and on the last afternoon we are out in the Zodiacs again cruising along the ice edge when some distance away we see a movement of white on the black water. We watch for it again, and there it is, and then another. Round, white shapes are bobbing about. Excitement mounts as we all want it to be something that it may not be! We motor closer, slowly. There it is again, and another; now there is no doubt; we have finally found belugas, the rare white whales of the Arctic. We slowly motor over to them. They are feeding near the ice front and, as we watch, they surface for air, roll their backs and go down again. This is a magical, thrilling moment. They are not big by whale standards. They probably range between about 12 to 20 feet long but are pure white all over. This is the first time I have seen them in the wild. We get within a few feet of where they have been seen and turn off the engine. The sea here is black with mud and dirt washed out from the glacier a few yards away, so we can not see down in to the water. We sit in silence, watching and listening for any sound or sight to indicate that they were about to surface. They surface close to the boats to see what we are then carry on feeding down below. They are so silent that they always catch us unawares and they surface and breathe before we have time to turn round to see them properly. They always beat us. A stage whispered 'There!' from someone and as we turn, so the soft-looking, pure-white back rolls and disappears from view. When you see belugas in places like Sea World, where you can see them underwater through viewing windows, they always look as though their skins are too big for them, like a diver in a white, rubber, drysuit three sizes too big. The smiling, inquisitive look that they always seem to have and the sing-song noise of their call (they were called sea canaries by early whalers), make them enchanting animals. But, they are also very rare and sightings are few and far between. They carry on feeding undisturbed by our visit. Reluctantly, we leave them and return to the ship to gloat about our sightings to those who did not come.

The nuclear-powered icebreaker *Yamal* emerges from the mist near Hooker Island having been to the North Pole.

Yamal

We had heard that the nuclear icebreaker *Yamal* was meant to be passing through Franz Josef Land and was possibly coming our way. She has just been to the North Pole and is on her way back to Murmansk. She is twice the size of *Capitan Dranitsyn* and with three times the power. She should be in the same area as us as we move into one of the north/south channels between the islands. Patchy fog lies in banks around the islands and the view to the north is masked. Captain Sergei stops the ship in an area clear of fog and we wait. Then, as we watch, *Yamal* emerges through the fog bank. Her squat red superstructure, black hull and the distinctive shark's teeth painted round her bows are easily recognisable. Everyone comes on deck including the crew. One of the waitresses from the Dining Room asks to borrow my binoculars so she could find her friend who is working on *Yamal*. She does, and there are lots of girlie squeals and waving to and fro as the two ships lie stopped about a hundred feet apart. Other crew members find their friends or relations on *Yamal* and vice versa. As they do so, little groups of squeals and males calling across the water rings out. We are the only two ships in thousands of miles of ice-covered ocean. You tend to forget that in Murmansk the sole industry is the sea. It is natural that the crews all know each other and live close to one another. They will have brothers and uncles, daughters and cousins working on the merchant ships and icebreakers, trawlers and naval ships that operate out of Murmansk. We all take photos of the other ship as we lie still in the clearing in the fog. After a while, the *Yamal* slowly heads off on her way back to Murmansk, leaving us for our last night in these beautiful islands. Tonight is to be Russian night and the crew do not let us down with a decorated dining room, colourful table linen and a wonderful Russian meal, with borsht, beef, potatoes and of course, vodka! All served with pride and a flourish.

Murmansk Again

So, after many days in the most fantastic of places, we head back across the Barents Sea on the two-day steam back to Murmansk. Now it is time to pack our cases and get ready for the trip home. We arrive back in Murmansk during the night and wake up to find ourselves alongside the wharf from which we sailed. We sadly leave the ship and are taken back to the airport by bus. Even though we were the only flight of the day, the Russian authorities were unable to decide how we should be processed and which check-in desk to use. So, after a delay of nearly one and a half hours, we finally get checked in for the flight and checked out of Russia. They then call us forward to get on the bus to go out to the aircraft. I have both of our boarding passes in my hand. As we leave the building, Doreen is immediately behind me but is stopped by the security guard. He has decided that this bus is full and as I step outside the door is firmly shut behind me. I get on the bus then realise that I am holding Doreen's boarding Pass. This could be a problem! I get off the bus at the foot of the aircraft steps. A tall, serious and unhappy-looking security guard with a tall-fronted, peaked cap is standing barring the way up the stairs. He demands to see everyone's boarding pass. I show him both mine and Doreen's boarding passes. He looks blank. I point at the terminal and say 'Wife'. He does not appear to have even heard me but just grunts and gives me a look that said 'You stupid tourist', and then lets me get on the plane. 'Oh boy', I am thinking, 'what happens now when Doreen gets to the aircraft with no boarding pass? Will they let her on? Even if they do, she is going to kill me. Oh well, at least I have had my holiday and if she is not allowed on and is carted off to the local salt mines she won't be able to shout at me anyway so that's all OK.' The next bus arrives at the aircraft with the remaining passengers. I watch from the aircraft as she gets off. She gets to the steps and is stopped by the guard. Now the fun will start! She shows the guard that she has no pass, smiles at him and points at the plane and says something to him. The guard just grunts and she walks straight up the stairs! No passport check, no boarding pass, nothing, just a smile! When she sits down beside me, I am given a look that says it all; 'You stupid tourist!'

CHAPTER 13

MV *Stockholm* – Spitzbergen – In search of Polar Bears

Glaciers

There had been rumblings and cracking sounds coming from deep inside the 'July 14th Glacier' for ten minutes or more, echoing around the mountains at the head of the fjord. Derek and I were leaning on the rail of the ship, savouring the smells from the galley and letting the afternoon drift toward dinnertime. We had heard noises from the glacier when we had been ashore earlier, but after one small icefall it had all gone quiet again. Now it had restarted. We watched fascinated, but all was still, the water flat and the glacier face remained intact. These noises seemed to go on forever without any ice chunks or small ice bergs calving off. The noises subsided again. Then, silently and without any indication that it was about to happen, a number of large pieces of ice, each the size of a small house, together with hundreds of smaller lumps of solid ice, detached themselves from the glacier face and slid and fell towards the water. Some slid straight in and others tumbled and tripped on the lower edges of the glacier before falling into the fjord. The slapping sound of the ice hitting the water reached us and the scene changed. Birds took flight, and the ice wall became a blur of action as the ice fell and the water splashed up before it all fell calm again. Then we saw the wave. It was at least 10 or 12 feet high and rising. We watched and wondered what would happen when the wave, which was already radiating and racing out from the glacier, reached our small ship with its 8-foot freeboard?

The '*Stockholm* Plan'

It was over a coffee at The Scott Polar Research Institute (SPRI) in Cambridge that the plan had been formed. We were attending a Polar Quest reunion, kindly hosted by the SPRI, for the UK clients of Per Magnus's company. Some of the expeditions that Per Magnus runs in Spitzbergen are on a small expedition ship called *Stockholm*. Over coffee, a couple of the ladies, Jill and Angela, who I had met earlier in the year in Spitzbergen on another trip, said that they wanted to get a group of twelve together and sub-charter the *Stockholm* from Per Magnus

MV *Stockholm*. A former Swedish Government vessel now converted for expedition work.

for a private expedition around Spitzbergen and would Doreen and I like to join the party? The plan was to go early in the season and take the ship from Longyearbyen and see how far we could get round the top of the islands and look for wildlife and scenery on the way. The trip had to take place at the very beginning of the season as the ship was fully committed after that. In spite of the short notice we said yes.

Svalbard was first mentioned in old Icelandic texts and means 'Land of cold coasts'. It is the official name of the Island group. Spitzbergen was the name given by the Dutch explorer Barents when he discovered the island in 1596 and Spitzbergen means 'pointed mountains'. Technically 'Spitzbergen' is the name of the largest island in the group of 'Svalbard Islands'. Longyearbyen, on Spitzbergen Island, was set up as a coal-mining settlement by an American called, strangely enough, Mr Longyear. The relics of the old mines remain and one of the mines is still in operation. The Russians also operate a bigger mine further down Isafjord at Barentsburg, which is a totally Russian settlement. Today, during the summer months, Longyearbyen is a busy starting point for expeditions all over Spitzbergen and further afield. It retains a strong frontier-town feeling with most of the shops selling rations, boots, supplies, spades and big parkas.

Doreen and I arrive in Longyearbyen from Edinburgh after an overnight stop in Oslo. The others travelled up from London later that day and arrive well after midnight. The hotel we have been booked into seems to be a theme hotel. It was, we thought, meant to resemble an old coal miner's hostel. The rough wooden top bunk bed I have is so designed that only a small and very flexible monkey can

The main saloon on *Stockholm* is a warm and welcoming area with polished wood and brass.

The main mess has a real feel of polar voyaging with old charts on the bulkheads and cabins opening off the mess and galley area.

climb up to get into it, as I certainly can't. I am certain that the designer chappy has never tested the access himself and in the end I give up and drag the mattress off the bunk and put it on the floor.

The next morning we all meet up at breakfast. There are twelve of us. It is fair to say that none of us are in the first flush of youth. Doreen and I had been on previous trips with some of the group but others we have not met before. There are Derek and Anne, who we met on the Greenland trip. There are Jill and Angela who organised the charter with Per Magnus. They are two independent ladies who live their own lives most of the year but join up each year for trips together to far-off places. Then there are those who have never visited the Arctic before. Sarah and Anthony, who seem to have been to all the hot and sticky places like the Amazon. Sarah's mother Barbara, who is a lovely lady and who one afternoon towards the ends of the trip, when it was announced that we were trying for yet another Zodiac landing, decided that she had had enough and, said 'Fine, You all go. I am staying here in the Saloon on my own with a very large whisky.' No one argued and in fact some of us were quite envious. Then there are Amanda and Alex, who have also never been to the Arctic but heard all about it from Gill and Angela, and want to see it for themselves. In addition, Per Magnus himself is coming as the expedition leader and, with him, his wife Katarina; who as a director has a large role to play in the running of the Company. Both of them, as well as Per the skipper and Lisa, one of Per Magnus's full time Arctic guides who is based in Spitzbergen, have all led many expeditions in and around Spitzbergen so there will be no shortage of ideas as to where we should try to go.

The *Stockholm* is berthed across the end of the commercial jetty, dwarfed by a large merchantman lying along the main jetty. We are warmly welcomed on board by the captain, Per Engvall, as well as by Annika and Kjell, the stewardess and the chef, who between them run all the 'hotel aspects' of the ship, and the rest of the crew. After the safety briefings, we set sail down the Isafjord towards the open sea and into a strengthening south-westerly breeze, which gives us a few white horses and a gentle roll for our first night at sea.

The ship is a real beauty. She is small enough to get into the bays and small harbours but big enough to offer some degree of comfort for her twelve passengers and seven crew. *Stockholm* was built in Helsingbors Shipyard in Sweden in 1953 as a lighthouse tender for the Swedish National Maritime Administration. She is 40 metres long and has a gross tonnage of 361 tons. After her life in the Baltic she was saved from the scrap yard and bought from the Swedish Government by her current skipper/owner Per Engvall. He restored her and saw the potential in her for small expeditions to the Arctic. He converted and updated her for expedition work and to meet passenger-carrying standards and Lloyd's ice-strengthened standard A1. He restored the ship's interior to how she had been when she was new. This included the restoration of the beautiful wooden-panelled bridge front and interior and the wood panelling in the main saloon. To enable more passengers to be carried, he turned the original hold space into passenger cabins and a central messing area and linked this area through to both the bow and

Polar bears outnumber humans on Svalbard. (C. McCutcheon)

stern areas. This allowed her to carry at least twelve passengers. By 1998 she was ready to go.

Entering the mess it instantly reminds me of seeing Captain Scott's ship, the RRS *Discovery*. The early polar expedition ships had a very similar layout, with a central wardroom mess and cabins opening off it. A central skylight makes it a bright and cheery mess deck. The atmosphere in the *Stockholm*, with the old charts and pictures of the Arctic on the bulkheads, combined with the rich use of wood and brass, gives her a warm and adventurous feel. The cabins are basic but cosy. Ours has two wooden bunks, (that were exceptionally comfortable), drawers and a wardrobe for stowage and a small shower cum toilet as well as a small porthole. This we have to keep firmly closed, as it is only a few feet above the waterline. The whole cabin is painted white and is spotlessly clean.

A gale has sprung up out in the Arctic Ocean but we avoid the rougher weather by sailing up the Forlandsundet, a wide strait between Prins Karl Forland Island and the mainland. Dinner is timed so that we are in sheltered waters by the time it is ready. Dinner on the first night is a delight. Norwegian smoked salmon, beef tenderloin with port and truffle sauce and some good wines.

Our first night's sleep is interrupted by our first meeting with the wildlife. At four in the morning there is a tap on the cabin door and Lisa tells us that we are stopping to watch a group of about twelve walruses on a shingle spit on the island. I struggle up on deck to find I am the last, apart from Doreen who decides to stay in bed. The spit projects out into the sound from Prins Karl Forland Island

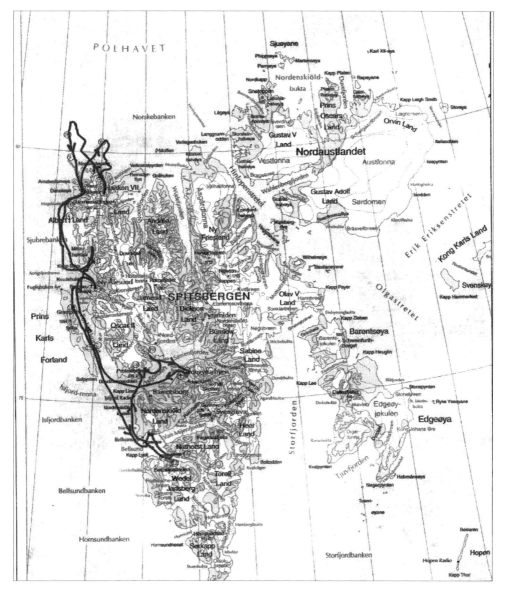

Map of Spitsbergen and the route taken. The route was, as always in the north, determined by the ice and not us.

and has an exceptionally steep shore. Because of this, and the fact that it is dead calm, Per edges the ship right up to the shore so that the bottom of the bow is just touching the bottom of the shingle bank and we, standing on the fo'c'sle, can almost lean over and touch the walruses on the shore. Not that we want to, the smell is enough and the continual belching and snorting is not conducive to getting any closer. Especially at four o'clock in the morning! A few bleary, red eyes peer up at us then close again. They are lying in a haphazard heap, overlapping each other with some asleep even though they have the tusks of others sticking in their side, or a flipper and folds of skins over their heads. Apart from an occasional glance they remain aloof and disinterested in our presence on their beach.

We continue sailing north up the strait, through the narrows and later that day we go into Ny Alesund. This village sits on King's Fjord, a long, wide fjord running south-east inland from the sea. The village was set up by sealers who were looking for fuel during the First World War. They found coal and set up the Kings Bay Coal Company. Its offices still stand above the tiny harbour/jetty. Unfortunately, a number of mining accidents led to the deaths of many miners and in 1962 the mine was shut down.

Two Norwegian whale catcher boats are alongside when we arrive. They are easily recognised by their crow's nests and harpoon gun on the bow. They are reportedly hunting for minke whales, which Norway is allowed to do for 'Scientific Purposes'. These obviously include selling raw whale meat on Bergen fish market. They are fine-looking boats. Both look new and are made of varnished wood and are obviously clean and well cared for. There is, however, no sign of the whalers themselves as they are probably sleeping down below. Ny Alesund is now a thriving polar research centre with scientists and students from around the world living there during the summer. It also boasts the world's most northerly post office, which sits among the other rust-red, painted wooden houses and buildings above the harbour.

It was from here that a number of attempts have been made on the Pole, particularly by air. A tall, metal lattice mast, which was the tethering point for an airship, stands on open ground about half a mile from the village. Amundsen and the Italian Nobile, together with the American, Ellsworth, set off from here in the airship *Norge N1* in 1926 and flew over the North Pole and carried on to land in Alaska. They were the first people to positively see the North Pole as well as the first to fly over it. A fine plaque and a bust of Amundsen have been set up at the base of the mast to commemorate the event.

Per and Per Magnus, are both keen to get up to the north so we reluctantly leave this delightful spot, leaving the two whalers resting gently against the quay. It has been a cold and breezy morning with snow showers blowing through. However, as we sail from the village, the sun comes out, illuminating a beautiful glacier on the eastern side of the fjord. As the sky clears, the sea instantly turns from grey to a sparkling blue. We sail out of King Fjord and up the coast of Albert 1 Land, the sun shining down on our small ship, which is no more than a dot in the vastness of the dazzling sea. After half an hour, the after deck resembles a cruise ship lido deck, with bodies lying in the sun everywhere. The only difference is that these bodies are not in swimsuits, but have heavy boots, parkas, hats and gloves on as well as sun glasses. It is a fabulous afternoon. The sun shines down and everywhere we look there is another fantastic view. We have a flat, calm, glistening, blue sea and white, snow-clad mountains and glaciers edge down to the sea under a clear blue sky. The gentle murmur of the engine continues as *Stockholm* heads further and further north. Spitzbergen might only be a speck on the map but when you see it on days like this, when you can literally see for miles and miles, you realise

Proceeding up the coast of Albert 1 Land on a brilliant sunny day.

what a vast wilderness it is; a wilderness of endless mountains and ice, empty of any form of human life. As the afternoon slips by, some people snooze on deck as the ship rolls along and the soft vibration of the engine helps relax us all. Some creep quietly below for a snooze in comfort and others sit in the bridge and chat with Skipper Per until drowsiness takes over and they also sneak off below. Per continues to sit contentedly in his chair in charge of his own ship, going where he wants to, in to the far reaches of the Arctic. I chat with Alec and Amanda up on the fo'c'sle, sitting under the bulwark and sheltered from the wind but still in the warm sunshine. They cannot believe either the weather or the beauty of the Arctic on their first trip. Like many in the Arctic for the first time, they expected snowstorms all the time. So, the afternoon drifts gently by, at every turn another spectacular view of Albert 1 Land, another glacier creeping to the sea, another ridge of snow-covered mountains climbing away deep into the interior. Another fjord, this time Magdalene Fjord, opens out to starboard, still, silent and empty in the sunshine.

The peaceful afternoon drifts by as we sail up the coast taking in the beauty of the islands. By early evening we reach the north-west tip of Spitzbergen and enter the narrow, twisting Sorgattet which separates Dane's Island and Amsterdam Island from the mainland. The towering black cliffs climb above us as puffins and little auks flap furiously along the cliffs to their burrows and nests.

This whole region was used by the Dutch, Scandinavian and British whalers in the seventeenth century and many of the place names reflect the history. This particular area is called Smeerenburg. Smeer is the Dutch word for blubber. So, this was Blubber Town. It is a low, flat area backed by low hills. It was set up in 1614 as a tented camp. They would catch the Greenland whales from small rowboats as the migrating whales passed through the islands and drag them ashore on the shingle beach and reduce them to oil in huge pots or coppers up to 2 or 3 metres wide. The Danes were also trying to establish a base here and there were disputes between the two nationalities. After the first years when they lived in tents, in 1619, the Dutch brought wooden huts, bricks and building materials and the camp became more permanent. Smeerenburg grew to sixteen or seventeen wooden buildings with cobbled lanes, brick-based boiling ovens and even a small fort in the centre of the settlement. It is reported that at the peak of the industry in the 1630s there would be up to 200-300 men living here in the summer, working for seven separate whale blubber bases, each financed by a different 'chamber' or company, from Holland.

The Bears are Here!

We round the beacon on the end of the spit that has, for years, guided ships through the strait. Then, as we are passing Slaadfjord, a small ice-filled fjord on the mainland side, Per alters course into the fjord looking for a mooring for the night and we break into the fast ice that leads up to the Sallstrom Glacier at the end. His plan is to spend the night anchored in the fast ice below the glacier. The glacier is large and dramatic and in the early evening the sun shines through the mountaintops onto the glacier, turning it a gleaming ice white and leaving the glacier front and the fast ice in deep blue shadows. We are watching the scenery when someone notices a slight movement on the ice against the dark shadows at the base of glacier. Then, as we slowly move into the thicker fast ice, through the binoculars, the slight movement resolves itself into two polar bears hunting along the glacier front. Eventually, when we are well into the thick fast ice, Per stops the ship. All falls silent, the sun slowly sinks lower and the bears continue their search along the deep-blue shadow of the glacier front as we relax on deck. The day is completed by another superb dinner and fine wine.

'The Bears are here!', Annika cries from the galley. We rush up on deck as quietly as we can, grabbing cameras and coats on the way. There, just a few yards in front of the port bow, are the two bears. One is a mother and the other is her cub, but probably about a year-and-a-half old. They are staring and sniffing, moving and stopping. Then, when they see us emerge, they snort quietly and wander away for a few paces, then turn and nervously wander in again. The main deck of *Stockholm* is low, with only about 8 feet of freeboard at the lowest point, so we are almost down at eye level with the bears. They come right up to the side. The mother's fur is a glistening white and champagne yellow while the cub's fur is pure

Stockholm edges gently into the fast ice in front of a glacier near Danskoya, north-western Spitsbergen.

The glacier front near Danskoya. The vast emptiness and remoteness of Spitsbergen is humbling.

A polar bear eyes up a
potential dinner.

white. It looks so soft as the sun shines through the individual hairs and fibres of
their fur. Four jet black eyes pierce and X-ray us, and everything they see, as their
black noses are constantly working to take in every scent. Four small, round and
rather cute ears listen to everything that is said (listening perhaps for an invitation
on board for dinner). The loudest noises on the ice are their giant, pigeon-toed
paws, as they gently crunch on the ice, and the sound of their breathing and short
snorts as they savour the smells from the galley. On board, twelve passengers and
all the crew are transfixed and silent. No one dares move or breathe in case we
scare them off. Slowly, they become bolder and stand with their noses right at the
deck level, peering through the rails. What will they do? Will they try to get on
board? If they decided to there was no way to stop them. One jump and they will
be on deck in a furry heap of hungry, prime carnivore. Will one of the peppermints
in my pocket be acceptable? The smells from the galley of the shrimp, marinated
in chilli and ginger, starter and the Asian fish dinner, with white wine sauce, as the
main course will undoubtedly be more attractive to them, so my peppermints are
probably safe. They do not appear to be threatening in any way, just curious and
interested, and they hold eye contact with us until a movement along the deck
distracts them. As we are watching the bears, an Arctic fox, half in and half out
of its white winter coat, trots round the ship. It is half the size of a normal fox.
It is obviously following the bears to collect any scraps from whatever meal they
find.

Finally, the bears grow bored and wander off across the ice astern of the ship,
still sniffing the air and looking for a better supper than anything a few tourists
can offer. We settle down to our coffee in the mess deck and let our heartbeats
return to normal.

Into the Ice

We sail again in the morning; having remained moored safely in the fast ice all night. No sooner have we left the fjord ice than we stop again to watch two male walruses on an ice flow near the fjord entrance. The early morning scene is magical. The two walruses are lying on an ice floe in the black waters of the fjord and behind them is the backdrop of the steep, snow-covered mountains and a glacier, all bathed in soft sunshine. As we move north through the strait, dead ahead of us, something is happening on a big ice floe. It is the two bears from last night and they have found their breakfast. They are devouring a seal that they have caught out on the ice. Blood covers the floe and it is easy to see that they have dragged the unfortunate seal onto a firmer part of the ice. The bears' faces are now bright blood red as they bury their heads in the seal's body and come out tearing and ripping pieces of flesh, blubber and entrails. Glaucous gulls scream and flap round the edge of the floe. Occasionally, one of the bears makes a move towards a gull to scare it away then returns to the seal's belly. Per edges the ship ever closer until, at about 100 yards, he feels we are close enough to see without being too close to scare them off so that they will lose the meal.

After a while, we move off and leave them to it – after all we have our own breakfast to get still. As we head out into the Arctic Ocean from the islands and turn east we can already see a wall of ice stretching right across the horizon. We are the first ship up this way this season so we have no detailed information from others who may have gone round before us. We steam towards the ice and enter it, with Per taking the ship in a careful but determined manner deeper and deeper into the pack ice, looking for a way through. Half a mile from the ship another polar bear is busy eating the last remains of a seal, with gulls circling him. He is a large male and he totally ignores us. He stays and chews at the last remains of the seal for some time before wandering off across the ice without a glance at us.

We try to see if we can find a route through the pack to the east all afternoon but there is no clear water. This is the fast winter ice that is still frozen to the land and has not yet retreated. Looking out across the ice through binoculars, the shimmer and reflections create hazy mirages that look like towering icebergs, or lines of icy cliffs of white skyscrapers in the far distance. As we had seen in Franz Josef Land, it is easy to start convincing yourself that there must be land and mountains out there. It is easy to see how the early explorers in the Arctic believed that there was a great undiscovered land to the north.

As it is still only early afternoon, we sail into Raudfjord, but heavy cloud prevents us enjoying the reported beauty of the place. Here, there is more fast ice, which is flat and clear of cracks and we are able to stop and go down onto the ice. The usual round of photography then ensues with people pushing the ship from the ice and stopping her with one hand, etc.

We sailed after dinner and as Per sees little chance of getting any further east he steams straight into the pack, heading due north. He is determined to get as far into the pack as he can and we have a sleepless night listening to the ice grinding past

Walruses lie on an ice floe off Spitsbergen.

Small sailing vessels at Longyearbyen, destined for the north of Spitsbergen. (C. McCutcheon)

Stockholm fast in the ice in a sheltered fjord allowed some leg stretching on the ice.

the hull, and feeling the juddering of the ship, as she smashes her way forward and as the ice falls off along the ship's sides. We imagine that there will be no paint at all left on the ship's sides by the morning. However, by morning and we are deep into the pack and up to above 81 degrees north. Soon after eight o'clock, Per stops the ship. The engines are shut down, silence falls and we go on deck to sit and watch as the Arctic world of the ice pack comes to us. It is a wonderful world into which we now find ourselves locked. Large floes of ridged and hummock ice lie all around. It is far too uneven and hummocky to venture out onto the ice as there are deep gaps between the floes that will be fatal if you slip and fall into the water as the floes are in slow, but constant, movement and they will close gently together over your head once you have gone through. Apart from that, the ridges are big enough to enable a bear to move very close to the ship without being seen and that will be a surprise that we might not want out on the ice. There is still no sign of any clear water or leads. The ship sits silent and still all day in the polar seascape while we let the atmosphere and the sensation of being where we are, in the ice pack north of Spitzbergen, sink in. I try to imagine Nansen and his men when they reached the point when their ship, *Fram*, was frozen into the ice off Siberia and they knew that she would not be released for another two or three years, by which time the *Fram* would have crossed the Arctic Ocean. This would be their world, a world of white, white and more white, apart from the total darkness of the too-long nights of the Arctic winters. They were no radios, no contact with the outside world, and

Two walruses escape the prying cameras.

As the vast emptiness of the frozen sea stretches across the ocean, a lone polar bear finishes his kill.

The mountains of Spitsbergen and the ice flows of the Arctic Ocean seen from the north.

no way for anyone to even know where they were let alone to help them. They were absolutely alone.

Nearby, two walruses emerge from between the floes and lie on a larger floe. They, as usual, are totally disinterested in us and more concerned about settling down for a sleep than any threat that we might pose to them. Eventually, they grow annoyed at our presence, even though we were here first, and both slide gracefully off the floe and back into the water without a splash. They surface, look back at us, and then vanish into the deep. A few of us spend the morning in the bows of the ship just watching and listening to the pack ice as it moves in the slight swell and listen to the grinding and groaning of the ice pack and absorbing the atmosphere.

In the late afternoon, Per restarts the engine and we force our way back out of the heavy pack and move back to the edge. Here, we stop and take the Zodiacs out for an evening ride round the larger floes, looking for seals. A large bearded seal lies on one with its head sticking out over the edge ready for a fast escape if a polar bear comes by. He is a bit surprised to see us appear in the Zodiac but other than that he never moves a muscle. We are within inches of him but he is just not bothered.

We stop and haul the Zodiac up onto a larger floe so we can get a better view of the area. We have already lost sight of the ship. She is out there somewhere but she has already vanished behind the floes. The sun breaks through the clouds and

shines on the distant peaks of Spitzbergen that lie low on the southern horizon
and are bathed in soft sun light, while the views of some of the mountains are
blocked out by the higher ice floes around us. As the sun drops behind the clouds
so it brings cold air to the scene and the sea turns from clear and blue to onyx
black and opaque and takes on a forbidding look. The sculptured ice statues of
some of the floes now look fragile and vulnerable, while in the sun they had been
dominant and strong, as the ever-changing Arctic light continually transforms the
scene. We feel the chill and launch the Zodiac back off the ice floe. We find our
way back through the ice floes to the *Stockholm* and gratefully climb back on
board.

South!

It is clear that the ice pack extends right round the northern tip of Spitzbergen
and that for all the captain's best efforts the *Stockholm* will not get through
to the eastern end of the islands. It had been a deeply cold and late winter in
the Arctic so we had expected the ice to still be quite far south. We are just
too early in a season. After some discussion, Per and Per Magnus decide to
head south and see some of the sights that lie off the beaten track south of
Longyearbyen. It seems strange to hear someone say 'We are going south to
80 degrees north'.

The July 14th Glacier

We work our way slowly back down the coast and a day or so later we stop
in Krossfjord, where the July 14th Glacier reaches the sea. We are soon in the
Zodiacs again and are kept company by two puffins that land by the boats and
spend ten minutes paddling along beside us about 10 feet away. They seem to have
decided to escort us round their fjord. After watching another group of puffins
perched outside their cliff-side burrows, we land on the beach about a mile from
the magnificent glacier. Its ice front is about 90 to 100 feet high and is jagged and
fractured. It stretches round the bay in an arc about a mile long. The ice at the top
has broken into crags, towers and spires of ice, leaning out towards the sea as if
waiting to dive in. Crevasses at the top edge open up as they reach the front of the
glacier. There are other sections where raw wounds of bright blue ice have been
left by ice that has broken away earlier. The light and sun gets behind these scars
and throw a brilliant blue hue through the glacier. As the sun shines across the top
of the glacier, some parts are a brilliant white while other parts that are shaded
are deep blue. Cracks run down the face and at the bottom there are a number
of small black caves. This fantastic mass of ice draws us to it like a magnet,
regardless of our leader's warnings to take care and not go any nearer. After a
short while, a few of us find ourselves at the extreme edge of the glacier face as it

curves round at the edges of the fjord to form an ice bay. We sit on a low, shingle beach about 20 feet from the water and with the sheer rock of the fjord side at our back. We can hear the great murmurings inside the beast. Muffled cracks and roars echo round the fjord, but it was all going on inside; on the outside, nothing moves, the frozen exterior is keeping the inner turmoils locked in. This goes on for some time and we watch and listen as the glacier groans and grinds a few yards away. Then, another series of louder cracks and roars ring out and then stop. It falls quiet again, but a piece of ice the size of a house, with hundreds of smaller chunks, silently just lets go of the glacier face. It slides silently and gracefully down the glacier face then trips and falls into the sea. We stare transfixed as it hits the water. 'Run! Run!' someone yells. At the same moment, a 6-foot high wave generated by this relatively small chunk is charging along the beach towards us, pushing other floating chunks of ice along in front of itself. Never have people in boots and parkas moved so fast. We run back along the beach and try to get up to the highest point and round the end of the cliff where we can clamber onto higher ground. We all make it, just, and escape, unscathed. Over our shoulders we see the wave rushing by at amazing speed and force. By the time it reaches us it has diminished to about 3 or 4 feet. The wave subsides, peace falls on the fjord and it is as if nothing has happened.

As we return to the ship, anchored safely a mile or so away, and get back on board we can hear the glacier still groaning and roaring away like distant thunder. We stand on deck and watch in awe as a huge section of ice, about ten times bigger than the one we had seen from the beach, collapses into the sea. The spray dies away and we can see the wave the calving has generated. It is a serious one, at least 12 feet high we think. Had we still been on the beach it would have gone well over the top of our boots. We watch as the wave races out from the glacier, rushing up the cliff sides and inundating the beach where we had been walking just a few minutes before. The wave clears birds and flotsam as it goes. What will happen when it reaches the ship? We are anchored in a wide part of the fjord and by the time the wave reaches us it has dissipated most of its energy and it is barely noticeable. We breathe a collective sigh of relief and recognise how, by not heeding the warnings given to us, we could have found ourselves in serious trouble. The message is 'do not to mess with glaciers'.

On the way south we land on Prins Karl Forland Island to study a small group of walruses that have hauled themselves up on the beach and are mostly sleeping. While most are dozing in a walrus heap, one of the young males is in the sea just off the beach and has clearly seen us land and beach the Zodiac. He decides to take a closer look at our Zodiac and swims slowly down towards it. Per Magnus spots the danger and runs back. The walrus reaches the Zodiac and sniffs at it. Then he raises his tusked head over the low stern of the Zodiac by the outboard engine and examines the boat. He then starts to try and get on board the Zodiac from the stern by putting his head into the boat. Per Magnus arrives at the Zodiac and climbs in at the bow, picks up a wooden paddle from the floor of the boat and with a couple of sharp slaps on its nose persuades the young walrus to go

The July 14th Glacier front and the narrow beach.

elsewhere for his fun. While Zodiacs are very tough and buoyant, they are not designed to act as flotation rings for a ton of walrus. If it had succeeded it would have probably destroyed the boat and certainly knocked the outboard motor into the sea.

By the next afternoon we are much further south in Kaulenfjord. We are relaxing in the saloon having a peaceful cup of tea and enjoying the warmth of sun shining through the windows, and I am thinking that perhaps no one would notice if I slipped away for a nap, when two polar bears are spotted on the fast ice by the shore. We rapidly take to the Zodiacs to have a closer look. As we gently approach, one of them moves off. The other one, however, is obviously in two minds and it decides to stay and see what we are. It then comes quickly out onto the fast ice and continues towards us and the ice edge with a swinging, loping gait and a look of purposeful intent. Is it going to dive into the sea to investigate us more closely? Should we get out of here fast? We watch in awe as it gets to the edge of the ice, then it stops and picks up the red remains of a seal carcass, which we had not noticed, and which the bears must have left there when they first saw us approaching. The bear has clearly remembered that it had left the remains of a seal on the ice and has returned to make sure we do not get it. We are able to sit in the Zodiac a few yards off the ice and watch this great beast as it comes out to the edge and collects the remains. It gives us a look that says 'This is mine, so clear off', then it trots off, with the remains of the carcass hanging from its mouth,

The world's most northerly train at Ny-Alesund. (C. McCutcheon)

to catch up with the other one, probably its mother, and together they wander off along the shore.

The day is spectacularly clear, the sun bright and warm, the visibility is endless and the scenery stunning. A few reindeer roam the lower slopes and Arctic birds are everywhere. The mountains all around the fjord glisten in the distance and the calm sea twinkle in the sunshine. Later that day we anchor in a bay by a huge shingle beach. Here, in the middle of nowhere, but not far from some old huts that had been used by whale hunters in the 1800s, we set up a BBQ at the top of the beach using some of the many thousands of tons of driftwood that for some strange reason have come ashore in this particular area. There is driftwood as far as you could see along the tops of the beaches. It is well dried and makes a grand fire. While the food and company are excellent, it is the aura that the place held that makes it magical. The perfect stillness and silence of the Arctic summer's night, the flat sea, the ship lying motionless at anchor off the shore and the mountains in the distance in the midnight sun. Everyone has come ashore and we leave the ship to herself for a few hours.

On our last day we meet up with some walruses, who decide to swim out and see us off. We spend a good hour drifting about them in the Zodiacs before we reluctantly move off.

So we ended this fantastic Arctic trip. It was made in many ways by the ship itself. The ship's warm and cosy interior, her history and the love that Per, her skipper owner, clearly had for her, all built the atmosphere on board and created

A walrus approaches the *Zodiac* looking determined. Will this one be friendly?

Evidence abounds of Spitsbergen's mining industry. (C. McCutcheon)

an environment where we all felt privileged and lucky to be where we were. The intimate nature of a small ship, with just a few good people living closely together, engenders a strong feeling of responsibility as we had to depend on each other if trouble arises. This feeling is impossible to get on large cruise ships as the more people there are on the ship the less responsible one feels as there will always be others there first to deal with a problem. On *Stockholm*, we all felt that we were a part of the crew and not just 'passengers'.

CHAPTER 14

Three Key Elements – Ships, the Sea and Ice

Ships

Since the day when I was handed out of the Mail Steamer to the waiting boatman, I have always found ships fascinating. If there are ships to look at, climb on board, or sail in, then I am happy. Why? It's hard to say exactly. There is no one single factor, but a combination of things. Their size is one thing: ships are always big especially when they are in port and you are close to them; even small harbour tugs have a solid, impregnable look and feel to them. Ships all seem to have their own character according to their role and they are living things and traditionally called 'She'. As ladies of the sea, their graceful and elegant lines make them a pleasure to look at. Some are more graceful looking and ladylike than others but, an elegant ship is a beautiful sight while a scruffy coaster can exhibit a tough no nonsense attitude.

In many ways ships are a contradiction. They are designed to do a job of work as cheaply as possible; to carry cargoes and make money. That they can also be attractive to look at is a great bonus. It is hard to believe that the graceful, sculptured hull forms of ships that have evolved in design over the centuries to better meet the elements; are made up from cold, hard, flat steel plates and that they are not created by an artist or sculptor. They could have evolved looking like square railway trucks which essentially do the same job! The wooden ships of old all started out as flat planks on the shipyard floor that were bent and steamed, carved and turned into the right shapes to do the job in the best way they could. Traditionally, steel ships were built from sheets of steel that were cut and bent, in to ribs and frames, and riveted together out on the open slipway. Today ships are assembled as kits, complete hull sections in covered assembly halls. Ships are made up of hundreds of thousands of individual components, sub assemblies, assemblies and even whole hull sections are now built separately and completed with all the internal equipments, fixtures and fittings before they are placed next to their neighbours in the building dock. These are then welded together to form the complete ship.

While ships can have a romantic aura about them, shipbuilding itself is not a romantic occupation. Ask any shipyard worker about working conditions in the shipyards, especially in the old days. Summer or winter they were outside in the wind and the wet, handling huge pieces of hard cold, sharp edged steel; climbing high in the unfinished frames of ship's hulls or working deep inside the machinery spaces. There was the endless noise of the riveting hammers and while modern welding is quieter, shipyards are still noisy and dangerous places to work. However, the workers have the pleasure of watching a new ship being created and most workers develop a strong attachment to her. From the laying of the keel block through to her launch they are a part of her and put part of themselves into her.

Launch Day is the highlight. It is the day they have all worked for. All the yard workers and their families, as well as local VIPs and other guests, gather to watch the launch. Local school children are given the day off and local businesses shut on launch day. The ship herself sits waiting, high and proud, her hull and superstructure freshly painted and gleaming; dominating the surrounding area until the final release from the land so she can slide down the ways and float free at last.

The shipyard directors and VIPs make their way to the special viewing platform at the bows. The smooth lines of the bow tower up, directly above the platform and dwarf them all. The ship's sponsor names and blesses the ship; the champagne bottle swings through an arc and smashes against the bow. The champagne fizzes down the hull and everyone cheers. All eyes watch for the ship to move, but she doesn't. She is still there. What has gone wrong? Then, when the triggers are released and the sliding cradle is free to move, gravity slowly exerts itself on the ship and then she moves. Imperceptibly at first, did it move? Yes it did and now it is definitely moving. The crowd cheers again as this steel monster of a fixed structure that has grown on this spot over many months and now dwarfs all the buildings around her, starts to move. Slowly, silently, she gathers speed. Faster and faster she goes and remorselessly heads for the water. A feeling of awe at the sheer scale of this moving mass grips all who watch and hushes the crowd. A lump rises in the throat as the ship is born but at the same time a fear grows in your heart that she is now going too fast. Nothing can stop her now. She is totally out of control. How can something so big move so fast? She is rushing towards the water, eager to be free of the land. As her stern reaches the river she pushes the waters out of her way sending great waves across to the other bank. She races past the crowds and then the huge drag chains start to work and clouds of rust dust rise from the masses of heavy chains that are attached to her sides. They scream and rattle as they are dragged down the ways behind her, slowing her and restraining her from careering into the opposite bank. Pieces of timber from her launch cradles pitch out from underneath her as she hurls herself into the sea like a child at the sea side on the first day of the holidays. As her bow clears the end of the slipway and reaches the water it dips and bobs up in a little curtsey of thanks to the shipyard and those who have built her. The ship is now afloat for the first time. After the excitement of her headstrong rush into the water she now lies at peace and benignly lets the tugs gather round her and gently take her to the fitting out basin for her final completion.

The other factor common in all ships is the feeling of power: either they have engine power or sail power with which to drive themselves through the seas, no matter what the weather. Whether it is a square rigger, an America's Cup racing yacht, a tug butting its way into a fresh gale or a destroyer at speed, there is a sense of power. Maybe it is the QE2 racing to New York at 29.5 knots through a Force 8 gale no matter what, or a Second World War battleship charging through rising seas, there always is a strong sense of power and supreme confidence. When a ship is at sea, moving under its own power and responding to the forces of the wind and waves, it is a living thing, a warm, vibrant creature and home to the crew that live and work aboard her. But, when it is tied up alongside without her crew, with no generators or engines throbbing away then it becomes a cold, damp and dead object.

Every ship is a unique capsule of life, a world to itself separated from and independent of life on the shore. Ships come in all different shapes and sizes, different nationalities and different cultures. All the ethnic and cultural differences between countries are apparent in their ships. Watching ships lights at night, as they silently creep across the horizon, I wonder not only 'What ship, where bound?' but, what language are they speaking and where is their home, when will they see their families again?

Some types of ship may be of no interest to you until you sail in them and then as you become a part of the ship a relationship develops. Like a human relationship, you get to know and trust a ship. You get used to her motion and learn to live in her. She in turn protects you from the elements and takes you to your destination. Attachments are formed as they become your place of work and your home and they carry you to wherever in the world they might be going.

Just as the launch of a ship is a cause for celebration so the death of a ship is a time for mourning. In Hull I was involved in de-equipping a number of the older trawlers before they went to the breakers yard and it was always a sad experience to see these fine old ships, which had sailed many tens of thousands of miles to and from the Arctic, safely carrying their crews outward and homeward hundreds of times, being towed away to be ripped apart by the oxyacetylene cutters of the breakers. Taking out the radars and radios, was a final confirmation of their fate. This was the point of no return for them. We would watch silently from the manager's window as the once proud and defiant ships, now stripped out and empty and forlorn, were towed out of the fish dock and down to the breakers, never to return. Most of us had memories of each of the ships and their crews and we all felt real pangs of sadness.

The Sea

What is it about the sea that gets into our blood and minds? After all, it is cold, wet and inhospitable; if we fall into it we can drown. The sea can make us seasick and feel like dying. The sea can be rough and it can destroy and kill ships and men. So why on earth should we like it? Perhaps, it is because the sea is a constantly moving, living thing; like the ships that sail across it. It has a life and moods of its own that forces an emotional response from us. The sea's moods directly affect our own and we tend to mirror the moods of the sea. If it is a cold, grey miserable day with white horse and a rising wind, we tend to feel gloomy and depressed. However, if it is a bright, sunny day with a sparkling sea then all feels right with the world.

On a fine day, the gentle waves roll slowly under a boat causing a soft, rocking motion that calms and relaxes us. The wooden thwarts creak quietly, loose ropes slap idly against a mast, or the engine trobs steadily on. The motion is therapeutic and eases our tensions and stress. We feel relaxed and, given a chance, we will nod off into a pleasant nap. The sea gives us the isolation from the land that we often need, the chance to get away from our shore life. The sea is a barrier across which shore side troubles cannot pass. There is always a lurch in the heart when, on departure, the gangway is removed and the last connection with shore life and loved ones is broken. Equally, there is a thill of excitement as we are now on our own. Now we are free! But also, now we and those left behind are alone: we are powerless to help those left behind, just as they are powerless to help us. They are on their own, just as much as we are. For that, we love or hate the sea.

The sea demands 100 per cent attention. Forget it, or take it for granted and it will punish you. It makes those who go to sea appreciate that the day to day events of life ashore are relatively trivial when compared with keeping your ship and shipmates safe at sea. The sea gives us total freedom and perhaps that is why, more than anything, we love it.

The sea is timeless. It is the same today as it was thousands or even a million years ago. It looks the same, it behaves in the same ways that it always has. What we see today is what our forefathers saw when they went to sea. The grey rollers of the Atlantic are the same now as when the Vikings sailed them. It is the same for all men of all nations of all times and we all have to learn to respect it or it will catch us out. But it is also our route to the rest of the world. From any piece of beach in any reasonably well built boat and an infinite supply of food and fuel, we can go, quite literally, to the ends of the earth. Nothing and no one can stop us. No passport controls, no security checks; nothing but total freedom.

The Polar Regions

The polar regions are remote, and the fact that so few people have ever been there makes them interesting. Hot places with their dust, dirt, sweat and biting insects have never really appealed to me; but I have always wanted to visit cold ones. I love the clean, freshness of the polar regions, the crackling of the crystal clear frozen air, the deep silence and the clear, almost endless, visibility.

I am not saying I like being cold! Liking the cold of the Arctic is not the same as saying I like being cold, in just the same way that liking being alone is not the same as saying you like being lonely. The cold when it gets hold of you is not a good feeling. When the temperature drops to -20 °C and -30 °C then the cold takes on a stronger character. One moment you are feeling warm in your multi layers and down parkas but then, without warming the cold will quite literally grab you. Maybe it is a hand or it will creep down your neck but the next thing you know is that you have this thing attacking you like a vice. The cold presses into your body. You can feel it enter your clothes, sneaking between your gloves and your sleeve. You feel that your clothes are invisible to the cold as it goes straight through them, as if it was penetrating the stitch holes. In a matter of seconds it has got you. It squeezes and goes on squeezing until your bones feel it. Your clothes feel useless, you may as well be naked! Then there is only one thing to do. Get warm somehow! Jump, walk, run, go inside anything to escape this vice like grip that has attached itself to you. Once your circulation goes, in cold like this, it is very hard to get it back by normal rubbing or blowing onto your hands. The secret, I think, is never to stand around and let yourself get cold in those low temperatures. Dress fully inside then go out and keep moving, doing whatever, but do not stand around! At the same time you should not work so hard that you sweat as the sweat will freeze on your skin the minute you stop working. The coldest that I have been in was -34 °C on a flat calm and sunny January day in Finnish Lapland. This would be almost tropical for the real hard men of the Arctic Commandos or real polar explorers. One minute I was warm and standing enjoying the view, the next the vice had grabbed me. With -40 °C, even -50 °C and below with gales force winds and chill factors, what must the cold in the polar winter really be like? A good idea can be found in Apsley Cherry Garrard's *The Worst Journey in the World*. This describes Scott's last expedition to the South but during the expedition three members of Scott's expedition, including Cherry Garrard, made a trip took from Cape Evans on the west side of Ross island to Cape Crozier on the east side, a round trip of over 200 miles, in the Antarctic winter, to search for emperor penguin eggs. Gales blasted them almost from the start and a storm blew their tent away with temperatures of -50 °C to -60°C. But they survived. How is a mystery to me.

The earliest books I read were often about the polar regions. In the golden days of polar exploration to get to the polar regions could only be done by long sea voyages whereas today it is possible to fly there, so the explorers of the early days had to be both explorers and mariners and often came from the Royal or Merchant Navies. To me those books conjured up a world far beyond our own. To see the sights that they first saw, the icebergs, the glaciers, the endless ice pack: and to experience some of the risks that they took, such as their ships getting frozen into the ice and having to overwinter in it, these were the feats that I daydreamed about when I should have been listening to school masters.

While most of my recent voyages have been as a passenger rather than as a crew member, for me that does not diminish the atmosphere or the excitement that a ship, or a voyage, can generate. It is true that as a passenger you are not a part of the crew and will always be one step removed from the decision making aspects of maritime life. In many cases you will not even be aware of what dramas may be unfolding on the bridge or down in the engine room. Even if you are aware of them then you will probably play no part in their resolution. But never the less, being a passenger is far, far better than not being on a ship at all. You share the same seas and weather; see the same ports and events as anybody else on board and you all share the experience of the voyage and the character of the vessel regardless of your role in it. Whatever happens to the ship happens to everyone on board not just the crew or just the passengers. Being a passenger gives you the luxury of deciding where you want to go and selecting a ship to get you there. As crew you can only sail on ships you are appointed to and can only go to the places the ship is sent.

People sometimes have fixed ideas about the size of ships and will say 'Oh I wouldn't go on anything that small'. Equally some say 'Oh you wouldn't get me on anything that big'. However, whatever the size or type of vessel, once you are on it and it is taking you where you want to go then it becomes your world and your home. You accept it and adjust to it as you do to living in a small flat or a large house. From trawlers to the QM2, from small minehunters to giant Russian icebreakers, they are all ships and were 'home' for a short time and I enjoyed the experience of being there and grew attached to the ship.

Ships that Pass with Time

Time passes and ships pass on due to the changing needs of man and the types of ship he needs. In the Antarctic in the nineteenth century it was sealers in small wooden sailing ships from America, the UK and other northern countries who first ventured south in search of the famed fur seals. The Antarctic continent itself had not even been sighted then and sealing was carried out on the many sub-Antarctic islands. Antarctica was first sighted by a British sealing captain, William Smith, in 1819 when he sighted snow covered land. Reports spread and in January 1820 the Russian explorer Bellingshausen sighted land and three days later land was sighted by the RN's Capt Brantsfield. He had been sent by the Admiralty, with Capt Smith, to investigate Smith's claims. The land seen by Smith was the South Shetlands but Brantsfield sailed on further and found the Antarctic Peninsula. Once the fur seals had been killed almost to extinction and the sealers left, it was the great explorers who held centre stage. They went south in old sealing or whaling ships or specially built vessels like the Amundsen's *Fram*. Men like Shackleton and Scott, Amundsen, Mawson, Biscoe and Ross and many other brave men from many countries who fought their way in, tried to survive the cold and the winds, achieve something for science or exploration and then fought their way out.

With the South Pole attained by Amundsen in 1911, and confirmation that the great southern continent was covered in a mass of ice, interest dwindled; so with the explorers passing another commercial prey was found, the baleen whale. In first half of the twentieth century the only ships that went to the Antarctic were the whaling fleets with catcher vessels and large factory ships, where whole whales were hauled on board up the stern ramp. Now, the whalers have gone and thanks to them most of the whales too. All that remains of those times can be seen at places like Grytviken, and Stromness in south Georgia.

Now fifty years on and it is the specialised ice strengthened expedition ships that pass down through the Roaring Forties into the great Southern Ocean. Ships are now carrying a new breed of crew and for the first time, passengers. Naturalists, ornithologists, lecturers, marine biologists and passengers keen to see and learn about these fantastic and remote regions and the wild life that lives there, rather than working men who joined a whaling expedition for the simple reason that it was good money.

In the Arctic it is a similar story, the first ships to explore the region were the fur sealers from Norway and Russia. Then came the whalers from Europe and Arctic whale camps such as Smeersburg and whaling captains such as the Scoresbys. When Arctic whaling passed its peak in the nineteenth century it was replaced by trawl fishing in the twentieth century. In the UK the old whaling ports such as Hull, Whitby, Dundee Aberdeen and many others became the centres for trawl fishing. Ships from the UK, France, Germany as well as Russia and East Germany, France, Poland and Portugal all sailed to the northern seas from the Grand Banks to Novoya Zemlya in search of cod and haddock and Greenland Halibut.

Again time and industries have passed. During the Cold War submarines and warships patrolled the northern seas. The Cold War is over, so we are told, but some think it is just a lull while Russia rebuilds her powerful submarine fleet. However, for the moment at least, it is big cruise ships and small expedition ships that sail across North Cape Bank in the Barents Sea past Bear Island to Spitsbergen. Very few trawlers are now seen in these once rich grounds. One wonders what sort of ships will be sailing these waters a hundred years from now. Perhaps the cod will have returned and large scale fishing will resume? Perhaps oil exploration will send drilling rigs and supply ships into these regions, who can say?

There are still many places I still want to visit, and some places I want to visit again. We are very fortunate as we now live by the sea and we can see ships passing by every day. From the VLCCs arriving at the oil terminal with tugs busying around to get them onto the berth, to product tankers and small container ships going up and down the estuary, to the occasional RN ship and large cruise ships that drop anchor nearby. I am a bit of a dreamer and often look at magazines and travel brochures and say to Doreen, 'Ah, now there's a voyage I would love to do'.

APPENDIX 1

The Tot

I was lucky enough to serve in the Royal Navy while the rum issue was still made. Although officers did not receive a rum ration, as cadets, it was part of our training to witness the issue of rum to the ratings. Rum, or the tot, was still very much a part of daily shipboard life and a deep part of the lore of the Navy.

The history of the tot began in the seventeenth century when drinking water, which was kept in the wooden barrels, could not be stored for any length of time as it soon spoiled at sea. So the ships carried beer for drinking as it kept for longer. Each man was issued with a gallon of beer a day. However, in the tropics, the beer also spoiled quickly so the Admirals in charge tried to find alternatives for the men to drink. In 1650, Admiral Blake decided to issue sailors with half a pint of brandy each day. In the West Indies in 1655, Admiral William Penn issued rum as an alternative to beer. After the conquest of Jamaica in 1687, rum replaced brandy, so starting a tradition that was to last nearly 300 years. A half-pint of rum, or two gills, was issued to each man in two portions of a quarter of a pint, one at noon and the other in the evening, instead of the gallon of beer.

Not surprisingly, drunkenness became an increasing problem and so, in 1740, Admiral Vernon, then Commander-in-Chief, West Indies Fleet, ordered that the rum be diluted with water by four parts (or one quart) of water to one part (half pint, or two gills) of rum. This not only weakened the drink but prevented sailors from hoarding their rum as, when mixed with water, it went off after a while. Admiral Vernon had a nickname of 'Old Grog', as he always wore a waterproof boat cloak made from a course material called Grogram, So, when he instigated his diluted rum mixture, it became known as 'Grog'. From grog we also get the word groggy, meaning unwell.

The new practice of issuing rum instead of beer spread throughout the Navy so, by the early 1800s, it was standard across the fleet. During the Napoleonic Wars, when the fleet was expanded by a large number of new recruits and pressed men who were not used to this level of alcohol, increased reports of drunkenness and ill-discipline led the Admiralty to gradually reduce the amount of rum issued per man over the following decades.

In 1824, after a trial on board HMS *Thetis*, the amount of rum issued was halved to a quarter of a pint (one gill) a day and the evening issue was abolished.

Rum was issued at 8 bells in the forenoon watch, just before noon and the time of the midday meal. The rum was a potent drink, 47.75 per cent alcohol. As discipline issues continued, the rum issue was reduced again in 1850 to an eighth of a pint (half a gill). The mix by this time had settled at a 2:1 mix; i.e. two parts water to one part rum. The senior rates got their issue served neat and the rum issue to officers was abolished in 1881.

After the Second World War and the advent of the modern high-tech navy, the constant use of sophisticated electronic equipment needed concentration and alertness and did not tally with the issue of strong liquor every day at noon. After many years of debate, including protests and speeches in Parliament, the rum issue was finally abolished on 31 July 1970, a day called 'Black Tot Day'. It was a sad day for many old salts as the tot had become a cornerstone of daily life at sea. The tot was used as a form of currency and tots were offered and accepted for doing someone else's duty or for other favours on board ship.

The money saved from the rum issue was used to set up a sailors fund, which is used for the benefit of ratings. A canned beer issue, however, continues for ratings, which they buy on board, while the senior rates now have bars in their messes.

APPENDIX 2

Seasickness

Anyone who has experienced it will recognise the symptoms: those lucky enough not to have ever experienced seasickness should read this with a feeling of thankfulness and sympathy for those that have.

Seasickness is real. Do not let anyone tell you that it is all in the mind. I have been seasick in all types of ship, from trawlers to the QE2, from yachts to cruise ships. I have, however, also been in horrendous weather in small ships and not been in the least seasick. I was never seasick in the RN Type 12 frigates, in the stern trawlers from Hull, nor on many small ships and yachts.

It is a personal thing and the symptoms vary from person to person. For me, seasickness is mainly caused by the irregular, vertical, pitching motion of the ship. It is seldom caused purely by the rolling, side-to-side motion, though in some extreme cases it can be. This is because the rolling is normally much more gentle and predictable while the pitching is variable, and often violent and sudden. It happens as the bow comes up and over a wave, then hangs in mid-air while the wave passes beneath the ship. The bow then falls into the wave trough until the ship is stopped suddenly as the bow hit the next wave and the ship recovers. Then it starts again.

When I feel seasick, it starts with a feeling that the stomach is trying to move about in time with the ship and is reacting to the motion. After a while I find myself feeling drowsy, perhaps yawning a lot and I just want to sit quietly and hope people do not want to talk to me. It then develops into a general feeling of queasiness. I start to find that my hand-eye coordination deteriorates as I grab for a hand hold but discover that it has moved fractionally and I miss it, so I lurch a bit more. I feel that my stomach then tries to move to counter the error. At this stage seasickness can sometimes be dealt with by getting out on deck into the fresh air and concentrating on something different. But, if the weather and motion continue then it progresses to a tightening of the throat, a feeling of being flushed, and then a cold, clammy feeling settles on the face and skin. By this point I are probably a paler shade of green. Eventually, after this has built up in intensity, the stomach starts to come up to the throat. Now is the time to get to the lee side of the open deck as the next happening is of a violent and liquid nature. Immediately after throwing up I often feel much better, but it is only a matter of time until the queasiness and vomiting starts again. This, after a time and many repeats, leads to a feeling of tiredness and extreme weakness until eventually, perhaps after a couple of days, the brain works out what is happening, then recalibrates itself with the surroundings and things calm down.

During seasickness, the overwhelming feeling I have is 'Get me off here', followed by a sincere prayer, 'Oh Lord, please don't let me die from this!' This leads to 'Oh Lord, please let me die, now!' The first time anyone is seasick, it is without doubt the worst feeling in the world.

It is always worst and most prevalent when you first set sail after any length of time ashore. Once your inner ear is in tune with the ship's motion all will be well. As I understand it medically, seasickness is caused by the messages sent to the brain by the sensitive balance nerves in the inner ear not being correlated with the information that the eyes are giving the brain; for example, the eyes see a chart table or a bunk that is stationery but the inner ear feels the vertical motion as the ship has moved up and down and so is telling the brain that the table should be in a different place. In addition, information sent to the brain from other motion-sensing parts of the body, such as skin receptors and muscles, also add to the confusion. The brain receives this conflicting information about what is happening and gets confused. This leads to nausea and sickness.

So, how do you cure it? Not by the old wives' tales of drinking a pint of seawater or swallowing fatty, greasy bacon. Some say that being able to see a level horizon, or the land makes it better. It can, as the eyes are then focused on a static object and the brain can to some degree ignore the inner ear motions. Certainly, being in fresh air is better than being in a small, noisy and stuffy cabin with low deck-heads, no portholes and smelly socks around! Being inside a small yacht is bad news. They are small, confined, airless areas and subject to the violent crashes when the yacht falls off the waves. Great intakes of marine smells such as diesel oil or of frying food in the galley do not help. Lying down with your eyes shut is best of all. It removes one of the brains inputs and helps you relax. Some say keeping busy helps and it does, but only when you are getting over seasickness, not when you are being ill.

Some say that the bigger the ship then the lower the chance of seasickness. This is not necessarily true. In the vastness of the open ocean all ships are tiny. I have felt seasick in the QM2. We had sailed from Southampton for New York and on the second day out, due to a storm in mid-Atlantic, we changed course to avoid the bad weather and sailed well to the south of the storm centre. However, we still encountered the swell created by the storm. Even in a ship of 150,000 tons and without any wind to speak of, when I was up in the forward public areas of the ship, the motion of the ship made me feel groggy and I retreated to the midships areas where I soon recovered. Being at the very forward end of a ship or at the very stern in bad weather is like standing on the ends of a swinging see-saw, so it is generally better to stay closer to the midships part of the ship.

In answer to 'It's all in the mind', I can offer two examples to make the point that it definitely is not. I have already mentioned the ship's dog, Rebel in HMS

Puncheston and his seasickness. In HMS *Nurton*, we found that after any leave period people tended to be seasick for the first couple of days at sea, so we did an informal survey among the crew. It is fair to say that Ton-Class minesweepers do not have the most highly-tuned performance hull design in the world. They have the underwater profile of a bathtub and the flotation qualities of a cork. We asked everyone on board to note down any ailments that they experienced after we sailed following a summer leave period. We found that everyone on board suffered 'something' that could be related to seasickness. It ranged from a few people just feeling a bit muzzy for a day, right the way through bad headaches, queasiness, odd bouts of sickness and right up to one able seaman who always was knocked out flat for two or three days after any long spell ashore. I was always sick to some degree in the first two days after leave; sometimes worse than others, but never badly enough not to be able to carry on working. However, it only lasted a couple of days and the lee-side bridge wing was only a few paces away.

As a 'reverse example' I can quote from my own experience. A number of years ago I had mumps as an adult. Not very usual, but it is not a problem in itself. A few days after the mumps had cleared up, however, I found that I started to lose my balance when I bent over and I developed a ringing in the ears. My doctor was fascinated. 'Not seen one like this before, let me go and get my colleague and show him.' While I sat there feeling terrible the two of them chuckled over a large medical tome and filled in their doctors' 'I Spy books'. They decided I had something called 'Nerve Deafness'. Apparently the mumps virus had settled into my left inner ear and totally destroyed all the nerves affecting balance and hearing so preventing any messages getting to the brain. These are the same nerves that send seasickness messages to the brain. My right ear was fine so the two balance systems were working against each other. I then spent three days sitting in my fireside chair, 40 miles from the sea, being seasick. I had to crawl about as I could not walk properly as my balance was destroyed. If I moved my head a little, everything carried on moving and I was sick again. I could not watch TV as even the movement of the picture set me off. In this case my brain was being told by my right ear that I was moving about and by my non functioning left ear that I was not! Result seasickness! I can assure you that while that might have all been going on 'in my head'; it was certainly not 'all in my mind'.

In recent years seasickness tablets that you can buy across the counter have made a huge difference. In the Fasnet Race of 1979 a huge storm decimated the race, many yachts were lost and 15 sailors lost their lives. It was claimed afterwards that those sailors who had taken a new brand of seasickness pill called Stugeron, were much less affected by seasickness in spite of the violence of the storm. Now, I always take them with me and if I know it is going to be rough or we sail out of port into rough weather, I take a couple before we sail and rarely need any more as by the time their effect wears off, my system has adjusted to the new motion. Since I started to take these I have never been troubled. Today there are a number of other new solutions on the market. Some people use wrist bands which work by applying pressure, through a plastic disc, to the acupressure point on the wrist and this reduces the symptom of nausea. Other forms of remedy use small medicated plasters or patches, stuck behind the ear. Both forms are now very common so must have something that works, although people do tend to wear them in flat calm conditions without a wave in sight and then say they work brilliantly. The true test is sailing out into rough weather before you have had time to get your sea legs. I recently joined a small coastal ship as it sailed from Kirkeness on the north coast of Norway straight into a northerly Force 9 winter gale. I took two Stugeron as we sailed and I was fine and enjoyed a good dinner even though the ship was bouncing around a lot. As I have never tried any of these bands or patches I cannot comment. It is a case of 'whatever floats your boat', if you will excuse the pun.

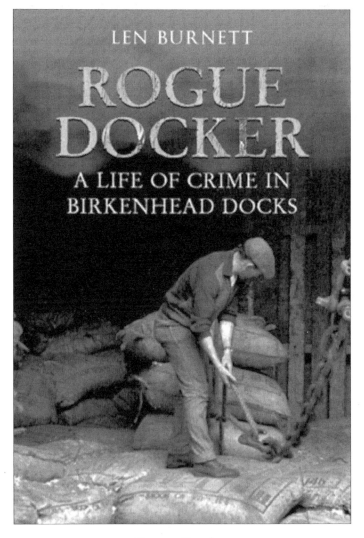

Rogue Docker
Len Burnett

978 1 4456 0259 2
160 pages